ALONG THOSE LINES

ALONG THOSE LINES

The Boundaries That Create Our World

Peter Cashwell

pcb PAUL DRY BOOKS
Philadelphia 2014

First Paul Dry Books Edition, 2014

Paul Dry Books, Inc.
Philadelphia, Pennsylvania
www.pauldrybooks.com

Copyright © 2014 Peter Cashwell

Printed in the United States of America

Library of Congress Cataloging-in-Publication Data
<TK>

For my parents

Richard Gordon Cashwell
and
Suzanne Sutker Cashwell

All boundaries are conventions, national ones too.
One may transcend any convention,
if only one can first conceive of doing so.

—David Mitchell, Cloud Atlas

A straight line exists between me and the good thing.

—Talking Heads, "The Good Thing"

Doing arbitrary tasks with great enthusiasm
is the key to a joyous life.

—Kelly Dalton

Contents

ALONG THOSE LINES

Prologue

Where I'm Coming From

Birds do the strangest things—Basketball, science, and dirt—A list of lists—The Fifty-Fifty Project

WHEN I WAS an impressionable child, I spent untold hours flipping through books about birds: field guides, Time-Life books, even that legendary selection from Random House's "Step-Up" series, *Birds Do the Strangest Things* by Leonora and Arthur Hornblow. With all this avian influence, it should come as little surprise that, once I'd grown up, I wrote my own book about the subject. *The Verb 'To Bird'* dealt with a wide variety of my bird-related obsessions, but astute readers may have seen within it the other huge component of my mental makeup: geography. The last third of the book, after all, focused primarily on my travels, because if you want to see interesting birds, sometimes you have to head in some interesting directions.

And I do have a very good sense of direction, perhaps to compensate for my lousy sense of smell. I make wrong turns on occasion, but those are usually mistakes of interpretation. I may not know which road to take, but I know whether I'm facing east or west. Heck, when I *dream* I know whether I'm facing east or west.

I don't know what gave me this sense of direction. Heredity is a likely candidate, since my father has it, too, but I also wonder about upbringing. Dad began his career in education as a geography teacher, and he and I both keep William Powell's *Gazetteer of North Carolina Places* within easy reach. (You never know when you may need a refresher on the location of Coldass Creek or Dog Loser Knob.) Moreover, tacked to the wall of my childhood home in Chapel Hill, right between the bathroom door and the dining room, was a large map of the United States. To say this map had an effect on my thinking is to understate the situation considerably; for years, I actually imagined each state in the same color it bore on my wall. Every time we crossed the border on the way to visit my grandparents in South Carolina, I expected the landscape to change to a more orangey shade.

State borders grabbed my interest in other ways. In March of 1971, I was only in second grade, but I was already developing a devotion to Tar Heel hoops. Under legendary coach Dean Smith, the University of North Carolina's basketball team was becoming a national power, but that year they'd lost the Atlantic Coast Conference title to the South Carolina Gamecocks. In those days, only one team per conference could qualify for the NCAA Tournament, so the Heels had to settle for the National Invitation Tournament, but they were soon on their way to New York to play in its championship game.

Fortunately there were few obstacles standing between me and a seat in Madison Square Garden. My dad worked in UNC's admissions office, so obtaining tickets wasn't difficult for him, and he had a friend at the Kent School in Connecticut, so we had a relatively nearby place to spend a few nights. No, the only real problem was Mrs. Koch, my teacher, who wasn't happy about my missing several days of class for the sake of a few basketball games. There wasn't really much she could do about it, but my parents mollified her by agreeing to have me perform a science experiment during the trip: I would gather soil samples from each of the states I passed through, and when we returned we'd see which was the most fertile.

Every time we crossed a state line, Dad dutifully pulled our big blue Chevy station wagon to the side of the road. My mom and I would then climb out, scrape some soil into a tubular Tupperware container, and label the tube with masking tape. Perhaps that array of Tupperware is how I came to be so aware of the layout of the eastern seaboard states: North Carolina, Virginia, Maryland, Delaware, Pennsylvania, New Jersey, New York, Connecticut, all in their neatly ordered tubes. The soil may not have had the exact coloration that my map did, but the pinks, blues, and greens of the plastic cylinders still formed a satisfying spectrum in my mind.

I don't recall much about the trip except that I took my first train ride (from Kent to Manhattan), I saw the Empire State Building lit up by night, and Carolina won the NIT behind 35 points from MVP forward Bill Chamberlain. The arrangement of the states, however, remained with me for years, long after we had planted a lima bean in each soil sample and discovered that, to everyone's surprise, the earth from the side of the New Jersey Turnpike produced by far the biggest, healthiest plant.

From then on, I found happiness in every sort of geography. I would read atlases for fun, delighting in the differences between the maps that showed political features and those that showed the physical terrain. I took a smug satisfaction in going fifty for fifty in our fifth-grade unit on state capitals, and I kept close track of every state I had visited: Florida, where I saw my first Brown Pelican when I was only four; Georgia, where my Uncle Buster ran Savannah's premier kosher bakery, Gottlieb's (our only source of bagels for the first decade of my life—the rest of the South didn't seem aware of them yet); Alabama, where I came close, but not close enough, to catching a flounder off the pier of the Grand Hotel; Massachusetts, where I visited Harvard's Museum of Natural History during (as I later realized) Stephen Jay Gould's tenure there. We followed the Tar Heels as well, flying to California for the 1972 Final Four; I got to go to Disneyland, but UCLA won the title—again. Happily, when we accompanied the Heels to Hawaii in December of 1977, they won the Rainbow Classic handily.

By the time I got to college, I'd added trips to Tennessee, Vermont, and New Hampshire, and I had every reason to believe that I would visit every state in the union by the time I was twenty-five. I had, of course, neglected to consider that it's far easier to visit a lot of states when the travel costs are being ponied up by one's parents. Also, it's a lot easier when they're doing most of the driving.

This was not, I must emphasize, a major motivation in my getting married, but I would have to say that my marriage did give me the chance to go to several states I probably wouldn't have driven to alone. In March of 1989, Kelly and I piled into the car to visit a friend in Missouri. This trip took us north from Chapel Hill into West Virginia, whereupon we took a hard left and headed through Kentucky, Indiana, and Illinois to the Show-Me State, where our host showed us such sights as our first hockey fight in St. Louis and the now-defunct lead mine in Bonne Terre. A few months later, we took a southern swing from South Carolina to Biloxi, Mississippi, where I achieved a moment of sublime ridiculousness (or was it ridiculous sublimity?) by successfully sending a mini-golf ball into the navel of a gigantic plaster Buddha. These trips, however, were not significant purely because they involved new states; by this time, I was engaged in a whole new activity: birding.

After my in-laws gave me a copy of Roger Tory Peterson's *Field Guide to the Birds of North America* in 1988, I started looking at birds with more care, and one of the side effects of this extra attention was my taking up a common bird-related activity, that of listing. There are lists of all sorts. The most common is the life list (a list of all the species that the individual has seen in his or her lifetime), but many birders keep separate lists for birds seen in particular places (the yard, the county, the state, etc.) or times (calendar years, vacations, migrations, etc.). Some birders go farther. In his excellent book *To See Every Bird on Earth*, Dan Koeppel tells not only of the mighty life list assembled by his father, Richard—a list over 7000 species long—but of Richard's list of the birds he'd seen *on television*. Part of me read this account with a frisson of horror, but part of me found it completely reasonable. After all, though I do not have it written down, I myself have a list of Major Ornithological Mistakes in Hollywood Movies.[1]

---

1. This list is not written down primarily because it's only two items long. First, there's the animatronic robin who sings along with Mary Poppins in "A Spoonful of Sugar"—an *American* Robin, which is a visibly different bird (*Turdus migratorius*) from the European Robin (*Erithacus rubecula*) you'd find in London. More egregious is the

Armed with my new Peterson guide, I'd begun keeping a list of life birds, and it was growing steadily, as was the list of states I'd visited. And when I got home from the Biloxi trip, I cheerfully jotted down not only the Mississippi Kite I'd logged in Florida, but the state of Mississippi itself.

It didn't occur to me for several years that there was a third list implicit in those two.

That third list finally appeared in late 2002 as I was putting together the pieces of *The Verb 'To Bird'*. Several of the chapters told of my birding experiences in various parts of the country: Iowa, Delaware, South Carolina, New York, and so on. In each of those chapters, I mentioned the life birds I'd encountered there, be they Dickcissels, American Avocets, Painted Buntings, or Canvasbacks. At some point a thought wafted through my brain (probably when I should have been concentrating on updating the species names to match contemporary American Ornithologists' Union standards): how many different states were represented on my life list? I brought the list up on the computer and these are the states I saw:

North Carolina—My birthplace, and the place where I began birding; nearly half the birds on my list were first seen in the Tar Heel State, beginning with the Northern Cardinal, the first bird I ever learned to recognize.

Florida—Here's where I saw my first Brown Pelicans when I was a child. It's also where I would see my first Swallow-tailed Kite, Chuck-will's Widow, and Magnificent Frigatebird years later.

Hawaii—Sadly, when I visited Oahu and the Big Island in the winter of 1977, I didn't see any of the rare native birds; instead, I saw two introduced species—the Common Mynah and the Red-crested Cardinal. Lifers, yes, but cheap ones.

"Pygmy Nuthatch" whose song gives away a hostage's location in Carmel in the first *Charlie's Angels* movie. In truth, the Pygmy Nuthatch (*Sitta pygmaea*) lives all over California and not just in one town, but that's not the glaring error. No, the glaring error comes when the bird is shown singing. Instead of a drab four-inch nuthatch, the songster is a large (over nine inches), brightly-colored (black and flaming orange) and obvious oriole, specifically the South American species known as the Troupial (*Icterus icterus*), which doesn't even live in California.

Indiana—Driving along Interstate 64 en route to Missouri on our 1989 trip, I logged a Rough-legged Hawk hovering over the roadside fields.

Illinois—A few hours further west, perched in a tree beside the interstate, my first Red-Shouldered Hawk appeared.

Missouri—Several days later, standing on a sidewalk in Desloge, I saw the slate-blue back of a male Merlin as it dove into the shrubbery across the street in search of prey.

Iowa—On one July morning in 1995, Iowa City resident Jim Fuller helped me log seven life birds, starting with the Dickcissel and ending with the Upland Sandpiper.

South Carolina—My parents lived there for ten years, so I got many chances to see the local avian population, from my first Tree Swallow to my first American Anhinga.

Virginia—My home since joining the faculty of Woodberry Forest School in 1995, and the hotbed of my birding activity in recent years. I picked up a Broad-winged Hawk during a 1993 visit, and I'd picked up lifers in the Commonwealth at a rate of roughly one per year since I moved here.

New York—Near Cold Spring Harbor in 1996, I saw a healthy supply of brand-new waterfowl, including Gadwalls, Canvasbacks, and American Wigeons.

Delaware—In 1997, a long day at Bombay Hook National Wildlife Refuge with my colleagues Tom Parker and Wallace Hornady got me a Snow Goose, a Black-necked Stilt, a Glossy Ibis, and even an American Avocet.

Connecticut—In the spring of 2000, our dear friend Elaine Carroll took the family to Hammonassett Beach State Park, where I spotted a quartet of Green-winged Teals.

New Jersey—I had spent several profitable mornings tooling around Cape May, the first in July 2000, with the Least Bittern, Short-billed Dowitcher, Worm-eating Warbler, and Marsh Wren, among others, to show for it.

All in all, I had collected a baker's dozen: thirteen states in which I had seen at least one life bird. It seemed a paltry total. Surely I could do better than that. Did the U.S. of A. stand pat with the thirteen original states? No! And neither would I! All I needed was a little time, a few bucks for gas, and a little luck. Not only would I visit every state, I would see a new life bird in each one. Fifty states, fifty lifers—I could do that.

Thus began the Fifty-Fifty Project, a personal quest to achieve something which was completely arbitrary, which had almost certainly been done before, and which was of no particular importance to anyone but me.

But for the next ten years, every time I crossed a state line, searching for the bird that lay on the other side of it, I was forced to think about what I was looking for and where I was looking for it—not merely about birds and places, but about the more complex ideas of species and states. And the more state lines I crossed . . . well, let's just say those weren't the only lines I thought about. Or the only ones that got crossed.

PART ONE

Space and Time

I would ramble all through time and space
Just to have a butcher's at your face.
—Robyn Hitchcock, "Kingdom of Love"

Maps and Legends

A line is a dot that goes for a walk. —Paul Klee

THERE IS NO such thing as a line.

Any discussion of lines must begin with that understanding. We can talk about the definition of a line, or its properties, or its uses, but if our conversation involves the mistaken belief that the line actually exists, we'll never get anywhere. The line is a convenient fiction, a metaphor given life, a conspiracy of geometers. And until we admit what a line is, we will never be able to figure out what one does.

This may seem paradoxical. It's certainly counterintuitive, as every one of us can claim familiarity with lines. Nonetheless, even those who work with lines on a professional basis can have difficulty getting a grip on them, and that difficulty starts with the definition.

The English word *line* is roughly a thousand years old. According to the *Oxford English Dictionary*, it was originally a reference to the fiber produced by the plant better known as flax. The Egyptians, Greeks, and Romans all knew flax well, and the Latin name for it was *linum*. From that plant the ancients got both the seeds we call *linseeds* and the cloth we know as *linen*, and centuries later English speakers got a name for any marking shaped like a thread.[1]

The concept of the line is far older than the word, but the definition has remained as slippery as linseed oil. Euclid's writings gave the world the first real idea of how lines behave, but even the founder of geometry was stymied when it came to defining one. The closest he came seems to be "breadthless length," which is functionally identical to "lengthless breadth" without being any more useful. Luckily, a more recent scholar, Eric Weisstein of *MathWorld*, has offered us this:

> A line is a straight one-dimensional figure having no thickness and extending infinitely in both directions. A line is sometimes called a straight line or, more archaically, a right line . . . to emphasize that it has no "wiggles" anywhere along its length.

The exact nature of "wiggles" was, alas, never explored by Euclid, and the word remains undefined by Weisstein, but at least we're starting to know some things a line *cannot* have—thickness, multiple dimensions, finite length. Ultimately, however, students of geometry are far more likely to rely upon their own imperfect, ill-defined concept of a line than on anything offered by geometers of any era.

Matthew Keating, a graduate of the University of Connecticut and the Teachers College of Columbia University, doesn't even offer a definition to his geometry students at Woodberry Forest School; he just asks them to accept the idea of a line and move on. "We use visual examples of lines, things they're used to—threads, ropes, and so on," he explains. "It's a model approach, not a definition. But once it's constant and agreed upon, you can move forward. We talk about collinearity without the word *line* in it."

Apparently I look puzzled at this, since of course the word *collinearity* not only means "being on the same line," but has the word *line* in it.

---

1. By far the best part of learning about linen production is discovering the wonderful vocabulary used to describe the pieces of the flax plant and the various processes for rendering it into cloth; it sounds like nothing so much as a series of sound effects from old *MAD Magazine* cartoons by Don Martin. I mean, how can you NOT want to read about *retting, scutching, shive, tow* (which rhymes with *cow*), and *heckling*?

Keating grins at me. "It's a recursive definition."

For an English major like me, a definition containing the word to be defined is not merely recursive, but nonsensical. For a math major like Keating, however, it's not a problem, and I understand his meaning: like the words *point* and *plane*, the word *line* has to be accepted before a line's behavior can be understood. Once that word is accepted, the practical value of Euclidean geometry is enormous, whether one is involved in carpentry, orbital mechanics, or even simple logic, but most of the things called *lines* by the people in such fields are technically nothing of the sort. Some of them lack straightness, becoming curves, or perhaps "wiggles." Some of them have a degree of thickness. The most common failure of a line to conform to the technical definition, however, is a failure to have infinite length.

Thus, even if Euclid had properly defined the word *line*, there wouldn't be much use for one in the real world, because the real world is finite and concrete. A collection of points extending indefinitely in a single dimension isn't something we can see or touch; it's arguable that we can't even conceive it. A line is a purely theoretical construction built out of an infinite number of smaller theoretical constructions, a pin on which even the most abstract of angels wouldn't be caught dancing.

Moreover, the shortest distance between two points is not truly a straight line, because a line must extend beyond both those points and across the entire universe in opposite directions. Only a small piece of it lies between those points. "Any two points define a line, and only one line," Keating explains. "But then we talk about *segments*. That's those two points and all points between." In practical terms, then, we can ignore the infinite parts, focusing on the bit between the important points—whatever they might be—and still call that bit a *line*. Yes, we really mean *segment*, but Keating's example still applies: as long as we all agree on the meaning of *line*, we don't need to meet a particular definition. The line is a tool of arbitration, and it's fitting that the decision about what a line actually *is* should be arbitrary.

This is not to say that lines have no impact on reality. Particularly when they are drawn on a map, they can be hugely significant, as any felon who crossed one and got arrested by the FBI will tell you. That significance, however, is not due to any natural condition, but due to human perception. Basically, a line is most important to human beings when it serves the purpose of separating reality into two sides—left and right, Central and Mountain, here and there. And if it performs this task, we call it a *borderline*.

Straight lines work as borders, but we often rely on Mother Nature to do the work of separating territories, and the curves (or perhaps "wiggles") of the Rio Grande, which serve to define the border between the United States and Mexico, are more her style. Sections of the river are wide enough to make crossing a difficult or even dangerous business; in other sections, the water is not wide, but the deep canyons it has carved into the rocks of the region still serve as a significant barrier to those who want to pay a quick international visit. Still, there are places where the Rio Grande isn't much of a barrier at all. In Big Bend National Park, tourists can stand in America and buy souvenirs that are brought across the river on horseback from the village of Boquillas. The watercourse is so narrow there that my son Ian and I were able to toss pebbles from Texas to Mexico, an idle pastime which is probably going to get either the National Parks Service or the Department of Homeland Security on my case now.

My point, however, is that even though this borderline has a very real river as a physical component, it does not separate the nations completely, nor does it always separate them effectively. In this, it is just like the parts of the U.S.–Mexico border that do not lie along a river. The jagged line drawn from El Paso to the Pacific (with a brief zig-zag at the Colorado River) ignores most of the geographical features it crosses, but it works exactly the way the Rio Grande does: though crossing the water may be more of a challenge, neither the river nor the nameless line would serve as a boundary if the people on both sides did not consider it one. This idea is worth considering because it's true of far more than just geography.

BORDERS GO WHERE people go. This is a fact made clear whenever an American crosses a state line. If you do so via an interstate highway, there's a fairly good chance that the border crossing will be marked by the presence of two things. First, there will likely be an enormous sign featuring the state bird and flower and proclaiming something like this:

WELCOME TO NEW AMNESIA!

The Vegetative State

Rufus T. Firefly, Governor

Please drive consciously!

Second, a short distance beyond the sign there will be a welcome center of some kind, full of toilets, vending machines, and map displays, and typically decorated so as to display the qualities the state wants to show off to its visitors. Tony Horwitz, Pulitzer Prize-winning author of *Confederates in the Attic*, has pointed out that these welcome centers show a lot about a population's self-image, and further that they belie the widespread but inaccurate idea of a monolithic Southern culture. As Interstate 81 crosses the border between Virginia and Tennessee, for example, one can see on the Virginia side a great structure of brick and white wood, with latticed windows, gables, and a steep roof, all of it generally reminiscent of Colonial Williamsburg, suggesting that the Old Dominion's natives spend their days dipping candles or locking criminals in stocks. On the Tennessee side, by contrast, the building looks rough-hewn, apparently made of chinked logs surrounding a stone hearth and chimney, with quilts, rocking chairs, and other trappings of the frontier on display. Here the South is a land of log cabins, the home of Daniel Boone or Davy Crockett, a place full of humble folk seeking their fortunes in an untamed wilderness. In other words, Southerners may claim distinction from Northerners, but these interstate welcome centers show that not even Southerners can agree on what the South is really like.

But should you cross a state line on a smaller road, one maintained not by the federal government but by the state or county, you will see no such grand evidence of division. There may be a sign or two noting the presence of the border and explaining any changes in traffic laws, but for the most part, in this place the line's presence is seen as less significant. Why? Because fewer people cross it here.

In fact, unless a significant number of people cross a border in a particular place, the two states may not acknowledge the line at all. This is a purely practical consideration; as geographer H. J. de Blij puts it in *Human Geography: Culture, Society, and Space*, "Demarcating a lengthy boundary by any means at all is expensive, and it is hardly worth it in inhospitable mountains, vast deserts, frigid polar lands, or other places where there is virtually no human presence." The process of demarcation, therefore, is limited to those sections of border where the people on one side or both feel a need to announce the line's presence in a highly visible or even physical manner—a fence line, a wall, a series of lookout towers. If there's no one to see it, the show does not go on.

Indeed, as de Blij explains, those in the area may be the last to know about the border. Demarcation, when it occurs, is the third step that a boundary line goes through, following two more abstract processes:

> Imagine a frontier area about to be divided between two states. First, agreement is reached on the rough positioning of the border. Then the exact location is established through the process of **definition**, whereby a treaty-like, legal-sounding document is drawn up in which actual points in the landscape are described (or, where a straight-line boundary is involved, points of latitude and longitude). Next cartographers, using large-scale maps and referring to the boundary line as defined, put the boundary on the map in a process called **delimitation**.

A borderline, then, is originally no more than a dream, but it is eventually established to reflect the desires of both sides, or at least those of the more powerful party. It is crucial, however, to avoid the delirium of thinking that this line in any way reflects destiny; it is imposed on the area *by* human beings *for* human beings. There are no supernatural forces involved.

Knowing what a borderline is, however, tells us relatively little about what it's good for. It can be used as a line of defense, but that's impractical unless it lies along a natural boundary of some kind—a river or ridgeline, say—or unless its demarcation is enhanced to an unusual degree, such as in the Korean peninsula's Demilitarized Zone.

Mind you, a defensive border isn't always effective, as the German troops who blew around, over, and through France's Maginot Line in 1940 could attest, but if there is no defensive buildup along the border at all, invaders are going to see the boundary as a virtual welcome mat. Hence, thanks to Genghis Khan and the Golden Horde, we see the most impressive act of demarcation in human history: the Great Wall of China.

Nowadays there are relatively few borders that mark defensive positions in a military sense, but there are still a variety of reasons why the people on at least one side of the border might want to discourage crossings. And it will come as no shock to learn that the dividing lines on the map can reflect the dividing lines between people—the differences in such categories as religion, language, race, culture, economics, politics, ethnicity, class, or even sex. What may be startling, however, is how the act of drawing lines can reify those differences, turning a perception of difference into a factual one.

There is, for example, a part of the United States where the majority of the population shares a language, a religion, a culture, and an ethnicity (though minorities in all these categories are present). The members of this majority have similar political traditions, enjoy similar foods, and base their economies on similar activities, but they are nonetheless divided by a border, one that is arbitrary but also very real: the line between North Carolina and South Carolina.

To an outside observer, the differences between Carolinians may be all but invisible, and confusion is common. Back in the 1980s, for example, the Police were touring America and performed a show in Greensboro, North Carolina, for an audience of appreciative Tar Heels. At one point, lead singer Sting acknowledged the horn section, noting that one of the brass players was a local boy—from South Carolina. The Tar Heels quickly became less appreciative.

Despite their numerous similarities, residents of both states tend to view each other as inferior. South Carolinians take pride in the fact that their state is older, having ratified both the Articles of Confederation and the U.S. Constitution before its northern neighbor, while North Carolinians note their state's greater size and population. I have heard my fellow Tar Heels dismiss the other state as "Baja Carolina," as if it were a superfluous peninsula jutting off the mainland, and we have long taken a certain ironic pride in our state's tradition of rejecting pomposity, at least in comparison to its neighbors. ("A vale of humility between two mountains of conceit" is a description of North Carolina commonly attributed to Civil War-era governor Zebulon Vance, whose impatience with the hotheaded secessionists in South Carolina and Virginia may have inspired the metaphor.) And of course, there is no quicker way to start an argument between North and South than to claim superiority for the style of barbecue served in one's native territory . . . even though both use the same meat (pulled pork) and a vinegar-based sauce. The iconic South Carolina sauce, however, also contains mustard, which all of North Carolina eschews.[2]

Such differences between the Carolinas may seem to a large degree both artificial and arbitrary, depending as they do upon an imaginary line drawn across the map. But as we have already observed, all lines are imaginary, established only because human beings need them for purposes of division. It would be a mistake to pretend that merely because the line doesn't really exist, the differences on either side of it do not exist either.

NOWADAYS, THE BORDERS between states are largely fixed, to the point where changes in the flow of the Mississippi have left some land that was originally on the Tennessee bank on the Missouri bank and vice-versa. Despite this, human ingenuity is constantly at work, tinkering with those borders in hopes of making them better—more aligned with physical geography, perhaps, or more reflective of cultural distinctions, or maybe just less goofy-looking.[3]

---

2. We will ignore for the moment the equally contentious division between North Carolina's two regional varieties of barbecue, Lexington style (pork shoulder with a sweeter sauce based on tomatoes) and eastern style (pork pulled from the whole hog, with a tangier vinegar-and-red-pepper sauce).

3. My own suggestion for fixing several problems in the "goofy-looking" category would involve letting Maryland have Virginia's piece of the Delmarva Peninsula, while West Virginia absorbs Maryland's tenuous western counties (Garrett and Allegany) and Virginia takes the panhandle counties of Morgan, Berkeley, and Jefferson from West-by-God. It'll never happen, but it would make each state's borders look considerably less bizarre.

Nor does the neatness and roundness of our current figure of fifty states, a number which has now stood longer than any previous American total, persuade every observer that we should stand pat at fifty, particularly given the enormous differences in size, shape, and, in some opinions, distinction that can be seen among the states. Geographers from big square western states might well laugh at the fact that Connecticut and Rhode Island have two senators each, while those on either coast might well wonder if we really need *two* Dakotas (each of which has fewer people than Rhode Island, and which combined have less than half Connecticut's population).

A recent guest entry by Tim De Chant (creator of Per Square Mile, a blog about density) at *Scientific American*'s website examined the question of our current borders and found them wanting:

The borders separating the United States' 50 states are perfectly idiosyncratic, outmoded, even arbitrary. Obvious examples of their obsolescence abound: The New York metropolitan area has grown to encompass counties in four states. Kansas City is really two different municipalities divided by the Missouri-Kansas border. Chicago's Metra commuter rail stretches into neighboring Wisconsin, just as Washington, D.C.'s Metro trains and buses collect riders from Maryland and Virginia.

Rather than urging the redrawing of the states based on some aesthetic principle, however, De Chant reported that a group of researchers had taken a more scientific approach using data from the website WheresGeorge.com, which has been tracking the physical movement of individual bills of U.S. currency since 1998. What they discovered was that currency tended to circulate within twelve distinct regions, including a large one that incorporates the Midwestern states—basically Indiana, Illinois, Missouri, and every state north of them—and a tiny one that occupies a Delaware-sized chunk of ground around Augusta, Georgia. By far the eeriest feature of the Where's George map is that the entire western portion of the country is essentially one region, lying south and west of the Dakotas, and including Oklahoma, Texas, and Louisiana to boot. In fact, it's not unlike the maps commonly seen in field guides to distinguish the birds of the eastern and western United States—maps where the dividing line is commonly the 100th meridian, which runs fairly close to the western borders of the Dakotas. As De Chant points out, these new regional borders are unlikely to be realized, no matter how economically practical their layout may be, but the project does demonstrate one important element of today's borders: in the twenty-first century, a borderline is less often used to mark a line of military involvement than one of economic involvement.

The biggest and most interesting example of this new style of borderline can be found—for the moment, at least—strewn like vermicelli all across the face of Europe. Where once the continent's borders were set directly on the lines the ruling powers intended to defend against invaders, they are now more or less permeable to the citizens of those other lands, so long as those citizens bring money. The European Union is the name for this experiment in economic cooperation, and as of this writing, the experiment's success or failure remains in some doubt. The idea behind the E.U. was to allow each nation in Europe to maintain its autonomy in political, cultural, and linguistic matters, but to combine their economic powers behind a single currency—the euro—in order to better compete with such enormous markets as the U.S. and China. In practical terms, however, some of the less stable economic actors in Europe (e.g., Greece) have created problems for some of the more stable economies (e.g., Germany), suggesting that perhaps the E.U.'s borders are more permeable than prudence might dictate.

The execution of the European Union's plans might not be perfect, but the idea itself has merit. After all, one of the most successful economies of the last 200 years is one that combines the small economies of semi-autonomous states using a single national currency. Granted, the dollar is far from the only thing South Carolina and North Carolina have in common; they share a national government, a language, a climate, a culture, a majority religion, and an irritation that some people still confuse them with the Dakotas. None of this is true for neighboring E.U. members such as, say, France and Italy. In most cases, crossing a European border means entering an area with a new national language and/or religion, not to mention stepping over a line whose placement was at one time settled not with surveyors' tools, but at the point of a gun, or a sword, or in some cases even a sharp stick and a handful of gravel.

Suppose for a minute, then, that North and South Carolina were separated by more than an arbitrary line on a map. Imagine instead that Carolinians spoke two different languages, worshipped different gods (or the same god in different ways, which almost always produces even more distrust and hatred), and had even warred on each other[4] on several occasions over the last millennium or two. You can imagine, then, a certain amount of resistance to the idea that you and your neighbors should join together with the people across the border—yes, those same mustard-eating sandlappers your granddad gave a good whuppin' at the Battle of North Myrtle Beach back in '61—in a vast economic enterprise, particularly when there is not a strong central government giving order to that enterprise and demanding cooperation. Still, the fact that the Carolinas have managed to cooperate economically (even to the point of mutually supporting a single NFL team, the Panthers, whose home in Charlotte lies close to the border) suggests that Europe's attempt to combine forces can be successful.

On the other hand, it is perhaps worth noting that a situation similar to the E.U.'s also existed in the U.S. at one point: the post-Revolutionary period of the Articles of Confederation, when the states were so loath to give up any autonomy that the central government did not even have the power to levy taxes. That situation lasted for all of six years before the country abandoned the idea, but not by abandoning the established borders between the states. Instead, the fledgling nation created a more powerful federal government under the Constitution, a government strong enough to tax, to control interstate commerce, and eventually to unite even the most rebellious states under its sway.

The borderlines between the states remained on every map and in many Americans' minds, but after 1865, the lines were so weak they couldn't even stand up to the power of grammar. As historian Shelby Foote noted, before the Civil War, the noun "United States" was plural, but the Reconstructed Union was a decidedly singular institution. The

---

4. Probably over barbecue.

war made the states' borders so permeable that we have spent the past century and a half saying, without any hesitation at all, "The United States *is*."

And when you get right down to it, that fact tells you all you really need to know about borders. If we don't act as though a word is plural, it's not. Similarly, if we don't act as though there's a line between two places, they're not two places. Like the rules of grammar, borders exist only in our minds; we put them there to help us think about the geography that already exists, just as we impose grammar to give shape and order to the language that people are already speaking. The lines around a territory don't show us what is there, but rather how people behave there.

We say there is a border between territories, but no noun, no actual thing, is really present—only an action, or a state of being. A verb. The territories *border* each other. But even then, the grammar isn't entirely correct; the territories aren't doing any bordering at all.

The real subject of that verb is *we*.

State of the Union

American pie—Physical and political—West-running lines—London Company calling—The landless states—A house divided—"He was James K. Polk, Napoleon of the Stump"—The Great Compromiser and the other guy—Boundary manipulation

> *We're Americans, with a capital A, huh? You know what that means? Do ya? That means that our forefathers were kicked out of every decent country in the world. We are the wretched refuse. We're the underdog. We're mutts!*
> —John Winger (Bill Murray), Stripes

WHAT MAKES US America?

Straight lines.

Every one of the forty-nine mainland states has at least one straight border. Colorado and Utah have nothing *but* straight borders, and the slight wavers in Wyoming's northern boundary with Montana are so minor that most observers don't know the state isn't a perfect rectangle. Even Hawaii, shaped by the sea, separates its counties with straight lines drawn invisibly between the islands.

The nations of Old Europe, by contrast, do not use rulers to mark their home territory. Instead, they rely on rivers, mountain ranges, or meandering poplar-lined drives in order to divide the French from the Spanish, the Austrian from the Italian, the German from the Swiss. Europeans lived in Europe long before the rise of nation-states, so they were content, once the nation-building urge had come upon them, to let their physical geography determine their political landscape. Granted, once the boundaries were drawn, there was ample conflict over which irregularly shaped bit of land ought to be included on which side of the irregular line, but so far as I know, questions of European nationality have rarely if ever been settled with the tools of Euclid.

America, however, was divided up by explorers and entrepreneurs, men who put property ahead of geography, particularly when it came to turning the natives' geography into their own property. When a king or a soldier or a businessman claimed a bit of New World territory, it was usually territory where few white people yet lived. Existing nations didn't especially care whether their new territories' borders made geographic sense, since no sensible person would want to *live* in such an intractable wilderness. What mattered was the presence of exploitable resources within those borders. As a result, the simplicity of the straight line, often extending from a coastal point into the infinity of the interior, became a popular choice for colonial borders. Those borders and the slices carved by a knife into a pie are not fundamentally dissimilar.

The greatest pie-slicer in European history, however, was neither a pastry chef nor a surveyor, but rather a pope. Alexander VI, born Rodrigo Borgia, made his cut in his 1493 bull "Inter caetera divinae," hoping to settle the territorial disputes of the two major exploratory powers of the day, the Portuguese and the Spanish. Lisbon had spent decades seeking routes around Africa into the Indian Ocean, but was also more than willing to jockey with Madrid for new territories on the far side of the Atlantic. (Not until 1497 did the Italian Amerigo Vespucci, exploring for Portugal, recognize these territories as a new continent, an insight for which the Spanish rulers, of all people, gave him a lifetime appointment.) Before long, Spain would claim Argentina, the Yucatan, Mexico, and Panama, though for sheer hubris, nothing would ever top Balboa, who set his foot in the Pacific Ocean in 1513 and claimed all the lands bordering it.

In anticipation of the competing claims on all these areas, the pontiff chose not to make a detailed survey of the terrain features or cultural divisions among the natives; instead, from thousands of miles away, he simply took a straight-edge to the map, drawing a north-south line lying 100 leagues to the west of the Azores and Cape Verde

Islands. A number of as-yet-undiscovered lands were thus assigned to the two kingdoms, with the Spanish, among whose number the Pope included himself, getting the better end of the deal: the right to all non-Christian lands west of the line. Portugal was granted the non-Christian lands to the east. Alas, this undeniably bold attempt to settle the dispute failed, but its failure is instructive in several ways.

First, this is a textbook case of confusing two distinct types of geography. Physical geography (sometimes called "natural geography") is the study of our planet's land, water, air, natural resources, and life-forms, as well as the processes (erosion, flooding, volcanism, etc.) that affect them. It is often a descriptive science, one which involves taking careful stock of what is actually present in the real world, and one where connections to "hard" sciences such as geology and hydrology are numerous. By contrast, political geography (sometimes called "human geography") is a field closer to the "soft" science of sociology, one concerned with asking people questions, particularly questions about what can be done with the things we find in the world (and the not inconsiderable issue of who gets to do it). It deals not so much with the space surrounding people as with the ways in which human beings organize and understand that space.[1]

The two forms of geography may seem at odds, but they are undeniably linked; as H. J. de Blij puts it in *Human Geography*, "[I]t often is difficult to discuss human geography without also referring to the physical stage on which the human drama is being played out." It would be a mistake, however, to give stage directions to a piece of scenery, or to tell an actor, "Stand here and look orange until Scene 3." Treating a physical location as a political one, or vice-versa, is a similar mistake. Indeed, until the physical geography of a place is known at a fairly detailed level, any attempt to apply the tools of political geography will lead to inconvenience at best and open conflict at the worst. If

1. An analogy that may be useful here was provided for me some years ago by Daniel Patterson, professor of folklore at the University of North Carolina. In discussing the noteworthy departures from fact in one folksong, "The Ballad of Gregorio Cortez," Dr. Patterson said, "History tells you what happened; folklore tells you how people *feel* about what happened." If we view physical geography as the study of what is there, and political geography as the study of how people think and feel about what is there, perhaps we're not too far off the mark.

nothing else, people who do not know a place (such as those in another hemisphere) will feel very differently about it than those who do (such as those who are exploring it in hopes of living in it and/or using its resources). Pope Alexander's line was a bold stroke, yes, but it was a philosophical failure, a collision between theory and practice, a confusion of the physical and political (or the natural and human) forms of the discipline.

CONFUSION ASIDE, ALEXANDER'S second and more practical problem was that the two disputing parties were not satisfied by his pie-slicing. The use of a line wasn't a problem, but its placement infuriated the Portuguese, who felt there was too little land on their side. They were somewhat placated, however, by the 1494 Treaty of Tordesillas, which moved the line 270 leagues farther west. They were even more placated in 1500, when Pedro Cabral, blown off his planned course around the Cape of Good Hope, raised the Portuguese flag over a vast new territory on the proper side of the line: Brazil.

But those more keenly aware of philosophy than Alexander will no doubt recognize that he had a third problem, one which relates to the logical fallacy known as the False Dichotomy. Yes, the two major naval powers of the day had been satiated for the moment, but the Pope had not recognized any other nation's designs on the New World. The French, Dutch, Swedish, and English were simply left out of his considerations altogether, and none of them wanted to be left without a slice of such an enormous, rich, and appetizing pie. Henry VII of England reached for his slice first, ignoring the Pope's jurisdiction (as his son would later do in a much more pointed and universal manner) and sending John Cabot to explore the northern reaches of America. Cabot, an Italian who originally went by the name Zuan Chabotto, took two attempts to reach the far shore of the Atlantic in 1497, but the records of his voyages are so scanty that no certainty about the location is possible. Newfoundland's Cape Bonavista is officially recognized by both Canada and the UK as the place where Cabot made landfall, raised both the Venetian and Papal flags, and claimed the new land in Henry's name before returning to England. A few years later, Cabot and his third expedition to America would vanish entirely.

What King Henry thought about having Pope Alexander's flag raised over his new-claimed territory is unrecorded by history, but it is interesting to note that the English largely eschewed the idea of an Alexandrian north-south boundary line when it came time to divide their holdings in what would eventually become the United States. Instead, they and the people who settled those holdings preferred their own cartographic innovation: the infinite west-running line.

Even three centuries after Cabot's landfall, such lines ran from the Atlantic shore along the borders of territories from Georgia to New England, stretching toward an indeterminate ending somewhere in mid-continent, where white men's property laws were still considered unimportant (or at least unenforceable). Eventually, however, mapmakers put an end to such lines—quite literally—and sealed up the western borders of the Atlantic states so as to create new territories beyond them.

The process of settling the termination of those borders was a sticky one, but it gets surprisingly little consideration in most American history classes—at least in those classes not taught by Matthew Boesen. A graduate of Yale and the University of Virginia now on the faculty at Woodberry Forest School, Boesen has made a special study of Anglo-American constitutional history (particularly the Massachusetts Constitution of 1780, on which he wrote his doctoral dissertation), and he is firmly of the opinion that colonial boundaries were a considerable stumbling block in America's early attempt to set up a government.

"The earliest colonies were granted by the king as royal charters: gifts of lands to his favorites," he explains. "The charters were all written after the basic Atlantic Coast was known, but the interior was still a mystery. And Virginia was the first and most significant charter."

The colony of Virginia had been established in the days of Queen Elizabeth I by Sir Walter Raleigh, but its exact parameters were not set until the reign of her successor, James I. Like Pope Alexander, King James did his pie-slicing from far away, and like Pope Alexander, he ended up satisfying nobody. The Virginia Company of London (known commonly as the London Company) was originally granted rights between Cape Fear, North Carolina, and Long Island Sound, but soon after its first serious attempt at settlement, in Jamestown, Virginia, in

1607, its charter was adjusted, and the adjustment was significant. Because the new charter established that the company's claims extended "from sea to sea," Virginia's territory was suddenly spread all the way to the Pacific, covering over half the North American continent. The southern border now ran from Cape Fear to California, while the northern border went northwest from the New Jersey coast to the shores of Alaska. With the extension of a single pair of lines, Virginia now had claims to land that would eventually be part of every state in the Union (except Florida, Louisiana, Hawaii, and the New England states) plus a considerable chunk of Canada. It was what Boesen calls, with the technical precision of a trained historian, "one big-ass land grant."

Over the next century or so, England carved its colonial territories in America primarily out of that big-ass land grant, but not exclusively. Some colonies whose borders did not extend into the indefinite lands of the west were considered "landless," though their fixed boundaries did not prevent them from making territorial claims outside those boundaries. As Boesen explains, "Some colonies were clearly defined on four sides. You knew all the boundaries of Connecticut in the 1660s. It was the same rectangle it is today, but it did claim its 'western reserve.'" That reserve included a chunk of what is now Ohio (which is how Cleveland's Western Reserve University got its name), plus territory in modern-day Indiana, Michigan, and Illinois. Massachusetts' western border clearly abutted New York, but that didn't stop the Bay State from staking claims to land in Michigan and Wisconsin, or for that matter the majority of Maine.

Other colonies—the "landed" ones—had open-ended grants, most of which suggested that their northern and southern boundaries, whatever they might be, extended at least to the Mississippi River. North Carolina claimed for itself what is now Tennessee, while South Carolina asserted its right to a narrow strip of land running across northern Georgia, Alabama, and Mississippi. New York boldly claimed all of Michigan, Ohio, and Indiana, plus most of Kentucky, central Tennessee, and what would eventually become West Virginia. (The Empire State was already in possession of Vermont.) And of course Virginia merely sat, smiling quietly, holding its big-ass claims on all of the above and more.

This was the situation confronted by the new-minted United States in 1776: a classic conflict between the realities of physical geography and the aspirations of political geographers. It was all very well and good to declare independence from the British, but the British crown had enjoyed the luxury of ignoring the competing claims of the various colonies until it was good and ready to settle them. If those colonies were to form a nation together, however, it was crucial that each one know exactly what form that nation would take and who would own which parts of it.

The disputes between states with open-ended land claims and those without, not to mention those with conflicting claims, "almost broke the country," according to Boesen. "In the 1770s and 1780s, the smaller landless states—Maryland, Delaware, Connecticut—said 'We cannot become a nation of equals if we allow these landed states to keep their land claims; the big ones will sell the land to settlers and create a revenue stream we won't have. Then they'll lower their taxes, and we'll lose our citizens by migration. We'll *begin* as equals, but landless states will be at a competitive disadvantage.'" Moreover, the landless states had a powerful legal argument: all of these land claims were based on grants from the British throne, an authority which the fledgling United States no longer recognized.

The disagreement came to a head when the new nation attempted to establish a national government under the Articles of Confederation. "At that point, Maryland said, 'We're not going to ratify it until the landed states give up their claims,'" Boesen explains. "In 1781, the last landed state, Virginia, gave up its claim and Maryland ratified the Articles." This was by no means the final act of cession among the original states—Virginia held onto its claims north of the Ohio River until 1784, and both Connecticut and Georgia still had claims in the west into the nineteenth century—but the precedent had been established: the borders in the west would be drawn up not by the interested parties in the various states, but by the national government.

In Boesen's opinion, this agreement was the key to creating a unified nation out of a group of squabbling colonies, more important than paper money, or credibility in the international scene, or any other issues. Because the people of the time saw themselves as citizens of states—"Massachusetts is my country," as John Adams put it—and not as Americans, erasing western land claims was a crucial element in putting each state on an equal footing. It also left the national government in a position to establish what would be done with the land between the old colonial borders and the Mississippi.

The dividing of that land into what Boesen labels the Big Ten and SEC sections of the country was accomplished through the three Northwest Ordinances of 1784, 1785, and 1787. These laws established methods for surveying property, governing territories, and bringing new states into the Union, methods that were used until after the Civil War. They were also, according to Boesen, "the most important and last thing the Articles of Confederation actually did." The third Northwest Ordinance went into law on July 13; the Constitutional Convention had already been in session for two months, and it would submit the final draft of the new document to the delegates for signing on the seventeenth of September.

The line dividing America's colonial history from its national history was a decision to stop squabbling over boundaries; perhaps it's fitting, or perhaps ironic, that the boundary between our first and second national governments was a set of laws that established how boundaries ought to be drawn.

THE GRADUAL CESSION of the Thirteen Colonies' western claims was a significant moment in American history, but it was far from the only time that lines played a major role in the human geography of our nation. For many years after the Northwest Ordinances were enacted, a pair of boundaries within the U.S. served as both a practical means of demarcation and one of the most pointed symbols of division ever, one celebrated by everything from folksongs to *Huckleberry Finn* to the legend of Harriet Tubman: the line between slavery and freedom.

There were actually two important boundaries for American slavery, one natural and one purely man-made. The Ohio River's southern bank was slave territory, while the free states of Ohio, Indiana, and Illinois lay on the north side. In slave spirituals, references to the River Jordan are frequent, typically as the border between the side of miserable toil and the side of the Promised Land; you don't have to be a Freudian to see the geographic symbolism there. The human-created Mason–Dixon line, meanwhile, divided free Pennsylvania from the slave states of Virginia (later West Virginia) and Maryland, though that division would become more complicated as time went on. Still, the combination of the Ohio and the Mason–Dixon effectively divided the nation, slave and free, from the Delaware Bay west to the Mississippi River.

But in 1803, the young U.S. of A. acquired its first territory beyond the Mississippi, an act that both doubled the size of the country and served to further divide it. The Louisiana Purchase, as well as the later acquisitions of territory stretching from Texas to California to Puget Sound, left the nation with a host of new questions to answer, and as Boesen puts it, "The question of how to draw the boundaries out west was the question that split the country."

In the early years of the nineteenth century, there was relatively little demand for the abolition of slavery, even in the north.[2] Nor was it common in those days for a northern politician to demand that the southern states abandon their "peculiar institution." The existence of southern slavery may not have been popular, but it was generally accepted.

What most northerners objected to was the *spread* of slavery. Boesen notes that in early 1861, Abraham Lincoln, despite his later reputation as the Great Emancipator, publicly supported a Constitutional amendment that would have protected slavery where it was, while ensuring that the spread of it stopped. (He was also notoriously hesitant to take steps to free slaves after his election to the presidency. Not until he saw a strategic wartime advantage in emancipation did he declare an end to slavery, and even then he ended it only in the states that were in rebellion.) The first decades of the nineteenth century were a period when the opposition to slavery was comparatively muted. In these years lines were drawn, erased, and re-drawn in order to maintain the precarious balance of interests between North and South—and in the end, the balance was upset because no line was drawn at all.

2. The slaves themselves, of course, were rarely asked their opinion.

Boesen sets the scene: "After the Louisiana Purchase, states are usually added to the Union in pairs, so that the South can have parity in the Senate. The House is flowing increasingly to the North due to population changes. By 1819, eleven southern and eleven northern states exist." This was the moment when the question of slavery's spread came to a head, as the nation proposed to admit a new state: Missouri, which lay entirely on the far side of the Mississippi River. "West of the Mississippi," says Boesen, "there were no benchmarks, no Northwest Ordinances, no rules in place."

The Missouri Compromise was the first attempt to establish such a rule, and it used two familiar mechanisms: the first was the continuation of the paired-admission strategy the nation had been using for years, allowing the admission of the free state of Maine in 1820 to balance the admission of Missouri in 1821. The second mechanism had an even longer history in American political geography: a west-running line. As proposed by Illinois Senator Jesse B. Thomas, Missouri would be admitted, but afterward no new slave states would be permitted north of its southern border—the parallel at 36° 30′—except the state of Missouri itself. Unable to stop the spread of slavery, the North was at least able to contain it, though of course it did nothing to bring emancipation to those already enslaved. All it did was stave off the inevitable conflict over the Peculiar Institution.

"The line created a rhetorical ceasefire," Boesen summarizes. "It calmed tensions." For two decades, at least, it did just that, and moreover even indicated where the next slave state would be: just south of the borderline, in Arkansas, which was admitted in 1836, with its free-state counterpart, Michigan, joining up a year later. A clear and decisive tool had been needed in order to divide the unorganized frontier into manageable political units, and Thomas's line had served that purpose—for the moment.

As he gets to this part of his story, Boesen begins warming up a bit; his gaze grows more intense, the pace of his speech more rapid. There's something about this historical period that grabs him, and he's not alone. We're preparing to launch into the story of James K. Polk.

Among historians of the American presidency, Polk is a figure of no small fascination. Boesen claims that he is often ranked fifth on the list of greatest presidents, with Lincoln and Washington duking it out for the top spot and some combination of FDR, Thomas Jefferson, and Teddy Roosevelt fighting for the bronze. In truth, this may be something of an exaggeration on Boesen's part, as Polk seems more often to be jockeying for a ranking of somewhere between 8th and 12th, depending on the poll. Somehow, though, Polk almost always manages to slip into the top quartile and often into the top ten, up where most of his competitors' faces appear on U.S. currency. How has a faceless one-termer managed this?

Well, it helps that his is a Cinderella story about a kid out of nowhere—or Nashville, more accurately—who ended up as a surprise candidate for the White House. A graduate of the University of North Carolina, a former Speaker of the House, and the recent governor of Tennessee, Polk was tapped by the 1844 Democratic National Convention as a compromise candidate after Martin Van Buren failed to draw sufficient support on the first eight ballots. Unequivocal in his belief that the United States should expand from sea to sea, absorbing Texas, the southwest, the Oregon Territory, and anything else it could get its hands on, Polk united the Democrats behind him by promising to serve only one term, and in November he defeated Kentucky's Henry Clay—one of the brokers of the Missouri Compromise—to become the eleventh president. In 1845, he oversaw the formal annexation of the former Republic of Texas, but this would not be enough to satisfy expansionists, particularly those favoring slavery. The ongoing negotiations to obtain the Oregon Territory from Great Britain were another issue of concern for expansionists, as any states carved out of it would almost certainly be free; cash crops like cotton, tobacco, and indigo simply wouldn't grow in the Pacific Northwest's climate.

"Then comes the Mexican War of 1846," says Boesen, practically rubbing his hands in anticipation of discussing a conflict full of naked ambition, trickery, and no small amount of irony—a historian's dream. "It's a war based on a conflicting land claim. Texas has seceded from Mexico, saying its southern border is the Rio Grande, but Mexico says the Nueces River is the border. Polk steps in, orders troops into the disputed area, and gets Mexico to start shooting. After eleven Americans die, Polk says American blood has been spilled on American soil, and Congress declares war.

"In other words," Boesen summarizes, "a slave-owning president basically manufactures a war with Mexico which we win handily. We acquire a big chunk of southwestern territory. And in 1848, somebody asks 'Is this slave or free?'"

The obvious answer would seem to be to look at the line established in 1820, but as Boesen points out, that wouldn't work: "The issue is that the Missouri Compromise referred only to land obtained from France and Spain—not from Mexico." Thus, the Treaty of Guadalupe Hidalgo, which ended the Mexican War, not only enlarged the U.S. yet again, adding what would become California, Nevada, and Utah, as well as parts of Arizona, New Mexico, Colorado, and Wyoming, but also threw the nation back into conflict over the expansion of slavery.

James K. Polk, meanwhile, had been as good as his word: he had taken the Southwest from Mexico, bought Oregon off the British, built an independent treasury, and kept his promise not to seek a second term. When he stepped down in March of 1849, replaced by Mexican War hero Zachary Taylor, he left the U.S. a transformed nation—one that stretched from the Atlantic to the Pacific, and from San Diego Harbor to the 49th parallel. Moreover, it was now populated by citizens with vast new territories to settle, by soldiers who had known the heat of battle first-hand, and by slaves who might now be sold off to even more distant lands. Whatever your opinion about the wisdom or the morality of his actions, you cannot deny Polk's impact on the United States.

He would be dead of cholera a hundred days after leaving the White House.

Back in Washington, however, the issue of what to do with all this new territory was creating just as much heat as the question of what to with Louisiana had created back before the Missouri Compromise, and its solution evaded Congress, despite various suggestions on how to settle the matter. Four possibilities dominated the discussion:

One: declare slavery illegal throughout the whole area. It had the advantage of matching up with the nation's professed beliefs in human liberty, but it was unlikely to earn the approval of the slave states.

Two: declare slavery legal throughout the whole area. South Carolina Senator John C. Calhoun offered a Constitutional argument for this position, saying the Fifth Amendment's protection against seizure of property without due process should permit property—i.e., people—to be kept even in the new territories. Other slave-state natives favored this option, unsurprisingly, but free states viewed it in roughly the same way the slave states viewed Option One.

Three: extend the Missouri Compromise line to the Pacific. This would offer some benefits to both sides and frustrate both sides in roughly equal measure, as well as harkening back to the days when the two factions could act in the best interest of the nation as a whole. And heck, it had worked before, right?

Four: let the people living in the new territory decide. This option was known as "popular sovereignty," a phrase that seems entirely reasonable and in complete accord with democratic principles (if you ignore the fact that the only people who could vote were white men). Blessed with an appealing name and a politically defensible appearance, popular sovereignty would end up carrying the day—and would eventually lead to the bloodiest conflict in American history.

As Boesen puts it, the central problem was abandoning the long-established idea of a border between slave states and free states. "They opted NOT to draw a line in 1850, which had worked well in 1820. And that led to the ultimate complications preceding the Civil War."

HOW DID THE LACK of a boundary line between slave states and free states lead to civil war? Not smoothly. President Taylor, born in Orange County, Virginia, was himself a slaveholder, but he surprised everyone by favoring Option One above, declaring that all the new territories should be free. Before the American people could wrap their heads around this, however, Taylor suddenly fell ill and died on July 9, 1850.[3]

His successor, Millard Fillmore, was a great deal more inclined to compromise on the issue of slavery, which allowed Henry Clay (dubbed

---

3. The combination of cherries and milk that Taylor supposedly consumed just before he died acquired a certain negative reputation as a result, but the cause of death remains unknown, despite ample speculation as to cholera, typhoid, gastroenteritis, and even assassination by arsenic poisoning.

"The Great Compromiser" by sympathetic historians) and Stephen Douglas (dubbed "One of the candidates for the Biggest Fuck-Up in American History" by Matt Boesen) to offer a series of proposals for settling the issue of how to divide the nation's new territories. By September, it was clear that the ultimate winner was Option Four: popular sovereignty.

The Compromise of 1850, as the Clay/Douglas proposals became known, included the admission to the Union of California, a free state without a corresponding slave state. The rest of the land ceded by Mexico was divided into the Utah Territory to the north and the New Mexico Territory to the south, with both organized on the principle of popular sovereignty; when their populations grew large enough, they would vote on the issue of slavery. The exact nature of the territories' landscape was still largely unknown to those in Washington, who would certainly never see cash crops being grown in either place, but for a while, at least, the appeal to popular sovereignty seemed a resolution just as good as the line from 1820 had been. That line, however, had been drawn without Stephen Douglas on hand. In 1850, the nation wasn't so lucky.

Boesen shakes his head and tells the story. "Douglas is a senator from Illinois who wants to develop the west and have Illinois be the hub of the transcontinental railroad. The question is where to build it, and this lands him in the slave controversy. There are basically four possible routes, two ending in Chicago: Seattle to Chicago, San Francisco to Chicago, San Francisco to St. Louis, and Southern California to St. Louis. The southerners favor the latter option. Douglas works with the southerners in order to get his preferred option—San Francisco to Chicago—but in return for their votes, the southerners demand he repeal the ban on slavery in the territories." To achieve his ends, Douglas pushed through an 1854 law that effectively repealed the Missouri Compromise: the controversial Kansas-Nebraska Act, which allowed the residents of the two eponymous new states to vote on slavery, despite their lying well north of the 36° 30' line. Northerners were infuriated, considering the Act a violation of a long-standing agreement.

The increasingly unclear borderline between slave and free territory was starting to be a problem, and the presence of other lines wasn't doing much to help. The state line between Missouri and Kansas proved particularly troublesome. "People in Missouri live right next to Kansas and flood over the border," Boesen says. "They discover great farmland—that never happened in New Mexico and Utah—so now they decide it's time to out-populate the other side." A war of immigration began, with settlers in both the pro-slavery and anti-slavery camps heading into the grasslands of Kansas in hopes of influencing the population's voting. Others opted to remain in Missouri, but were more than willing to cross the border temporarily in order to cast votes in any elections that might interest them. With the very presence of a person in Kansas being tantamount to a statement on the nature of slavery in the territories, it was almost inevitable that the territory would soon be known as "Bleeding Kansas." Abolitionist John Brown would go on to far greater fame in Harper's Ferry, Virginia, three years later, but in 1856 he and his followers struck a first blow against slavery in Kansas, avenging an attack on free-soilers by hacking five pro-slavery settlers to death with broadswords. One of Brown's sons would shortly be killed in a retaliatory attack, and the blood would continue to flow for years.

"Popular sovereignty leads to unprecedented violence," says Boesen. "They've been yelling since before 1820, but now popular sovereignty—the act of *not* drawing the line—is leading to open conflict. Kansas is the tinder that gets going, and from there, there's no lull, just escalating tension." That tension would of course reach its peak at Fort Sumter in the spring of 1861, and over half a million Americans would die as a result.

Boesen, more than many, appreciates the irony that the placement of lines on a map—a theoretical construction of geography—can result in very real lines of soldiers fighting over them. "Polk, a pro-slavery president, tries to manipulate boundaries—mainly the southern border of Texas—which leads to war. The war leads to an attempt to eliminate a boundary between slave and free. And that decision to abandon boundaries leads to war."

It's easy to laugh about the foolishness of placing a border here or there, particularly when you're chasing birds that give no thought to them whatsoever, but that's a luxury reserved for creatures who deal only in natural geography. For those of us who have to deal with human geography as well, it's important to recognize that a borderline is a geographic tool. It's a tool that can help you carve out a compromise, but it's also one that can take you to the extremes of frustration, or sometimes, if you're lucky, the extremes of satisfaction. It's not always the best tool for a given job, but there are jobs for which it is highly useful. And if you don't use it for those jobs, there's a very good chance that someone will try to do them with some other tool. Badly.

Driver's Education

North of Calvander—Anticipation—It is wrong—"The map is not the territory"—As above, so below—Under the sea—Ocean views—I am a pale shadow—The line of descent

> *Writing is like driving at night in the fog. You can only see as far as your headlights, but you can make the whole trip that way.*
> —E. L. Doctorow

WE WERE SOMEWHERE north of Carrboro, north of Calvander, even, when Dad pulled the car to the side of the road, set the handbrake, and turned off the ignition. "Forget everything you've learned," he said. "I'm going to teach you how to drive."

Part of me wanted to protest. I had, after all, just earned my North Carolina driver's license. I had finished both my classroom instruction and behind-the-wheel instruction with flying colors several months before, and not thirty minutes earlier I had earned a perfect score on the driving test.

Dad, however, was not about to let the N.C. Department of Motor Vehicles tell him who was or was not capable of driving his car. The car in this case was a light blue 1974 Volvo sedan whose fuel injection system had never entirely satisfied him. It spent considerably more time in the shop than he felt a relatively new car ought to, which was perhaps one reason he usually let Mom drive it, preferring, as he had for many years, to sit behind the wheel of whichever Oldsmobile he had bought from his fraternity brother in Lexington.

The Olds wouldn't do the job today, however, because Dad's purpose was not merely to test me on my existing automotive knowledge, but to teach me something altogether new: how to use a stick shift. When I got my driver's license in 1979, American manufacturers had been putting automatic transmissions into cars for over twenty years. (Europeans were and remain less enthusiastic about automatics; nearly eighty percent of the cars sold in Europe in 2006 were manual-drive vehicles.) Oldsmobile, like other General Motors imprints, had been one of the leaders in introducing automatic transmissions, starting with the "Hydra-Matic" transmission in 1948, and over the years Dad's brand loyalty had ensured that at least one of the vehicles in our driveway would be an automatic. Knowing this, I had vaguely supposed that whenever I needed a car, the other drivers in the house would rearrange their plans so that I would be able to use the Olds. It had certainly seemed to me like the simplest solution to the problem.

My father, however, defined "simple" rather differently. Like many sixteen-year-olds, I considered simplicity whatever required the least effort on my part; Dad saw it as whatever caused the fewest people the fewest problems. As a result of this definitional argument, I now found myself on a country road in the middle of Orange County, preparing to ensure that I knew how to operate whatever car might be available for me to use.

In a way, this lesson was a microcosm of the philosophy that my father has always held where driving is concerned: anticipate. Instead of focusing solely on what you see around you, consider as well those things that may not have happened yet. As you approach that overpass on the interstate, consider the chance that you may encounter a truck seeking to merge on the far side. As you pull up behind a car at a stoplight, consider the chance that it might roll back slightly as it begins its forward motion. And as you make your way down the road, consider the chance that you may have to pull off it quickly if the guy in front of you slams on his brakes.

The lessons my father has imparted to me regarding driving are multitudinous indeed, but in many ways, those two skills—how to manage a stick shift, and how to anticipate possible problems—have been the most important. Indeed, they have led me to learn a few other things on my own, some of them with ramifications that lie far outside the realms of traffic law or automotive safety.

For example, seven years after I learned to handle a manual transmission, Kelly and I got married. We honeymooned in England, where the cost of renting an automatic was prohibitive, and I was thus presented with a choice. I could do all the driving for the next two weeks, having both long familiarity with a clutch and some experience driving on British roads; the alternative was teaching Kelly to drive a stick. With her left hand. On the unfamiliar side of the road. My well-honed skills in anticipation were useful in making this choice, as I was able to anticipate the likely result of spending our honeymoon in such a teacher-student relationship: divorce.

I put 2300 miles on our rental car.

The benefit of all this driving—from London to Windsor to Cambridge to Suffolk to Boston to Manchester to the Lake District to Oban to Skye and back—was that I got very comfortable operating a right-hand drive car on the left side of the highway. And that comfort led to my next important lesson: how to view the lines on the road.

When you first take a driver's ed class, the lines in the middle of the road have a power not unlike the lines on your first sheets of notebook paper, which tell you when you've made the stem on your lower-case *d* too short, so it looks like a lower-case *a*, or when your sentence is starting to rise off the bottom line like a kite in a high March wind. These, like the ones in the road, are guidelines—lines that exist in order to tell you You're Doing It Wrong.

But once you've spent some time behind the wheel in the UK, you start to realize that there is no wrong way to drive—there is only an *unsafe* way. If everyone else on the road is driving on the right side of the yellow stripe, driving on the left side is the unsafe way. By contrast, when you visit this Sceptred Isle, everyone else is going to be driving on the left, so for safety's sake you'd better do likewise.

The problem, of course, is that long practice makes it very easy for even well-educated people to ignore the foundations of what they practice. Many of us learn how to do something in a particular way and assume it's the best way; if we're not careful, we can begin to think it's the only way. We fail to consider the possibility that our method may have been presented to us because it's the easiest one to learn, or the easiest one to teach, or the one that our teacher happens to like best. It may have been taught to us in order to preserve a tradition, or to shake up a boring syllabus, or simply out of sheer inertia. But the lesson you learn when you spend time driving on the "wrong" side of the road is that we must never make the mistake of confusing a practical standard with a law of nature, or even worse, with a moral principle.

In other words, because of my father's driving lessons, I've learned to appreciate the difference between doing something wrong and doing something wrong—that is, between doing something bad and doing something badly.

ON MY CLASSROOM WALL is a world map, and it's one that has occasioned commentary from a number of viewers because, as they put it, "It looks *wrong.*" It's this—the Peters Projection World Map:

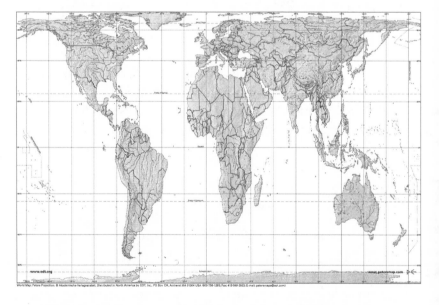

And of course, it IS wrong. Deeply wrong. Just not for the reasons most of them think.

The Peters Projection World Map, like any other map, is wrong because it's a two-dimensional image of a three-dimensional object: the planet Earth. Though you can create a 3D map of the world—in other words, a globe—it's not always the most useful or portable means of determining location. A flat map is much more convenient for most purposes (and a damn sight easier to fold up in a glove compartment), but you can't make a flat map of a more or less spherical planet without distorting something—either the shape of the continents or the size of them or both.

The most familiar type of flat map, the Mercator projection, was created in the sixteenth century for a very straightforward purpose: navigation. The map's lines of latitude cross the lines of longitude at right angles, meaning that the direction on the map is the same as the direction on the planet; if you're sailing due west and you turn ninety degrees right, you'll be going due north; turn another ninety degrees right and you'll be heading due east. As geographer H. J. de Blij puts it, "Thus the Mercator projection enabled navigators to maintain an accurate course at sea simply by adhering to compass directions and plotting straight lines."

Unfortunately, the practical advantages of the Mercator projection—showing directions clearly, as well as accurately reflecting the shapes of the landmasses it delineates—are accompanied by unintended consequences. For one thing, though the shapes of the various continents and islands are preserved, their sizes are badly distorted, which is why the island of Greenland looks far larger than the continent of Australia despite being less than one-third as big: landmasses close to the poles appear expanded in size, while those close to the equator appear to have shrunk proportionately. As a result, certain places on the globe look bigger (and therefore more important) than they really are, while others appear smaller (and therefore less significant). And since the bigger places include northern Europe and North America, while the smaller places include Africa, India, and Latin America, you can understand why a person of African, Asian, or Hispanic origin might view the use of the Mercator projection as a political decision, not just a cartographic one.

That's one reason I display the Peters Projection, which preserves size at the expense of shape. Anything near the poles appears flattened out horizontally, while anything near the equator is stretched vertically. The landmasses look a bit odd, but you can tell at a glance that Australia is a continent and Greenland only a big island, and that Europe is a tiny place (not quite 4 million square miles) in comparison to the massive expanse of Africa (nearly 12 million). With its neatly perpendicular lines, the Peters Projection even preserves the navigational utility of the Mercator. At a fundamental level, however, the Peters Projection is still wrong. Not only does it distort the shape of every landmass it shows, but its lines of longitude do not behave like the ones on the globe; instead of meeting at the poles, they run parallel to one another from top to bottom, suggesting that the world is not spherical at all, but shaped like a can of baked beans.

Why is it on my wall, then? Because it helps the viewer to remember that, in the words of philosopher Alfred Korzybski, "The map is not the territory." As Korzybski's predecessors agreed, from Plato to Kant, human beings have only limited ways of understanding the world around us; we can know only what our senses tell us, and both our sensory apparatus and the brain where all sensory information is processed can be mistaken. In order to prevent our senses and our brains from leading us astray, we devise tools to make our senses more acute and our understanding more complete, but no matter how many microscopes we build or how many thought experiments we devise, the world we perceive is perceived only indirectly. In other words, a map is a useful tool for understanding reality, but it is only a human tool, not the reality itself. The lines of the Peters Projection are no more right or wrong than the lines of any other flat map, or for that matter the lines on a British road. They only seem right or wrong to people who don't know how to use them.

As TOOLS GO, the line on the map has proven hugely useful throughout human history, but in fact, it's no more correct to say that borders are lines than it is to claim that territories are maps. Even when they're straight and seemingly linear, borders do not extend over the surface of the globe; they go up, and they go down as well. In truth, the boundary between two regions is a vast vertical plane, one that separates not only the surface territory on either side, but two things not on the surface: the air above it and the earth below it.

Throughout most of human history, the latter was far more important than the former, and though in recent years the air has become a battlefield just like the surface, both air and land conflicts are often concerned with what lies below the surface. As a result, boundaries must be carefully drawn even underground. In southeastern Missouri, for example, mining was long the foundation of the local economy. According to Desloge City Administrator Greg Camp, many homeowners' property lines extend downward only a certain distance (though the distance might vary from property to property). Below that point are resources that usually cannot be exploited by an individual, but which mining companies can extract at a good profit. The Bonne Terre Mine, for example, has been part of the National Register of Historic Places since 1974, but for a century before that, it was part of the nation's largest lead-producing area. Now it is open to the public so that tourists can see the workings of the place. Much of the mine is now flooded, creating the world's largest subterranean lake and a popular fresh-water scuba diving area, but even as one wanders around the uppermost levels (which are kept dry), one cannot help but realize how this man-made cave differs from a place like Carlsbad Caverns: above is not parkland and wilderness, but the streets, shops, and houses of a small town. While ordinary people file papers and mix concrete and make love, you have the eerie recognition that you are but one of the thousands of complete strangers who have walked around beneath them for over a hundred years. You suddenly know in your gut that the earth is three-dimensional.

That three-dimensionality is something worth considering when drawing a border, but not every surveyor has considered it, and the results have sometimes been problematic. One of the issues that led to the first Gulf War in 1991 was that of the Rumaila oil field, a massive reservoir of petroleum that lies near the Iraq–Kuwait border. Since soon after its 1953 discovery, the Rumaila oil had been viewed by Iraq as its own, though at least one map, drawn up by the Arab League in 1960, gave a part of it to Kuwait. Saddam Hussein's government, desperate for money to rebuild the nation after the decade-long devastation of the Iran–Iraq War, did not wish to share the Rumaila oil, and among its disputes with the government of Kuwait was a claim about a form of three-dimensional trespassing: slant drilling.

Slant drilling (also known as directional drilling) is the practice of drilling an oil well not vertically, but at an angle. This is useful in cases where oil lies below something (say, a town) that cannot be easily displaced for an oil rig. It can also create an uproar if the drill is used to cross a borderline below the surface. Iraq accused Kuwait of doing just this—sending its drills into the ground at a shallow enough angle to reach the Rumaila oil that lay under Iraq. Most experts discounted this accusation at the time, and following Iraq's defeat, the United Nations redrew the border to give Kuwait even more of the field, but it remains perhaps the most famous example of a border's extension below the ground.

In addition, the Gulf War provides two good examples of a border in the air: the so-called no-fly zones (NFZs). In 1991, concerned that Saddam Hussein might restart his persecution of Kurds in the northern part of the country, the allies drew an east-west line along the 36th parallel, from Syria to Iran, and proclaimed that no Iraqi aircraft were permitted to fly north of that line. A second NFZ was established in 1992 to protect Iraq's southern Shiite population. In both cases, the zone's border could be said to extend from the surface of the earth up into space, and flying across it several thousand feet into the air would be viewed as the same kind of hostile act as stepping across it on the ground.

This idea of the borderline as a vertical (and virtual) plane isn't quite intuitive, probably because we are so used to seeing borders drawn as lines on a flat surface, but there is one place where the idea makes more immediate sense: when the line is drawn not over land, but over water.

If you've ever taken a boat out of sight of land, you can appreciate the folly of attempting to draw a line on the ocean. It's the very definition of impermanence, as stated best by Keats' tombstone: "Here lies one whose name was writ in water." The surface holds no shape, heaving up and down and left and right, and determining one's position upon it requires either the most precise technologies or the most arcane skills. Moreover, other than boats, there is practically nothing of value on that surface—just an expanse of undrinkable water. Whatever good stuff the sea holds lies beneath the waves. And that's why nations are so eager to draw borders on water—to claim what swims in it, or what rests on the bottom, or what the earth below that bottom contains. Historically, the two most important reasons for creating a boundary at sea have been the same as those for creating one on land: military defense and economic control. In the former case, nations wanted to ensure that their dry-land territory was unassailable from the sea; in the latter case, they wanted to ensure that the resources in the waters close to their shores belonged to them alone.

This is not to say that the ocean's surface has no true borders of its own. In some ways, that surface is itself the most clear and direct border that a human being will ever encounter; it's the line between where you can breathe and where you can't. Rarely does trespassing on the far side of a boundary carry a penalty so final or so automatic.

The consequences of crossing a line *on* the water are nowhere near as drastic, but the placement of the International Date Line on the surface of the sea, rather than across a continent, is in itself an indicator that some borders work better on water than on land. It also brings up an additional question about boundaries: just how many oceans does the IDL actually cross?

This question would be easier to answer if there were a fixed answer to a more basic question: How many oceans *are* there, anyway? Instead, we get the answer we so often get in geography, and birding, and English grammar: *It depends.* Some authorities, such as MarineBio.org, consider Earth to have only one ocean, sharing its waters around the globe, and it is certainly true that you can sail from one to another without even noticing (unless of course you go through a canal, which rather gives it away). This concept is not some sort of newfangled touchy-feely thing, either; Greek mythology taught that the world was surrounded by a single salty river which they called Oceanos, and which they personified as one of the Titans, a son of Uranos and Gaea. Later exploration, however, revealed that there was a lot more water out there than any river would have, and new names were applied to various bits of it.

To name those bits, however, someone first had to draw the lines that separated them from the other bits. In some cases these smaller seas were simply enclosed (or largely enclosed) sections of the larger body of salt water, such as the Black Sea, the Red Sea, or the Mediterranean Sea, and the borders were easily drawn. But with some parts of the Mediterranean designated as separate seas (such as the Aegean and Adriatic), the question of defining such bodies became even more troublesome, and enumerating them all but impossible. Some western cultures settled on the number seven for purposes of counting seas, but today most maps of the world will indicate dozens of seas, some more enclosed than others, including the Arabian, the Caribbean, and the South China.

The number of oceans is considerably smaller—typically no more than five—but still debatable. Though they do flow into one another at the northernmost and southernmost points of the Americas (not to mention a certain spot in Panama), the Atlantic and Pacific Oceans are almost always considered separate. Most mapmakers designate the Indian Ocean as a separate entity as well, placing its waters roughly east of the Cape of Good Hope and west of Australia.

The disputes generally come when the poles are brought into the discussion. At the top of the world there is nothing but water, much of it frozen, and it is largely enclosed by Asia, North America, and Europe, not to mention the enormous island of Greenland. That water's general level of separation from the Atlantic and Pacific leads some geographers to call it the Arctic Ocean, the fourth body of water with that title.

The fifth, however, is not so easily defined. Some mapmakers recognize the ocean zone that surrounds the continent of Antarctica as a separate body of water, dubbing it the Southern or Antarctic Ocean; others see no line of division between the southern parts of the Pacific, Atlantic, and Indian and the icy shores of Antarctica. The International Hydrographic Organization, which oversees the question for its eighty member states, gave no official consideration to the Southern Ocean until the year 2000, when the IHO defined it as all waters lying south of the sixtieth parallel. Australia, however, has long called the sea directly south of itself the "Southern Ocean," and Australia's southernmost point (Tasmania's South East Cape, unless we count several islets populated only by researchers) lies at 43° south. That leaves a good seventeen degrees of latitude between South East Cape and the northern border of the Southern Ocean; at 69 miles per degree of latitude, we thus have an expanse of salt water that extends nearly 1200 miles from north to south and is about 2500 miles across at its widest point. To which ocean does all that water belong if not the Southern? Call me unreasonable, but it seems to me that we should be able to settle with some degree of certainty exactly where a chunk of ocean three million square miles in area—roughly the same size as Australia itself—actually belongs. Even if the borders of that chunk are writ in water.

I HAVE NEVER BEEN to the Southern Ocean or any of the waters near it, but I have spent a little time navigating boats. Most of that work was done on or near the Intracoastal Waterway between Chesapeake Bay and Atlantic Beach, North Carolina, typically with my father in command of the vessel. We've also spent more than a little time playing similar roles on dry land. Not everyone wants to travel with his father, but mine is an ideal companion for a variety of reasons. He's a birder, for one, not as obsessed as I, but still willing to put in miles and hours in order to view new species. He's at least as devoted to the North Carolina basketball team as I am, so he'll cheerfully put all touring on hold to watch a tournament game in a hotel room. He's also retired, which means he's usually free to hit the road during Woodberry's early-to-mid-March trimester break, a two-week stretch during which no other school or business in America (including my kids' and my wife's) has a vacation. Dad has therefore been my spring break companion of choice for some years now.

His best quality as a partner in travel, however, is his driving. I consider myself a good driver, capable of handling varying road, traffic, and weather conditions with confidence, and I have never yet (knock wood) caused an accident or been cited for a moving violation. I can handle a stick shift or an automatic, dance through a roundabout or negotiate a cloverleaf, parallel park a Chevy van or work a Nissan Titan out of a garage. I've driven in D.C., Manhattan, and Vegas, along every inch of I-95 from Miami to Boston, and through the nightmare that is the Atlanta-Charlotte corridor. I've braved the highways and alleyways of Italy. And yes, I've logged several thousand miles on British roads, shifting with my left hand and going against every instinct when it comes to handling sightlines. But behind the wheel, I am at best a pale shadow of my father.

There may well be men out there who know more about an engine's inner workings than Richard G. Cashwell, and there may even be men who have logged more driving time—but of the latter there are very few indeed. Between traveling for the University of North Carolina admissions office and the United States Marine Corps Reserve, Dad probably did more driving from 1965 to 1995 than anyone not actually paid to plant his butt in a car seat. Knowing this, whenever I'm in Dad's passenger seat, I am utterly comfortable, even in heavy traffic or bad weather. I know that his ability to anticipate and avoid trouble will keep me safe and happy, and that my occasional needs for pit stops, road food, and good music will be attended to almost immediately. We can talk about any subject under the sun, but we can also go mile after mile without needing to say a word. It's like being back in the womb, only with a better view, and with more diesel fumes.

In the realm of the family, as in pretty much everything else, there are lines, and the lines in that realm are the lines of descent. You'll often come across references to a line of kings, or an unbroken line, such as that proceeding generation by generation down from Christopher Columbus. The lines of descent upon which I myself lie are in some ways entirely straightforward and in others more than a little twisted.

Dad is a Tar Heel. He has picked tobacco for money and he has been to every one of North Carolina's one hundred counties, from Dare to Cherokee. He graduated from high school, and college, and grad school in North Carolina, settled there to raise his family, and eventually retired there. You can no more remove the Old North State from my father's being than you can pry his DNA loose from his cells. That's his territory.

But the map says he's from Cleveland.

My dad's mother, Lucille Marie Ruttkamp, was a Cleveland girl, one whose family had roots in the city's manufacturing success; her father worked for the U.S. Wire branch of U.S. Steel, while her mother's family owned the Raymond Piano and Organ Company. That kind of success is what drew my grandfather up from eastern North Carolina during the Depression.

Joseph Leon Cashwell, Jr., had spent two years at Wingate College before he moved to Cleveland, and while he was there, making a living pumping gas, he decided to finish his bachelor's degree at Western Reserve University. During his gas-station days, he met Lucille (whose family's reaction to her romance with a pump attendant remains sadly unrecorded) and married her some months later. And in 1936, on Joe's 27th birthday, he and Lucille became the parents of Richard Gordon Cashwell.

The fact of my father's Ohio birth is difficult for some to swallow, particularly for those who hear his accent or watch him at work on a plateful of country ham biscuits. Still, despite his dyed-in-the-wool Southernness, his first few years on earth were spent in Cleveland, and that period did have an influence on him. During baseball season, for example, he roots for the Indians, and he also handles snowy weather with equanimity, particularly when behind the wheel, which is something I cannot say about the vast majority of people in either North Carolina or Virginia, whose first response when a winter storm is forecast is inevitably to rush to Food Lion and stockpile enough milk to make snowcream for the entire planet of Hoth.

Still, it remains strange to see Dad moving around a place as un-Carolinian as Cleveland, pointing out the places where he used to play, or the hill where he learned to handle a sled. It was he who taught me, both directly and indirectly, about the line between perception and reality, but sometimes seeing that line up close is necessary in order to appreciate anew that even the familiar people who make up our ancestral lines are far, far less simple and straightforward than we might assume. Dad comes from within the borders of North Carolina, but at the same time, that's not where he's from.

Over the years, my father and I have driven thousands of miles and crossed dozens of state lines. We've seen eiders in the surf off the coast of Maine and ibises picking through the shallows of the Great Salt Lake, and we've been to places where people don't even recognize English's only viable second-person plural pronoun (*y'all*). But wherever we've gone, he has kept me mindful of two things. First, when you trace a line of descent, you may end up far off that simple path between two points, just as the road to learning about your Tar Heel ancestors may end up being the road to Cleveland. But second, and perhaps more important, when you travel that road, it's nice to have your driving instructor with you, reminding you as always to stay on the proper side of the lines.

History's Greatest Monster

Malapropisms, bowdlerizations, and smoots—The very best or the very worst—Spreading santorum—A Field Guide to Gerrymanders—From the New World—A small and niggling sort of shame

> *The last election, constituents were concerned that it didn't matter what they did, that more densely populated areas were going to outvote them. —Virginia State Sen. Charles W. Carrico Sr., January 2013*

A WORD THAT IS derived from a person's name is called an *eponym*, and English is rife with them. Practically every field of human endeavor produces them, and they are applied to everything from the philosophical principle known as Occam's razor (named after English logician and theologian William of Ockham) to the culinary breakthrough popularized (though certainly not invented) by John Montagu, Earl of Sandwich. The English language, a tool of unmatched nuance and flexibility, is commonly altered by its users when necessary, and when a particularly apt or vivid name comes along, particularly if there is not already a commonly known word for a particular definition, an eponym is likely to result.

Most names are attached to behaviors or objects in a haphazard fashion, often because of the example set by a real or fictional individual, and language itself is a field where eponyms are often created. One such is *malapropism*, meaning a word misused to humorous effect, in a way similar to that of the word-muddling Mrs. Malaprop, who discussed such unlikely phenomena as "an allegory on the banks of the Nile" in Richard Brinsley Sheridan's play *The Rivals*. There is also the *spoonerism*, a reversal of sounds (as in "The Lord is a shoving leopard") characteristic of the Reverend William Spooner, dean of New College, Oxford, who said many but not all of the comical things attributed to him.

Perhaps the most interesting literary eponym is a verb inspired by Thomas Bowdler's carefully edited 1807 version of the works of Shakespeare, published as the rather over-titled *The Family Shakespeare, in Ten Volumes; in which nothing is added to the original text; but those words and expressions are omitted which cannot with propriety be read aloud in a family*. (Among the words and expressions omitted so as to avoid traumatizing tender ears: "Out, damned spot!" and various cries to God; these became "Out, crimson spot!" and "Heavens!" respectively.) Nowadays we say that any work from which potentially offensive words or sections have been cut has been *bowdlerized*, but *The Family Shakespeare* was itself bowdlerized at a fundamental level before it even saw print: the true editor's name was considered too scandalous for publication. Instead, the credit for bowdlerizing the Bard was deliberately given to the wrong Bowdler. Yes, Thomas did write introductions to each of the plays in the volume that made him famous, and his name was the one that appeared on the title page, but it was his sister, Henrietta "Harriet" Bowdler, who did the actual work of cutting Shakespeare's presumed excesses.

The same social pressures that demanded a censored *Macbeth* also demanded secrecy about the censor. As American University literature professor Fiona Brideoake explains, "There was no way for a young unmarried woman to claim she had actually undertaken the significant intellectual labor of editing and compiling this major text." But that was hardly the only barrier standing between Harriet and her own undisputed eponym: in order to excise the naughty bits, she would have to admit she understood them.

In the realm of science, however, understanding is not merely expected, but celebrated, and those who understand the most are often celebrated in the most enduring fashion. Chemical elements, for example, are often named after prominent scientists, which is why we have *einsteinium, curium,* and *nobelium,* among others. Another common way of acknowledging a scientist's contributions to human knowledge is with a unit of measurement, which is how we got the *watt*, the *angstrom*, and the *newton*, not to mention the rather less celebrated *smoot*. The smoot is a unit of distance (equal to 67 inches, or just over 1.7 meters) named after one Oliver R. Smoot, a pledge of the Lambda Chi Alpha fraternity at the Massachusetts Institute of Technology, who in 1958 was instrumental in the act of measuring Harvard Bridge. By carefully laying himself down, one smoot at a time (at least until tiring and being carried by his fraternity brothers the rest of the way), Smoot helped his frat mark off his height in a series of measurements along the bridge, eventually determining that it was some 364.4 smoots in length (plus or minus one ear). This feat of measurement, carefully maintained with paint touch-ups by each year's Lambda Chi Alpha pledge class, was marked on its fiftieth anniversary in 2008 with the addition of a plaque to the bridge and the celebration of Smoot Day at MIT. It is only fitting that, following his 1962 graduation, Oliver Smoot went on to head both the American National Standards Institute and the International Organization for Standardization.

Inventors have often been memorialized in eponyms related to their inventions, which is why the British adopted the verb *to hoover* to refer to their use of vacuum cleaners, and why the engines created to fire due to compression, rather than to spark plugs, are named after their creator, Rudolf Diesel. (Possibly the greatest of all these is the eponymous term for an ice-resurfacing machine, better known as a *zamboni*.) In the realm of fashion, however, eponyms tend to celebrate not those who invent the style, but rather those who popularize it. General Ambrose Burnside is credited with popularizing whiskers on the sides of one's face—*sideburns*—while the advocacy of Amelia Bloomer for reforming women's dress led to the adoption of the term *bloomers* for several types of pants and underpants. Even the bodies inside the bloomers have eponymous pieces, such as the Achilles' tendon, the Adam's apple, and the Islets of Langerhans.

For politics, however, eponyms tend to celebrate either the very best or the very worst that those in the field can do, and in the former case, a successful politician stands a good chance of having his or her name attached to a geographical feature. While discovering a place (or more accurately "bringing it to the attention of western mapmakers") is the traditional way to get one's name on the map, as in the cases of the Bering Sea, the Straits of Magellan, and the continents of North and South America, it is hardly the only way. You can also have something named after you if you help liberate it (Bolivia) or if you simply own most of it outright (Pennsylvania).

In a great many cases, however, your name can become attached to a place simply because the locals admire you from afar, as with the island nation of St. Lucia (named after the patron saint of the blind) or the city of Cincinnati (named after the great Roman leader Cincinnatus). In America, this practice has been responsible for the presence of George Washington's name on everything from states (one) to cities (the majority of U.S. states have a town named after him) to universities (including George Washington University, Washington University of St. Louis, Washington and Lee University, Washington and Jefferson College, and Washington College, not to mention the University of Washington and Washington State University). The fact that Washington never visited most of them has not mattered one whit to his admirers.

Outside the realm of geography, however, political eponyms are not always so well-meaning, nor the politicians themselves so admirable. Consider Norwegian leader Vidkun Quisling, whose collaboration with the Nazis during World War II gave the world a new synonym for "traitor," or Captain Charles Boycott, a land agent in Ireland's County Mayo. Boycott's 1880 attempt to evict tenant farmers from his employer's land was considered so objectionable that the Irish National Land League called for his complete ostracism in the community. His servants were advised to leave his employ, his blacksmith and laundress denied him service, and even his postman stopped delivering his mail. Unable to hire workers to harvest the estate's crop, Boycott was forced to write a letter to the editor of the London *Times* to get assistance. A party of Ulstermen was soon sent (with armed escorts) to bring in the harvest, but not in time to save the word *boycott* from entering the language as a synonym for any kind of deliberate economic isolation.

A more recent political eponym was noteworthy for a variety of reasons. First, it was decidedly not welcomed by its namesake, who felt its definition was objectionable; this is unusual, but as *boycott* demonstrates, not unique. Second, he was not alone in his feelings; the definition in question was considered so objectionable that a number of publications, including *National Review* and *The Economist*, refused to print it—a reversal of the usual pattern of refusing to publish an objectionable word, but allowing its definition (often accompanying a euphemism) to see print. Third and most important, this eponym quickly gained notoriety because it ended up becoming one of the first-ever (and most enduring) "Google bombs." The practice of deliberately manipulating the Google search engine to take users to a particular website is one whose origins are uncertain, but in the early days of the millennium, it was adopted by Seattle columnist Dan Savage in order to promote an eponym that had begun without a definition: *santorum*.

The word itself came from the name of Pennsylvania Senator Rick Santorum, a socially conservative Republican who in a 2003 interview with an AP reporter casually equated homosexuality with pedophilia, polygamy, and bestiality. He also proclaimed his support for anti-sodomy laws and announced his belief that the Constitution assures no right of privacy—news to those of us who have read the Fourth Amendment, certainly. The interview, probably the first in which a sitting U.S. senator raised the topic of man-on-dog sex, created something of an uproar. Democrats and a number of moderate Republicans criticized Santorum's comments, as did Savage in a guest column for the *New York Times*, while White House Press Secretary Ari Fleisher responded with the rather odd point that President George W. Bush considered the senator an "inclusive" man. This last prompted one reader of Savage's (eponymous!) "Savage Love" column in *The Stranger* to write in with a suggestion: "[I]f Rick Santorum wants to invite himself into the bedrooms of gays and lesbians (and their dogs) I say we 'include' him in our sex lives—by naming a gay sex act after him."

Savage correctly pointed out that the senator was not merely targeting gay bedrooms; indeed, by objecting to the Supreme Court's *Griswold v. Connecticut* verdict striking down state laws against contraception, Santorum was advocating government control of heterosexual bedrooms as well. All in all, however, Savage fully supported the reader's idea: "There's no better way to memorialize the Santorum scandal than by attaching his name to a sex act that would make his big, white teeth fall out of his big, empty head." Thousands of suggestions were sent in, but Savage whittled them down to nine finalists and presented them in his May 29 column, telling the readers to vote for their favorite. By an overwhelming margin, the voters selected as the definition for the new eponym not a sexual act, but a related and rather unappealing substance: "the frothy mixture of lube and fecal matter that is sometimes the by-product of anal sex."

In the wake of the vote, Savage set up a website, santorum.com (also known as spreadingsantorum.com) to proclaim the existence of the new word, and he encouraged his readers to talk about it, link to it, and literally get the word out. By December 2003, his site was the fourth most popular result for anyone searching for the Senator's surname, and it would soon become number one. When Santorum was crushed in his bid for re-election in 2006, his unwelcome eponym was credited by some observers as a factor in the final 18-percentage-point loss. Savage himself disagreed, stating that, though the existence of santorum certainly offered no benefit, Santorum would have lost anyway. Still, as he observed, "We helped to make Rick Santorum into a national laughingstock—with an invaluable assist from Rick Santorum, of course."

Even today, as Santorum contemplates his political future, the santorum problem hasn't gone away. During his unsuccessful quest to win the 2012 GOP presidential nomination, it haunted him in a variety of ways; in February 2011, Stephen Colbert noted on the air that the Google bomb was still in place; in January of 2012, following Santorum's near-victory in the Iowa Republican Caucuses, the first result I got from Googling "santorum" was still Savage's white-with-an-unseemly-splotch-of-brown web page—despite the fact that it hasn't been updated in years; and even in August 2012, with Mitt Romney assured of the Republican nomination, the first Google result for "Santorum" was the Wikipedia page about the neologism—marginally better than Savage's actual page, but still a highly visible link between the Senator's name and the frothy mixture. Whether he will pursue political office in the future remains unknown, but as *Mother Jones* notes, when it comes to online searches, as a candidate Santorum is "kinda screwed."

GENERALLY, THEN, while non-geographical eponyms can be the result of contempt or disdain for politicians, geographical names are reserved for politicians who achieve widespread approbation—but not always. I have found one instance where political infamy and geography met to create a memorable eponym. The politician in this case was Massachusetts governor Elbridge Gerry, and his namesake was a geographical monster never before described—a creature both formidable and enduring.

Gerry himself was a formidable figure in the early days of the republic, a member of the Continental Congress and signer of the Declaration of Independence. In John Trumbull's famous painting of the Declaration's presentation, he is depicted in a reddish jacket, left hand to his chin, apparently staring at John Adams's right elbow. He was also a delegate to the Constitutional Convention in 1787, one of three who ended up refusing to sign the Constitution because it did not include a Bill of Rights. Following the document's ratification, however, he was elected to two terms as a Massachusetts Congressman before serving as an envoy to Paris under President John Adams. Upon his return to Massachusetts, Gerry made a number of attempts to win statewide office and was finally able to win the governorship of the Bay State in 1810. There he served two one-year terms before moving to Washington in 1813 to be James Madison's vice-president. Tapped for the job because the previous vice-president, George Clinton, had died of a heart attack in 1812, Gerry apparently followed his predecessor's example rather too precisely and died in office of heart failure on November 23, 1814.

It is not surprising that a man of Gerry's status and accomplishments should have been recognized in several places with eponyms. Perhaps it is somewhat surprising that the two towns recognizing him lie not in his home state, but in New York: Elbridge (west of Syracuse) and Gerry (southwest of Buffalo). By far his most famous namesake, however, did appear in Massachusetts: the monster known as the *gerrymander*.

The gerrymander is an unusual creature in many ways, but it shares with other monsters the trait of a slightly inaccurate name. Many people, for example, mistakenly refer to the patchwork man built from corpses and animated by chemicals and electricity as *Frankenstein*, though in fact that was the name of the scientist who created it; others mangled *Gojira*, the name of the giant reptilian beast that so frequently stomped on Tokyo, into the decidedly non-Japanese name *Godzilla*. In the case of the gerrymander, the inaccuracy is audible; though Gerry's name was pronounced with a hard *g* (as in *gate*), that of his monstrous namesake is typically pronounced with a soft *g* (as in *ginger*).

Had Gerry himself coined the name, perhaps it would be pronounced properly, but it was applied by an anonymous group of newspaper editors after seeing the results of the redistricting bill passed by Gerry's Democratic-Republican party (and signed by the governor) in 1812. Like many parties before and since, the D-Rs (known to contemporaries as "Republicans," but not actually related to the current GOP) took advantage of their majority in the state senate to redraw the voting district lines to their liking. In northeastern Massachusetts, they carefully circumscribed the areas of Essex County where the Federalists held power and combined them into a single district; the Republicans could then hold power more easily in the remaining districts of the county, giving them a solid majority.

The area in question was a long, narrow, C-shaped region extending from the coast of Gerry's hometown, Marblehead, up along the western edge of Essex County, through Salem, Lynn, and Andover, right to the New Hampshire border—at which point it abruptly curled back to the east, incorporating Methuen, Haverhill, Amesbury, and Salisbury before striking the coast again. Sitting in the midst of the *C*, quite divorced from the area surrounding them, were such towns as Gloucester, Ipswich, and Newbury.

Perhaps because of the sinuous curve of the circumscribed area, or perhaps because of the clawlike shape of the peninsulas where Marblehead and Salem lay, the overall shape of the district reminded the editors of the *Boston Gazette* of a fantastic reptilian creature of some sort—a dragon, perhaps, or a salamander. At some fateful moment, one of the editors (either Nathan Hale, unrelated to the famous colonial spy, or one of the Russell brothers, John or Benjamin) was seized with the urge to credit the beast's existence to Governor Gerry, and the gerrymander was born.

The term might have faded into oblivion on the spot but for the creativity of one of the *Gazette*'s artists, possibly Elkanah Tisdale, whose wood-block cartoon of a map featuring a winged, clawed, dragonish beast with an improbably long eastward-stretching neck appeared on page 2 of the March 26, 1812, issue under the heading "The Gerrymander." This lively visual representation of the new district drew enough attention to the Republicans' maneuver to launch the Federalists to victory in the 1813 elections, and the term *gerrymander*, as both noun and verb, remains enshrined in English to this day.

Nowadays, the word is used primarily in critical or dismissive comments about any attempt to redraw borders for *unfair* political advantage, though the practice itself has a long and storied history, and the question of what kind of advantage is "unfair" has had to be settled in court on more than one occasion. Clearly, many of the loudest complaints about gerrymandering come from those whose political oxen are being gored, but in many ways, the gerrymander is the most useful of creatures because of the lesson it teaches: that at their core, *all* political boundaries are gerrymanders. They are drawn purely for the sake of convenience. Whose convenience? If you answered anything but "the convenience of politicians," I have a field guide to gerrymanders to sell you.

MY OWN UNDERSTANDING of the gerrymander came from my look at another eponymous creature. In the natural sciences, eponyms appear primarily in the common names for various species, such as Thomson's Gazelle, Brimley's Chorus Frog, and Townsend's Fangblenny.[1]

In most cases, such a name reflects the first naturalist to describe the organism, though sometimes the naturalist might choose to honor someone else. Vaux's Swift, for example, was named after William Sansom Vaux, the vice-president of the Academy of Natural Sciences of Philadelphia, though it was his friend John Kirk Townsend who had actually discovered the bird for science. French naturalist René Lesson named Anna's Hummingbird after Anna Masséna, the Duchess of Rivoli, for reasons that no gentleman would speculate upon. This

---

1. Yes, really. Look it up.

practice of naming suggests two traits about eponymous species. First, such species tend to be relatively recent discoveries, historically speaking; you won't find them listed in the works of Linnaeus, but if they were first described after about 1760 or so, the discoverer may have chosen to apply an eponym. Lewis's Woodpecker, for example, was first described by Meriwether Lewis on his 1804 expedition with William Clark to explore the Louisiana Purchase; the closely related (but more eastern) woodpecker described by Linnaeus in 1758 is known as the Red-headed Woodpecker.

Second, such a species will almost certainly occur somewhere other than western Europe, though occasionally one will have been discovered in an isolated or somewhat inhospitable space like the Caucasus Mountains (home of Guldenstadt's Redstart) or the Madeira Islands (where Fea's Petrel breeds). The science of taxonomy began in Europe with the cataloguing of the species already known to Europeans; as scientists observed the life forms in other parts of the globe, they had a much greater chance of describing or even discovering a new species than those who remained at home. Among North American birds, for example, eponyms are nearly fifty percent more common than in Europe; of the 896 species described in the fifth edition of the *National Geographic Field Guide to the Birds of North America* (not counting the 71 extinct and accidental species), over 90 have eponymous English names, from Allen's Hummingbird to Xantus's Hummingbird. And this isn't even counting the American birds that are named after places or things that were themselves named after people—birds like the Carolina Wren, the Aztec Thrush, or even the American Woodcock. Given the distance from Europe and the fact that a large number of American birds were described in the 19th or even 20th century, no American birder should be surprised to encounter an eponymous bird.

There are some such birds, however, that are a bit harder to spot than others. You can see the bold and aggressive Steller's Jay with ease so long as you go west of the Rockies, and even the more secretive Cooper's Hawk can be observed almost anywhere in the country with patience and a little luck, but if you want a look at Kirtland's Warbler, you should expect to put in some effort. For one thing, there aren't many of them; in 2005, fewer than 1500 singing males were observed in their breeding grounds. This is actually a huge improvement over the situation in 1987, when there were fewer than 200 singing males, but even with numbers growing, it's not a large population. Moreover, the bird's range is extremely limited; the Kirtland's nests only in jack pine forests, migrates to the Bahamas for the winter, and is rarely observed during migration.

The good news about this limited range, however, is that if you decide you want to see a Kirtland's Warbler, they're relatively easy to find. This was what I kept telling myself during the summer of 2010, when I was starting to feel a bit of pressure with regard to the Fifty-Fifty Project. I couldn't stop myself from birding in familiar places near my Virginia home, but if I recorded a lifer in one of them, like the Long-tailed Duck I had spotted in Maryland that March, that was one more species I couldn't record in a new state. I started doing advance research, reasoning that if I wanted to check a state off the list, the best possible bird to see would be one that I couldn't see anywhere else. Quickly I realized that Kirtland's Warbler was the perfect bird. Not only had I never seen one, there was only one state in the Union with enough jack pine forest to serve as its breeding habitat: Michigan.

This was new territory for me—literally. I had never been to the Great Lakes State, let alone into the section of the Lower Peninsula where jack pines grow. I was also leaving my comfort zone with regard to birding. Plain and simple, I was willfully and knowingly violating my own principles by displaying a naked greed for the Kirtland's. The essence of birding, I have long felt, is being open to your environment; the best birder is one who goes to a place and observes whatever might happen to be there. To go out with the desire to see a particular species can be something of a trap; even if you're successful, you miss the joy of seeing something unexpected, settling for the mere relief of filling the slot you'd already created for the bird. Worse, if you're unsuccessful, you end up disappointed by what you didn't see and fail to appreciate the beauties of what you saw.

And here I was, having roped my father into making a four-day, 1600-mile round trip, knowing that I was not only devoting a ridiculous amount of time and money to this journey, but expecting ultimately to feel nothing more than relief. If I was lucky.

In the end, I was lucky. Out in the low scrubby jack pines, not one of which rose over twenty feet high, I was able to hear the distinctive call of the Kirtland's, get a brief glimpse of the male's yellow belly, and take what is probably the worst photograph of a life bird ever taken. But standing there in the cloudy, muggy, July morning, knowing what I'd done, I didn't feel relief. It wasn't an emotion I'd ever felt on a birding trip. There was nothing here like the triumph of tracking down a Roseate Spoonbill in Louisiana, or the delight of discovering a Common Goldeneye in the icy waters of Ohio. I couldn't help but feel as though I'd taken advantage of the Kirtland's Warbler. For my own selfish purposes, I'd come to a place where the borders of the jack pine forest hemmed in a bird that couldn't nest elsewhere, and I'd done it at the time of year when it was nesting. This wasn't birding. I might as well have been meeting a train.

What I felt, when it came right down to it, was shame. A small and niggling sort of shame, yes, but shame nonetheless. To achieve my goal, I'd crossed a line, and I'd crossed it knowingly. The only reason I felt entitled to check Michigan off my list was that a few minutes later, I heard a strange, metallic chitter like that of a big insect, and the jack pines parted to reveal a Clay-colored Sparrow, a wholly unexpected life bird.

So today, when I see the Kirtland's Warbler in a field guide, I don't see it as a familiar friend, the way I do when I recall my first look at New Mexico's Scaled Quail or Alabama's White-winged Dove. I see it as a reminder of just how easy it can be, when you want something badly, to gerrymander your soul.

The Starting Lineup

What it is is football—How to get paid to watch sports—Interview with the umpire—Quantum baseball—A Platonic ideal—A short trip to Cooperstown—Framing devices

> *Any umpire who claims he has never missed a play is . . . well, an umpire.* —Ron Luciano

THERE IS AT LEAST one place on earth where no one is under any illusion that the lines are natural; everyone knows these lines are purely human constructions, dividing up the surface of the Earth in a manner both arbitrary and artificial.

And naturally, this is also the area where people get the most worked up about where those lines lie.

I'm speaking of the playing field. Or if you prefer, the pitch, the diamond, the court, the alley. The vast majority of sporting events involve lines in some fashion, and in some cases determining what lies on which side of a line is the same as determining victory. This is especially true in races of all sorts, which involve both a starting line and a finish line, and field events like the shot put and the javelin throw, which are won by measuring the length of the line between the athlete and the hurled object. Tennis is played between fault lines and sidelines. Baseball has first-base and third-base lines, ice hockey red lines and blue lines, and basketball end lines, half-court lines, foul lines, and three-point lines (which are partly arcs, admittedly).

To many Americans, the most bewildering lines are the ones on a soccer field, partly because of terminology. The long lines along the sides of the field are not officially known as sidelines, but *touch lines*; the lines at the ends of the field are sometimes dubbed end lines, but are technically *goal lines*—even the parts that are outside the goals. (Those outer portions are also known unofficially as *by-lines*.) There are lines six yards inside the goal lines, forming the goal areas, and eighteen yards from the goal lines, forming the penalty areas. None of this seems strange. But the first time an American sees a soccer ball roll onto the touch line with no stoppage of play, there's a moment of shock.

Soccer's international governing body, the Federation Internationale de Football Association, known universally as FIFA, explains the matter thus, according to what it calls, oh so unpretentiously, the Laws of the Game:

> The ball is out of play when . . . it has wholly crossed the goal line or touch line whether on the ground or in the air.

It's that "wholly" that makes the difference. In soccer, the line itself is part of the playing field; the out-of-bounds area doesn't begin until the far side of the line. For that matter, if the ball is resting on the grass beyond the line, but part of it is still hanging above that line, play will continue.

In most other sports, the sideline is itself part of the alien area beyond the boundaries of play. For example, in football—by which I mean the sport that over ninety percent of the world's people call "American football"—neither the ball nor the player possessing it may touch that line in the slightest. The referee looking at the ball carrier's foot had better see a smidgen of green between the shoe and the white chalk sideline, or else he's obliged to blow his whistle and bring everything to a halt.

Not every line on a football field is so disruptive. In fact, the entire object of football is to cross one of them: the goal line. If you can carry the ball over it, you will obtain six points for your team. And on the way to that ultimate goal, the officials set up a series of ever-shifting lines in ten-yard increments. The offensive team gets four attempts (or *downs*) to move the ball the necessary ten yards, and if it succeeds, it gets another four downs to go ten yards more; this is called making a *first down*. Because these first-down lines are not fixed, however, they must be indicated by portable markers on the sides of the field; this means that occasionally the question of whether the ball has been moved past that line must be settled by having the markers brought onto the field for an official measurement. Luckily, the field is marked with lines and segments of chalk or paint every few yards, which make progress easier to judge.

In the grand scheme of things, there is no significance to these lines. But in football, America's most popular sport, the question of whether the ball (or at least its nose) has crossed the line or not has become so crucial that television broadcasters have resorted to superimposing a computer-generated first-down line across the audience's view of the field. This digital marker has no official status, though, and on a close call the old-fashioned metal posts, linked by ten yards of chain, must be hauled out onto the field as they have since the days of Red Grange and his open-faced leather helmet.

The eyes examining these chains and posts, as well as every other marking on every other field of competition, belong to those we call *officials*, or sometimes *referees*, *umpires*, *judges*, *scorers*, or something less suitable for family publications. To serve in such a capacity is a thankless task, one that will at best leave half the spectators indifferent and at worst leave all of them incensed, but it is also a necessary task. Without officials, the rules of the game cannot be enforced; but to enforce them, those officials must have an intimate knowledge not only of the game's rules but of the game's lines.

Greg Jacobs knows those lines intimately. A childhood following the teams in his home town of Cincinnati left him steeped in the minutiae of baseball and football in the same way that Skyline Chili is steeped in allspice. In addition to breathlessly following the exploits of local legends like Anthony Munoz and Barry Larkin, he learned how to keep a scorecard, which gave him a useful skill to exploit when his schoolyard days were over. In 1997, he began working for STATS, "the world's leading sports information, content and statistical analysis company" according to its website. Basically, STATS reporters watch games—originally only Major League Baseball games, but now over 55,000 competitions per year in 85 sports leagues all over the globe. In front of his TV set, wherever it may be, each reporter logs the data for his assigned contest—every pitch, pass, run, shot, wicket, lap, serve, bout, goal, etc. That information is then crunched by STATS and provided to the leagues and media outlets like Yahoo! and Fox Sports. In the process of watching over a decade's worth of games, Jacobs discovered a few things. First, he discovered that he knew enough about sports to write two introductory texts for young fans, *The Everything Kids' Baseball Book* and *The Everything Kids' Football Book*. Second, he realized how much he hated the majority of sports broadcasters; for every interesting and informative announcer who enhanced the game with clear explanations and choice observations, there were seemingly dozens who cluttered up the broadcast with non sequiturs, faulty reasoning, self-aggrandizement, and ignorance of the rules. (The unforgivable broadcasting sin, in Jacobs's mind: interrupting the coverage of a contest in order to interview a player's family member.) Putting his mouth where his mouth was, so to speak, Jacobs decided to begin broadcasting games himself; since 2004, he has provided online play-by-play for the varsity baseball, soccer, and football games at Woodberry Forest School.[1]

But as a corollary to his increased understanding of sports broadcasts, Jacobs also acquired a greater appreciation for the people who officiate the contests. His experiences running Woodberry's intramurals program gave him insight into the sometimes difficult realm of in-game rules interpretation, and his occasional disagreements with testy student-athletes led him to desire a stronger foundation in making those interpretations. In 2008, the chance to obtain one appeared. Given a winter sabbatical from WFS, Jacobs spent five weeks in Florida at the Harry Wendelstedt Umpire School, one of only two institutions in the U.S. dedicated to training professional baseball umpires.

---

1. In his daily life, he chairs the science department and teaches physics at Woodberry Forest, where he has won recognition as one of the nation's top high school science teachers, and is co-author of McGraw-Hill's *5 Steps to a 5* guide for the AP Physics B and C courses. And for purposes of full disclosure, I should note that I am a co-announcer for most of his webcasts.

When he graduated, he and his classmates were fully qualified to begin careers as minor league umpires, with the chance of moving up to the majors in seven or eight years.

His wife, son, and students persuaded him not to take that particular career path, and he returned to the classroom soon after, but he still keeps his hand in by umpiring the occasional middle-school or high-school game in the Woodberry area. And if you want to understand how the lines on a baseball diamond work, you want a teacher who's had a lot of practice explaining simple concepts like torque, vectors, and Bernoulli's Law. Why? Because baseball rules are a lot harder to understand.

"It's complicated," is the first thing Jacobs says when I ask him what seems to me a fairly straightforward question: *How do you determine whether a ball hit up the third base line is foul or fair?*

And it *is* complicated. For one thing, there's a question about who's *making* the call. Until the ball travels all the way to the base, it's the plate umpire's job to judge the question, but once it gets beyond the base (a.k.a. the *bag*), the umpire in charge of third base is the final arbiter.

If the ball doesn't cross the line and doesn't reach the bag, what should the plate ump call? "Between the first-base and third-base lines, if the ball settles and is never touched, it's fair."

What if the ball is touched before it settles? "If it's touched while it's in fair territory, including the base line—if *any part* of the ball is on or above the line when it's touched," Jacobs explains, "then it's fair."

What if the ball goes past third base? "A ball that bounds past the bag in fair territory is fair. If it bounds off the base or directly over the base, it's fair—the bag is fair territory. And past the bag it doesn't matter where it's touched." In other words, once a fair ball gets beyond third base, it's fair regardless of where it's touched. And regardless of where it's been, too—a ball that bounces in foul territory short of the base can then spin over the bag and *become* fair.

What if the ball isn't "bounding"? "For a ball that flies past the bag, it only matters where the ball first touches the ground." In other words, if it flies into fair territory—including the lines—it's fair.

And what if it flies all the way out? "Any ball that hits the fence and goes over, or flies over it in fair territory, is a home run."

Well. That's pretty clear. What if it hits the foul pole?

"The foul pole is fair."

This is why I am not a physicist.

THE OTHER PROBLEM with the lines on a baseball diamond, of course, is that some of them aren't really there—at least not physically. Instead, they're drawn invisibly in the mind of the observer. The difficulty there, of course, is that different observers will inevitably draw different lines, which is why it's important to recognize that the only lines that matter are the ones drawn in the mind of the umpire.

In cases involving foul balls, the lines are clearly visible to everyone, and the spectator has little difficulty observing the events under discussion. In a sense, this is Newtonian baseball, where the rules are clear, the lines of motion are easily detected, and the scale is large enough that we can intuitively understand how everything works.

As in physics, however, there is another, deeper sort of baseball, one that operates at a smaller scale, with invisible lines, by rules that seem highly variable, or sometimes even contradictory. This "quantum baseball" comes into play on practically every pitch, and leaves that pitch in a superposition not unlike that of Schrödinger's cat: both dead and alive, until the observer opens the box that contains it and causes one of the two outcomes to be reified.

This state of uncertainty is created every time a batter lets a legal pitch go by him into the catcher's mitt. Because the pitch is legal, there can be no balk. Since the catcher controls the ball, there cannot be a passed ball or wild pitch. And without the batter's swing, there can be neither a hit nor a foul. There can be only one of two things: a ball or a strike. But even then, there is no way to know which until we see what's in the box—or, more precisely, until the umpire sees what's in it. The umpire's box is invisible to everyone but the umpire, but the rest of us do at least know where it is supposed to be: right over home plate, inside the set of invisible lines that define the *strike zone*.

According to MLB.com, the strike zone is defined thus:

> The STRIKE ZONE is that area over home plate the upper limit of which is a horizontal line at the midpoint between the top of the shoulders and

the top of the uniform pants, and the lower level is a line at the hollow beneath the kneecap. The Strike Zone shall be determined from the batter's stance as the batter is prepared to swing at a pitched ball.

As Greg Jacobs notes, even MLB's definition leaves some nuances to consider: "The top and bottom parts are established in the swing, as the batter swings at the pitch," not in the stance he might take while waiting for the pitcher to throw. "When he's swinging, he may duck down and lower the top line of the zone." The story that Reds legend Pete Rose would stand scrunched down at the plate in order to make his strike zone smaller is just a myth—or at the very least, it wouldn't have affected the umpire's call, even if Rose believed it would.

The vertical limits of the strike zone are thus somewhat variable, but what about the horizontal limits? "Some part of the ball must pass over some part of the plate," says Jacobs. "Even if it just clips the corner, it's a strike." The border area on the outside of the plate, known colloquially as "the black," is not officially part of the plate, and thus is not part of the strike zone.

How then does the umpire determine whether the ball has passed through the strike zone? "The best way to have a consistent top line on your strike zone is to put your eyes on that line," says Jacobs. The ump thus squats down until his eye is as close to that shoulder-to-waistline midpoint as possible, preferably lined up on the inside corner—the side of the plate closest to the batter. From that vantage point, he tracks the ball all the way from the pitcher's hand to the catcher's mitt. Wendelstedt's instructors warn their students to avoid "tunneling," the tendency to blink or stop following the ball as it comes out of one's main visual field. An umpire is supposed to keep his head still, but to move his eyes so that they are focused directly on the ball until it hits the mitt. "You don't want to call a strike until it's in the mitt—not as it's crossing the plate," says Jacobs.

Wendelstedt schools its students on the legal definition of the strike zone, but most of what they learn early on has little to do with that definition. "You are never ever evaluated on the quality of a ball or strike. You're evaluated on stance, head position, keeping your head still, watching the pitch," says Jacobs. "They don't care if you're right or wrong. They want you to be in the right place, with body language that's strong and clear. You'll figure out for yourself how to be a consistent ball/strike umpire. They're giving the fundamentals."

The strike zone, then, is not a universal constant that each student is drilled on during his training. Instead, it's more like a Platonic ideal; all the Wendelstedt School can do is train each umpire to develop the habits that will help him more fully understand and approximate the true Strike Zone as he gains experience. No less an authority on biology (and baseball) than Stephen Jay Gould has spoken out on the strike zone, framing the issue this way in *Questioning the Millennium*:

[E]ach pitched baseball crosses home plate in a particular location of undeniable factuality—but the definitions for balls and strikes are human decisions, entirely arbitrary with respect to the physics of projection, however sensible within a system of rules and customs regulating this particular sport.

Jacobs may spend his days teaching students how to analyze factuality, but he agrees that the human element is integral to the determination of balls and strikes. "A good umpire develops a strike zone over years of trial and error. You're consistent within a game; a pitch in a particular spot is always a strike or ball." But after calling a game with a certain zone, if you find out that teams are complaining, you might adjust your zone for the next time, so that you don't call those same high pitches strikes.

In other words, the strike zone is like most other things defined by lines: subject not only to the vagaries of individual judgment, but to the consent of those affected by it.

Each strike zone also varies according to the size and shape of the batter. The most extreme example of this variation would be the strike zone of the legendary Eddie Gaedel, who played for the St. Louis Browns in 1951. Hired on a Friday by Browns owner Bill Veeck, whose willingness to do anything for publicity was already well known, Gaedel took the field on Sunday for a first-inning at-bat against the Detroit Tigers, drawing a walk on four pitches. After reaching first, he was replaced by a pinch runner and went to the dugout, never to return. It was his only major league at-bat, yet his jersey now rests in the Baseball Hall of Fame.

The reason his jersey is on display in Cooperstown is the same reason Gaedel drew the walk: he stood only three-foot seven, giving him a strike zone only one and a half inches high (at least according to Veeck). The shortest Major Leaguer in history, Gaedel also retired with the highest on-base percentage in history (1.000) and is the only player ever to wear the number 1/8.

So, other than the stature of the batter, the complaints of the managers, and the umpire's position, equipment, and league affiliation, is there anything else that can influence the dimensions of the strike zone? The alignment of the planets, perhaps?

Bah. Greg Jacobs is a scientist; he scoffs at astrology. Nonetheless, he will admit to at least one other element that can affect the strike zone: the catcher. Consider the so-called "12–6 curveball," a ball that arcs straight downward with topspin, dropping faster than gravity tells it to, seemingly from 12 to 6 on a clock face. What happens if it drops down into the back of the strike zone?

"It might legally meet the definition of the strike," Jacobs admits. But if it's going down so sharply that the catcher must reverse his glove to catch it, the umpire will probably call it a ball. Why? Because the catcher's "framing" of a pitch has a significant influence on the call. Generally speaking, at the Major League level, the more a catcher changes the location of his glove in order to catch a pitch, the less likely an umpire is to call a strike. "If the catcher sets up on the inside corner, and he has to chase the pitch to the outside corner, the umpire almost never calls that a strike. If the catcher sets up way outside and the pitch comes in, same thing." Similarly, the catcher always wants to catch the ball with his glove in the same position it began in; if he twists his mitt, the pitch will almost certainly be called a ball. Jacobs is quick to note, however, that this is not the case for schoolboy teams: "At the lower levels, this is not so true, because the catchers have no skills. At the eighth grade level, the strike zone is a mile wide and very low, or you'd be there all night."

Umpiring, then, has similarities to a wide variety of human activities, including birding. In fact, Jacobs says the process is somewhat like learning how to bird (something his son Milo began doing at an early age): "Get in the right position, and don't worry about the ID. Just be able to describe what you see." In addition, both umpiring and birding often have less to do with being correct than with knowing where to look and being authoritative. As Jacobs summarizes, "If you're in the right position, you'll be right more often. And even if you're wrong, you'll be able to sell the call properly." And that, in a nutshell, helps us see how lines work in sports: the same way they work everywhere else. They're not impartial arbiters of what is right and true, but tools used by human beings to persuade other human beings about what is right and true. The foul line doesn't tell us what is foul and what is fair; only an umpire—a human being—can do that.

The Four Corners Offense

The clock is your enemy! —Al McGuire, former basketball coach, Marquette University

I'M SURE THERE'S some form of obsessive-compulsive disorder which is defined by a preference for things that are neatly blocked off by perpendicular lines, just as I'm sure that those with that particular syndrome are among the very best LEGO artisans. Still, I must warn right-angle fanciers that they are unlikely to derive any sense of satisfaction from a visit to that region of America known as the Four Corners.

As we have seen, using a straight line as a boundary is a resort to the arbitrary, a deliberate dismissal of the area's physical geography. What, then, is there to say about a place where such borderlines not only lie, but actually cross? The lines making up the intersecting borders of Utah, Colorado, New Mexico, and Arizona are not merely arbitrary, but proudly, even absurdly arbitrary.

As borders go, they are also rather flimsy, as they create vulnerability for each of the four territories involved. A military position that projects sharply into enemy territory is known as a *salient*, and it can be difficult to defend because opponents can attack it from three directions. If Utah goes to war with its neighbors, its southeast corner will automatically become a salient, likely to be caught between the combined forces of the Colozonicans and pinched out like a candle wick. This is probably why intersecting borders occur only within nation-states, where military conflict is less likely.

Nowhere in the world do national borders intersect each other, even when they're not straight, though admittedly, it's a near thing in southern Africa; at the Kazungula Ferry across the Zambesi River, Botswana and Zambia share a border less than 500 feet long, thus preventing, just barely, the existence of a Four Corners-style meeting with Zimbabwe and Namibia. And despite the liberal use of straight borders within the U.S., Canada, Australia, and Argentina (all large nations colonized by pie-slicing Europeans, I note), these former colonies have for the most part eschewed Four Corners-style intersections for the borders of their states, provinces, and territories. The rarity of such intersections is perhaps the clearest indicator of how they serve nothing but convenience. They have no relationship whatsoever to the surrounding landscape, to the traditional territories of the native peoples, to the history of the region, or to anything else. They are in short a deliberate fuck-you to the entire concept of physical geography.

Being one who delights in the judicious use of profanity, I could easily have become obsessed with the Four Corners for that reason alone, but in truth my obsession with them stems, as so many things do, from my twin loves of both geography and Carolina basketball. Geography geeks have a natural fascination with the uniqueness of this place—the only spot in America where you can touch four states at the same time! In fact, I still recall an episode of *The New Dick Van Dyke Show*—the early-70s revival with Hope Lange as Dick's wife, rather than Mary Tyler Moore—where Dick's neighbors fire up the home movies of their trip to the Four Corners. Bernie Davis (played by Marty Brill) proudly points at the unseen movie screen, announcing, "There I am, lying with my right hand in Utah, my left hand in Colorado, my left foot in New Mexico, and my right foot in Arizona!" And then he turns off the projector. That's the whole movie.

Perhaps, then, only a truly deranged geography geek would find such a vacation appealing, but I am not one of these—or not *solely* one of these, at least. I am also a graduate of the University of North Carolina, and any Tar Heel will immediately associate the name "Four Corners" not with a feature of the American West, but with a feature of the Carolina basketball team's game plan.

Former UNC coach Dean Smith was an innovator in a number of ways, but there was a unifying principle to his offense: that it's better to attempt easy shots than hard ones. That principle explains why Carolina teams routinely make a high percentage of their shots—because they work very hard to shoot from very close to the basket, rather than bombing away from the outside. Layups and dunks, both of which can be obtained in a fast-breaking offense, are ideal high-percentage shots. Similarly, shooting free throws is easier than shooting when you have defenders trying to stop you, so Tar Heel teams generally prefer to take the ball inside and either score or get fouled, rather than staying outside, where you both settle for a lower-percentage shot *and* lower the odds of getting fouled.

This is not the only way to win a basketball game—a team that shoots well from outside can be very successful, though a bad shooting night can be disastrous—but it has been the way preferred by UNC coaches for the last half-century.

It's also responsible for one of Dean Smith's signature game plans: the Four Corners offense. Developed back in the days when there was no shot clock (a timer requiring that a team shoot the ball within 35 seconds of taking possession), the Four Corners was an offense that allowed a team with a lead to hold onto it—even if the lead was a slim one. Thus, once the Tar Heels got that lead, the point guard would walk the ball up the court, holding up four fingers, and the Carolina faithful would roar with anticipation.

Each of the other Tar Heels would move to a corner of the forecourt, usually drawing his defender with him. This left the middle of the floor wide open, and if the point guard was a skilled ballhandler (such as All-American Phil Ford, under whom the offense reached its apotheosis), he stood a very good chance of faking out his defender and driving in for an uncontested layup (High-percentage Shot Option #1). If the other defenders rushed in to stop him, they were likely to put him on the foul line (High-percentage Shot Option #2) or give him an open man to pass to for a layup (High-percentage Shot Option #3). And since the Four Corners was a delay offense, intended to use up the opponent's time for a comeback, the longer the Heels held the ball without attempting to shoot, the more antsy the opponent would get. The antsier they got, the more likely they were do something stupid, like lose track of a Tar Heel making a backdoor cut for a layup or a dunk. Yes, the Four Corners was a delay, but it was also an offense, and an offense that won games. Basically, once the point guard held up four fingers, UNC fans knew they were going to see exactly three things: easy inside shots, free throws, and a Carolina victory.[1]

Needless to say, a boy who grew up with a poster of Phil Ford on his bedroom wall—e.g., yours truly—would find the name "Four Corners" enchanting on a level that no fan of some other basketball team could. (Entrepreneurs in Chapel Hill certainly liked the name, affixing it to the front of a downtown eatery that has operated for over thirty years.) And when such a fan was also a geography geek, the name had added enchantment. It took me a while—until the spring of 2008—but I was determined that I would someday walk in Bernie Davis's footprints. Or at least lay my ass down where his had been.

The first kink in my plan to sprawl across the Four Corners was my father. He's usually a big help when it comes to these trips, and not just because he pays for the hotel rooms. No, he's a Marine Corps logistics officer at heart, and he delights in nothing more than setting up schedules, movements, and routes in order to achieve the goals of the mission—how to distribute the necessary bullets, beans, and bandages, as he puts it.

Unfortunately, he's also insane. It's not a debilitating form of insanity, and in some instances it even helps him function better in society, but the fact of the matter is that the man likes to drive too much. I mean WAY too much. And when I announced to him that I had two weeks off from work and wanted to see the Four Corners, his response

---

1. The misuse of the Four Corners against Duke in 1979, a strategy that ended in a 47–40 win for the Blue Devils following the Heels' scoreless first half, is the exception that proves the rule; in this instance, Smith used the Four Corners simply as a delay, rather than as an offense, and it didn't work.

was to suggest driving there from Chapel Hill, which Google Maps reports as a distance of 2,301 miles.

"If we push it, I think we can get there in three days," Dad said cheerily.

I gently pointed out that I didn't want to spend the majority of my break traveling TO the Four Corners area and back, but would instead prefer to spend it traveling AROUND the area. Somewhat glumly, he agreed and arranged for a flight to Las Vegas.

BEFORE WE COULD confront the lines that meet on the ground at the Four Corners, however, we had to work with an entirely different kind of lines: the ones that divide time.

For once, humanity can look to Mother Nature as a model delineator. She may not use lines to divide space, but she does provide a line (in this case one called a *terminator*) between day and night. A terminator, which curves when it falls on a curved surface, is visible on any planetary body lit by a single source, but the one people are most familiar with is the terminator on the moon. When the phase of the moon is anything but full or new, the terminator is visible even at a distance of 240,000 miles, dividing the lit part of the lunar sphere from the dark part. It's a line duplicated on everything from the Turkish flag to the Bacardi logo, and one drawn by millions of schoolchildren whenever they sketch a night scene.

Earth has a terminator, too, and astronauts and satellite cameras can view and photograph it. For that matter, those of us on the ground who feel the urge to get an up-close and personal view of it can do so simply by standing outside and watching it cross over us; we call this event "sunset" or "sunrise."

Like most of Nature's seemingly precise lines, however, Earth's terminator gets a bit fuzzier if you examine it closely; even in a tropical place like Mandalay, where the dawn comes up like thunder, there is still a period of semi-darkness just prior to sunrise and another just after sunset. These twilight times demonstrate that the dividing line between night and day is hardly as clear as, well, night and day.

With the terminator's example, however, humanity has put an enormous amount of effort into carving the day into smaller sections, using shadows, water, bells, counterweights, springs, cogs, gears, fly-wheels, and even radiation to help draw the dividing lines. And when they weren't enough, we went back to the old standby of drawing a line on a map. If you examine many maps of the U.S., for example, you'll discover a vertical (and frequently dotted) line that starts near the southernmost point of Lake Michigan, close to the Indiana-Michigan border; it quickly swings west to follow the Indiana-Illinois border, then suddenly cuts southeast across the toe of Indiana and through the middle of Kentucky, then turning south through Tennessee to the Alabama-Georgia border and down across the Florida Panhandle to the Gulf of Mexico. This is the dividing line between the Eastern and Central time zones.

The concept of "time zones" is a relatively new one. Most places on earth used to set their clocks (or sundials, prior to the invention of clocks) according to the sun; whatever time it reached its highest point over a certain place became known as *noon*. This worked beautifully, but only so long as everyone stayed in one place. Once people began traveling and communicating over great distances, it didn't work so well, and eventually the need for precise scheduling over great distances became a major concern. In seventeenth-century England, for example, a standard time had to be established so that ships could measure longitude accurately; this was accomplished with the creation of Greenwich Mean Time (GMT), which was based on noon at the Royal Observatory in Greenwich. In the late 1840s, British railroads began using GMT as their standard, and the phrase "railway time" became synonymous with it. In 1880, GMT was legally adopted as the standard time for the entire island.

American and Canadian railroads had a different problem, however, owing to the far greater distances their tracks had to cross, not to mention the creation of forms of communication that could travel faster than the sun crossed the sky. Local noon on an island, even a big one like Great Britain, will vary only somewhat; the sun is at its height in southwestern Land's End less than thirty minutes after it reaches its zenith on the eastern coast. In the U.S., however, local times have far more variability, even discounting the far-flung areas of Alaska and Hawaii; noon in Boston arrives a full three hours before it hits Los

Angeles. That's more than enough time for a railroad car of frozen food to begin thawing, or for the patience of a mother meeting her children to become completely lost.

Thus, American and Canadian railroads had to set not only a single time for all stations where the sun was roughly at its height, but also *another* single time for stations in an area to the west, and still another single time for stations to the west of *that*, and so on. Adopting this practice assured that passengers and freight would arrive and depart according to a uniform schedule, but not everyone found it a useful innovation in non-railroad matters. It was not until 1918 that Congress passed the Standard Time Act, formally setting up the United States' four time zones in almost exactly the familiar configuration they retain to this day: Eastern, Central, Mountain, and Pacific.

To imagine what life would be like without this Act's passage, one can consider the example of China. Though the People's Republic extends from east to west even farther than America's lower 48, there is only one official time: Beijing Time, which is eight hours ahead of GMT. Thus, when the workday begins in the port of Shanghai, it should in theory also start for workers in government offices that lie further west than Nepal. This would be like having a nationwide firm's Los Angeles office open its doors at 5:00 A.M. and close at 2:00 in the afternoon, all because of the Boston office's 8–5 working hours. In the face of this inconvenience, Xinjiang Province, the semi-autonomous westernmost part of China, unofficially observes a standard time two hours behind Beijing's, but if the regime in Beijing ever gets tense, expect rush hour in Xinjiang to begin at oh-dark-hundred.

Outside of China, time zones have proven such a useful and successful innovation that they are almost universal. Unfortunately, the familiar refrain of "except for" must once again be raised, and in this case the exception is one that my father and I were about to confront head-on.

When we boarded our Vegas-bound plane in Raleigh, we were observing Eastern Standard Time (which, if you're curious, is five hours behind GMT, or the more precisely correct *UTC*, "Coordinated Universal Time"). We had a layover in Houston, and to prevent missing our connecting flight, we reset our watches to the local Central

Standard Time (six hours behind UTC). From there we flew over the Mountain Time Zone entirely, landing in Las Vegas at the very edge of the Pacific Time Zone (UTC minus 8). We spent the night in Sin City, where I blew a dollar at slots just to say I'd done it, and headed for Zion National Park the next morning. Crossing into Utah, we moved into Mountain Standard Time (UTC – 7), spent two days exploring, and then settled into our hotel room in Cortez, Colorado, for the evening. That night, however, was the night to "spring forward," so we reset our watches to Mountain DAYLIGHT Time (UTC – 6). That Sunday we finally made it to the Four Corners Monument itself, where I dutifully lay with my limbs strewn across four states, before jumping back into our rented truck to head to our lodgings in Monument Valley, Arizona.

After a good long look around the Valley the next morning, we headed west toward the Grand Canyon, at which point we discovered the "except for" we had not expected: the fact that the entire Mountain Time Zone observes Daylight Savings Time . . . except for the state of Arizona. The Navajo Nation, however, *does* observe Daylight Savings Time, and since Monument Valley lies within the Navajos' territory (which itself lies in three states), we had not missed any important deadlines. Nonetheless, Arizona itself remains proudly in Mountain Standard Time even when the rest of the Mountain Time Zone has sprung forward. Somewhat aghast, we left the reservation and reset to MST (UTC – 7).

And two days later, we got back to Vegas (now on Pacific Daylight Time, which we were relieved to realize is the same as Mountain Standard), flew into Houston (Central Daylight, UTC – 5), and at last returned to Raleigh (Eastern Daylight, UTC – 4).

To sum up: in ten days, our watches reported eight different times: UTC – 5, – 6, – 8, – 7, – 6, – 7, – 5, and finally – 4.

When my hour comes round at last, I just hope the Great Timekeeper has been keeping careful track. He may owe me a couple of days.

THE UNDERLYING ABSURDITY in all of this, of course, is that time zones, like the hours that define them, are a purely arbitrary creation. They exist because human beings need a common point of reference in order to get things done. If we can't all agree on a time, anything requiring cooperation becomes difficult at best, impossible at worst. (This can be demonstrated with ease by getting someone to help you lift a heavy object without either of you saying "Lift on three" aloud.) Time itself is a naturally occurring phenomenon, but it's not terribly useful in its raw form. Thus, human beings are just as likely to divide up time as they are to divide up space.

As Randall Monroe points out in his brilliant webcomic *xkcd*, "Calendars are just social consensus . . . Nature doesn't know the day of the week." He urges us to make today Saturday—forever—but the very fact that he has to ask us to agree on this eminently sensible proposal illustrates the basic problem with any task involving human beings: getting a consensus. Sure, we all know we need a common point of reference for time, but there is considerable disagreement about the best way to pick it. In other words, we can't even form a consensus on the best way to form a consensus.

If one is looking for consensus, one can find it in a variety of areas; historians will generally agree that the Allies won World War II, and astronomers are nowadays just about unanimous in believing that the earth revolves around the sun. Unfortunately, these are not my fields; no, I obtained my professional expertise in the teaching of English.

There are over 400 million native speakers of English, plus another billion or so who speak it as a second or third language. The danger here is that many of these billion and a half people confuse experience with expertise; yes, they've written or spoken English, often for many years, but that experience doesn't make them authorities any more than the experience of being born makes you an obstetrician.

And worse, even the presumptive authorities have difficulty agreeing on many aspects of English grammar. One grammarian says, "It is not permissible to end a sentence with a preposition," while another says, with equal passion and equal authority, that a preposition is a perfectly legitimate thing to end a sentence with. Some grammar experts assert emphatically that the "to" should never be separated from the verb in an infinitive, while others are willing to boldly insert an adverb where none has gone before. I once worked grading standardized essay tests, and we had access to no fewer than 34 grammar texts to assist us in the course of our duties—which meant, of course, that we had 34 different (and often contradictory) sets of rules about the proper and improper placement of commas.

Nor has it escaped my attention that the most famous rule in English spends more time discussing its own exceptions than laying down the rule itself:

> *i* before *e*
> Except after *c*
> Or when sounded like *a*
> As in *neighbor* and *weigh.*

Worse, this rule is not even accurate—you can have a seizure, or purchase a heifer at your leisure. And when you consider the issues of s*cie*nce and spe*cie*s, it's clear that this so-called rule is defi*cie*nt. Weird, isn't it?

Perhaps because of the presence of such rules and authorities, it took me a long time to realize that my preferences in English are largely that: preferences. They stem from my own beliefs about what constitutes successful communication, but alas, I cannot be the sole and absolute judge of whether a given piece of communication is successful or not. Thus, if two people think that the word "impact" is a verb meaning "to affect," they can communicate that meaning to one another; eventually, if enough people share their belief, the word's definition will change, even if we English majors scream and tear our hair.

You might expect, then, that with my professional life so inexorably tangled in questions of differing opinion and uncertain authority, that I might seek an avocation where consensus is the watchword . . . where the lines are clearly drawn . . . where authorities are unassailable. And yes, I might have picked such a field. Unfortunately, I picked birding.

The great ambiguous questions are usually "Why" or "How" questions: *Why do bad things happen to good people? How did the universe begin? Why am I such a misfit?* By contrast, "What" questions generally have simple answers. *What is your name?* There's usually only one answer. *What is your favorite color?* Again, fairly straightforward. *What is the capital of Syria?* Damascus! This is why "What" questions are the staple of *Jeopardy!* competitions; when Alex Trebek reveals a screen reading "This Middle Eastern city is the capital of Syria," nobody ever hits the buzzer and says "*Why* is Damascus?"

In birding, too, "What" questions predominate. *What is the state bird of Virginia? What call does a Carolina Wren make?* And of course, the main question on any birder's mind: *What is* that *bird called?* Nonetheless, only one of these seemingly straightforward "What" questions has anything like a straightforward answer, while uncovering the other answers can be at least as stressful as determining the proper placement of a comma following an introductory prepositional phrase; even if you can find out the answer, it's often difficult to persuade a layman that there's any value in learning it. But let's consider the questions anyway.

What is the state bird of Virginia?

The Northern Cardinal. So much for the easy one.

What call does a Carolina Wren make?

The Carolina Wren is a lovely reddish-brown above and a rich buff underneath, with a white eyebrow stripe, a short tail, and a voice so loud that it can be heard in states that don't even border the Carolinas. But what does it say in this ridiculously loud voice?

This is where a simple "What" question gets complicated, because translating birdsong into English often leads to some ludicrous statements. It's difficult to look someone in the eye and report that the White-throated Sparrow says, "Old Sam Peabody Peabody Peabody." In recent years, birders have tried to duplicate the calls phonetically, but this strategy isn't always terribly successful, either; "sooooo seeeeee dididi dididi dididi" doesn't really sound any better than "pure sweet Canada Canada Canada." And while it's true that once you hear a Bobwhite's eponymous call you'll never forget it, seeing it rendered as "pup WAAAYK" probably won't help you identify it in the field.

The Carolina Wren's call is thus a matter where consensus is all but impossible to achieve, despite the fact that everyone who has heard it agrees on what the bird actually sounds like. A quick Google search will reveal that numerous birders have asked online about a bird that goes "cheeseburger cheeseburger cheeseburger." David Sibley believes it goes, "pidaro pidaro pidaro," or perhaps "TWEEpudo TWEEpudo TWEEP." The Cornell Lab of Ornithology's award-winning website, All

About Birds, however, agrees with the field guides of Roger Tory Peterson and the National Geographic Society: the call is "Teakettle teakettle teakettle."

So what call does a Carolina Wren make? The only correct answer is "A really, really loud one."

*What is **that** bird called?*

This is the most basic "what" question in birding, but it's perhaps the most frustrating as well, because birds collect names the way windowsills collect dust. The Bobolink, for example, has a Latin scientific name, as all birds do: *Dolichonyx oryzivorous*. It has also collected quite a few vernacular names over the years, often in a bewildering series of recombinations: Skunk Blackbird; Skunk-head Blackbird; White-winged Blackbird; Meadowwink; Meadow-bird; Rice-bird; May-bird; Reed-bird; Butter-bird; and even Bob-lincoln, who was present at Lee's surrender but did not accompany his father to Ford's Theater. "Bobolink" is the official American name, but you won't always hear it, because birders love to assign nicknames. They'll call Turkey Vultures *TVs*, and you may hear Sharp-shinned Hawks referred to as *sharpies*. In field notes, birders often whittle names down to two-letter pairs, making Herring Gull into *HeGu* and Atlantic Puffin into *AtPu*. Thus, even if you know exactly which species of bird you're looking at—a situation which is fraught with its own difficulties, as we will see—there may be no consensus about what to call it. And the nature of the controversy can change, seemingly with the seasons.

The organization that assigns official bird names in North America, the American Ornithologists' Union (AOU), has been assigning them since 1883, and I don't think I'm the only birder ever to wonder if 130 years isn't plenty of time to get them right. Alas, like every organization, the AOU is subject to politics, and there are often disputes between the two main parties, the "Lumpers" and "Splitters," about the dividing lines between species. Depending on who's in power, a species may find itself being split in two or being lumped together with another species. For example, the Baltimore Oriole (*Icterus galbula*) and the Bullock's Oriole (*Icterus bullockii*) were two different species for years, the Baltimore in the eastern part of the U.S., the Bullock's in the western part—but then a Lumper administration came to power in the late 1960s. Noting that the two species often produce hybrids where they meet, the Lumpers declared them to be a single species, the Northern Oriole, and assigned them both the Baltimore's Latin name. Within thirty years, however, the Splitters retook the AOU throne, brandishing DNA analyses and reports that the Baltimore-Bullock hybrids were not reproducing, and declared the two species once again separate, restoring *Icterus bullockii* to full status. Not that the Splitters stopped there: they also split the Rufous-Sided Towhee in two, creating the Eastern Towhee and the Spotted Towhee. And in 1997, the AOU split the Solitary Vireo into *three* separate species, the Blue-headed, Cassin's, and Plumbeous Vireos. Will this state of affairs last? Tune in again in 130 years.

WHETHER JUSTIFIED or arbitrary, the ways in which we divide things up can lead to conflict, as any border skirmish will demonstrate, but it is sometimes surprising how much emotional stress can be caused by the divisions we place in time. Sometimes the stress comes from a simple disagreement about exactly where the division lies, yes, but at times the stress can develop even when there is complete consensus. For example, many young couples have found themselves intensely concerned with a certain twenty-eight day cycle; in general, they agree completely on the proper time for the cycle to begin, but there may be a great deal of stress based on the consequences of either its arrival or its failure to arrive at that time.

In *Questioning the Millennium*, Stephen Jay Gould theorizes that our brains often latch onto mathematical regularity because so much of nature actually does follow regular mathematical patterns, such as the inverse squares that underlie the law of gravity, or the hexagonal efficiency of a honeycomb. Unfortunately, Gould points out, "Our searches for numerical order lead as often to terminal nuttiness as to profound insight." In my experience, the search for consensus operates in the same way.

What I've learned, then, is that to a large degree, chronology is the same thing as geography, and birding, and grammar: an attempt to get human beings to agree on a system in order to understand something that human beings didn't design. As Derek Jennings once said,

"Like the rings of Saturn, English grew through accretion over a very long time and only appears uniform and structured from a distance." Now that Saturn has rings, we can assign them names and talk about whether a given chunk of ice belongs in ring A or ring B, or establish the dividing line between those two rings, but we can't take credit for putting that dividing line there. Similarly, the birds were here before we were, and though we can argue about their names or their family relationships, the arguments don't reveal anything about birds—only about what we think about birds.

So that's what I do. Every day. I show up in the morning at a time that we all think is the time to start class. I spend my working hours teaching students what writers think about us, and what we think about writing. And at a time that we all agree is the time to stop class, I go out and do the exact same thing, except with a pair of binoculars.

There are no lines; there are only places that people think lines should go.

What God Has Put Asunder

The Lord is One—Acts of division—The longest afternoon of my life—
Sailing the Sea of Talmud—Fishing for capybara—I wouldn't think
of it—Surveying the moral landscape

> *Terminus is the only god to whom Jupiter must bow.*
> —*Neil Gaiman,* Sandman

GOD IS A LINE.

Well, maybe not, but you must admit God and lines have a
lot in common—so much so that Western monotheism without lines is just about as unthinkable as Western monotheism
without God.

Consider the geometry inherent in Judaism, Islam, and
Christianity. The line's defining quality is its oneness. It has
only one dimension—length. In the most basic statement
about the nature of the Divine, the Torah states plainly, "The
Lord is one." Moreover, in its purest form, the line is unique—
no other line on a plane or in space can duplicate it without
becoming it—and the Quran declares, "There is no god but
God." And of course, a true line is infinite, having no endpoints, and the infinite nature of God is proclaimed in everything from hymns ("Eternal Father Strong to Save") to the Old
Testament ("The eternal God is thy refuge,"[1] Deuteronomy

---

1. To me the most beautiful English translation of the Bible is the King
James Version, from which I have taken the excerpts in this chapter, but
you're welcome to consult your own preferred text, even if it's written in
Hebrew or Arabic.

33:27) to the last chapter of Revelation: "I am Alpha and Omega, the beginning and the end, the first and the last."

The singularity of the line, however, is not the only quality it shares with the fundamentals of Western religion. A line's nature may be singular, but its purpose, as we have seen, is dualistic; the line is the tool you use to divide.

That lines are drawn by human beings for human purposes ought to be fairly apparent at this point, but there are many who believe certain lines were not only drawn for non-human reasons, but set down by non-humans as well. Adam, for example, was assigned to name the animals, but that task presupposes some kind of existing difference between them; in order to give different names to the goose and the swan, after all, he had to recognize some distinction between them. The nature of these distinctions is a matter for later consideration, but let's note that, according to the Abrahamic religions, the very first job given to humanity by its Creator was the job of drawing lines.

The most common lines in the worlds' religions, however, are the lines drawn between right and wrong. Sometimes the line defines a very straightforward taboo—the Hindu prohibition against eating beef, for example—but in religion, as in so many other areas of human understanding, it's hardly uncommon to discover boundaries that have been bent, smudged, broken, or even erased. It is also possible to discover instances where lines are drawn, and redrawn, and redrawn again, with seemingly infinite care.

JUDAISM IS THE oldest of the Western world's major religions and the one whose tradition of setting boundaries has the deepest and most complex history. In fact, the first actions taken by God in the book of Genesis are acts of division: taking the formless void and separating it into organized parcels—light here, darkness there, waters here and land there. By the end of the first chapter, heaven has been divided from earth, night from day, and male from female, but one crucial division is not made until the early verses of chapter two:

2   And on the seventh day God ended his work which he had made; and he rested on the seventh day from all his work which he had made.

3   And God blessed the seventh day, and sanctified it: because that in it
he had rested from all his work which God created and made.

In short, here YHWH[2] draws a distinction between the seventh
day—*Shabbat*, in Hebrew, and in English *Sabbath*—and the rest of the
week. That day is set aside for contemplation of the divine, for spending time with the family, and above all for rest. Despite the Creator's
early example, however, there were Jews who demonstrated an inabil-
ity to put aside their workday concerns, which prompted the Lord to
make somewhat more specific points about Shabbat in the book of Exodus. First, as Moses tells the Hebrews in 16:26, there will be no manna
in the wilderness on that day; second, in 20:8–11, there is an explicit
commandment—one of the Ten—to "remember the Sabbath day, to
keep it holy"; and third and most pointedly, in 31:13–18, YHWH gives
Moses specifics about not only the rule, but the penalty for violating it:

13   Speak thou also unto the children of Israel, saying, Verily my Sab-
baths ye shall keep: for it is a sign between me and you throughout your
generations; that ye may know that I am the Lord that doth sanctify you.

14   Ye shall keep the Sabbath therefore; for it is holy unto you: every
one that defileth it shall surely be put to death: for whosoever doeth any
work therein that soul shall be cut off from among his people.

And in case you didn't read carefully, God repeats:

15   Six days may work be done; but in the seventh is the Sabbath of
rest, holy to the Lord: whosoever doeth any work in the Sabbath day, he
shall surely be put to death.

Got that?

---

2. The common Jewish practice of using this four-letter construction, the *Tetra-
grammaton*, rather than God's full name, is in itself an act of drawing fine lines of distinction; for purposes of communication, one must be able to refer to God without
confusing the reader, but using His full name is considered at least irreverent, and at
worst a potential violation of the Third Commandment. The use of *YHWH* thus leaves
the writer just on the safe side of that line, having written a name that isn't the Name. So
strictly has this line been toed over the years that modern scholars do not know for certain how God's name is properly pronounced; "Yahweh" is the most common guess, but
as cartoonist Larry Gonick observes, it could just as easily be "Yahoo-Wahoo."

Keeping a particular day of the week holy for everyone, however, takes more than a purely personal effort. As a result, certain remnants of the Bible's rules about working on the Sabbath remain enshrined in American law, though the timing has shifted to reflect the Christian majority's schedule. For observant Jews, Shabbat begins at sunset on Friday and continues until sunset on Saturday. For most Christians (with the exception of Seventh Day Adventists), the Sabbath is observed not on the seventh day of the week, but the first: Sunday, the day on which Christ was resurrected. To some degree, the secular concept of the weekend stems from the idea of a Sabbath, and some of the specific legal prohibitions against weekend work seem religiously motivated. These laws focus primarily on certain specific forms of work and often go by the puzzling term "blue laws," a name taken from the laws which supposedly governed colonial Connecticut (though there is little evidence that such laws existed by that name).

While government departments, banks, schools, and offices are usually closed on Sundays (and often on Saturdays as well), businesses that cater directly to consumers—restaurants, stores, gas stations, etc.—are more typically open. At least one highly profitable enterprise—the National Football League—does the majority of its business on Sunday. But as bibulous NFL fans can attest, perhaps the most bewildering Sabbath-related strictures remaining in America are those governing alcohol, though in fairness, not all the confusion and contradiction involved stems directly from the tradition of the Sabbath. In some places, alcohol cannot be purchased on Sundays at all; in others, it can be sold by the drink in bars and restaurants, but grocery and convenience stores cannot sell a six-pack to a thirsty football fan; and in others, you can buy whatever you care to swill down and get thoroughly ripped before kickoff. Cross a state or county line on a Sunday, however, and you're likely to find yourself in an area where your assumptions about purchasing alcohol are invalid.

Mind you, these assumptions can be smacked down on any day of the week, depending on where you are. Some states allow wine and beer to be sold in the same place, but require liquor to be purchased elsewhere; sometimes wine and liquor are sold in the same place, while beer must be purchased elsewhere. Sometimes the amount of beer you can buy is regulated; sometimes the amount of alcohol in the beer is strictly regulated, while at other times it is allowed to vary from the nominal (Coors Light, 4.2% alcohol by volume) to the brain-smacking (Founders Kentucky Breakfast Stout, 11.2% ABV). No matter where you grow up, you will at some point find yourself stymied by the liquor laws in some other locality. I remember well how shocked I was the day I was pushing a cart through a Missouri supermarket and came around the corner to discover the liquor aisle. (In Virginia and the Carolinas, bottles of anything stronger than beer or wine are sold in government-regulated Alcoholic Beverage Control stores.) I will also never forget the longest afternoon of my life, which was spent driving around the Poconos with my brother, attempting to find and purchase a six-pack of beer, acts that the good people of the Keystone State had made not merely illegal but downright impossible.

Tom Cowell of *Philadelphia Weekly* describes Pennsylvania's alcohol policy as "an absurd, patronizing and pointless rip-off that by rights should be blown up." I am not in a position to argue. As Dave and I learned, after the expenditure of much time, effort, and gasoline, you cannot buy a six-pack of beer in a Pennsylvania supermarket, nor in one of the state-owned Wine and Spirit stores that often occupy strip-mall stores near supermarkets. You can buy a case from a Liquor Control Board-approved beer distributor, and you can buy two six-packs from a tavern, but these options require both a lot of inconvenience and a lot of cash. When the minimum purchase is a twelve-pack, the purchasing of beer will remain the domain of the well-off, or at least that of any group of teenagers with at least fifteen bucks and one fake ID among them. But even on weekdays, Pennsylvania's alcohol laws are as straight as a Kansas interstate compared to the Bible's laws regulating the keeping of the Shabbat.

THE ORIGINAL BOOKS of the Old Testament were of course written in Hebrew, and the Hebrew word that King James's translators eventually replaced with *work* was *melakha* (plural *melakhot*). The correspondence is not precise. In his lively guide to comparative religion, *The Joy of Sects*, Peter Occhiogrosso recounts a story originally told by the great scholar and civil rights activist Rabbi Abraham Heschel, one which offers a fuller understanding of *melakhot* and the peculiar nature of the Shabbat:

> [A] renowned rabbi . . . while strolling in his garden one Sabbath, noticed that the branches of his apple tree needed pruning. Although he took no action, he did make a mental note to do so after the Sabbath. But when he returned to the garden, he found the tree withered. God had apparently destroyed it to teach the rabbi that even to think about doing work during the Sabbath goes against the spirit of the law.

Among the forms of "work" forbidden on Shabbat are using the telephone, driving a car, or handling money, and the rule applies even if you don't do any of these things as a career. As rabbis would later point out in the Talmud, a *melakha* is not merely a task requiring effort or resulting in recompense, but any action that relates to creativity, to workmanship, or even to exercising dominion over one's environment. All the types of work involved in the construction of the *mishkan*—the Tabernacle, or portable Temple carried by the Hebrews in the wilderness—are forbidden on the Sabbath according to Exodus 31 and 35, but in a more general sense, *melakhot* echo the activities of the Creator during the first six days of creation.

To truly explore the concept of the *melakha*, however, one must turn to the collection of oral law, commentary, and anecdotes that make up the Talmud, the second-most important book in Judaism, and a work so vast and complex that it is sometimes referred to as the "Sea of Talmud"—and that's by the people who study and use it. For non-Jews, the cross-currents, icebergs, and maelstroms are even more bewildering and intimidating. Nonetheless, certain organizing principles can be understood: the two main categories of material in the book are Mishnah (laws gathered from oral tradition and ordered in the third century) and Gemara (rabbinical commentary on the Mishnah, gathered over several centuries afterward). The Mishnah itself is divided into sixty-three treatises which are gathered by subject into six orders, indicating that Jewish scholars have spent more than a little time drawing dividing lines, sometimes lengthy and recursive ones, all over the corpus of Jewish law.

But if we look between some of those lines, at the second group of Mishnah treatises, we can learn a few things about proper observation of the Shabbat. This group, known as Moed, provides no fewer than thirty-nine categories of *melakhot*, some of which are fairly straight-forward: planting, reaping, sewing, and writing are examples. Others can become extremely complex and require extensive discussion, such as the issue of how to deal with a bowl of trail mix; picking out raisins from the mix might or might not be permissible, depending upon such issues as whether one prefers the raisins or the non-raisin parts of the mix, or what one does with them after picking them out. Several of the *melakhot* involve this process of "winnowing," or separating what is desirable from what is not; since the Lord divided sea from dry land on Day Three, on the Shabbat an observant Jew is not even supposed to pick the small bones from a piece of fish. The boundary between the seventh day and the other six is so strong that even the practice of drawing lines is forbidden.

For many goyim (and, I suspect, more than a few Jews), the most bewildering of the Shabbat rules involve transferring things from one "domain" to another. In effect, things cannot be taken from a pub-lic space to a private one, or vice-versa; in practical terms, this prohi-bition against "carrying" means an observant Jew cannot take things across a property line on the Sabbath. This prohibition is in force even in a shared area like an apartment complex; though it may be a sin-gle property to the landlord, the Talmud recognizes each individual dwelling as a separate domain.

The difficulties this presents are numerous and potentially trouble-some. How can a mother take her baby out in the stroller? How can a woman bring flowers to a sick friend? How can an old man go for a walk without his cane?

Rather than leaving each family trapped in its home for the entire Sabbath, the rabbis found a solution in the concept of the *eruv* (plural *eruvin*). An *eruv* is literally a food item, usually bread, that is shared by the people dwelling within a wall, thus making the enclosed area a single dwelling for carrying purposes. Eventually, however, the word came to refer to the enclosure itself. Rabbinical teachings about the city of Jerusalem in the book of Jeremiah expanded the use of *eruvin* even more. The prophet's specific prohibition against bringing burdens into the gates of the city suggested that carrying them *within* the city was permissible—clearly, then, an *eruv* could extend over enormous distances.

Nor did the wall or fence have to be a functional one; the borders of the *eruv* could be symbolized by stakes and ropes, or (as is most common today) by utility poles and wire. Thus, so long as an apartment complex is surrounded by a wall or fence, even one that keeps nothing in or out, the individuals living inside it can treat the courtyard within as part of their own homes.

I'm sure some readers are ready to jump on the idea of *eruvin* as some kind of cheating—as though the rules of Shabbat were comparable to those of an Olympic event, and the use of an *eruv* were equivalent to stepping out of bounds without penalty. This is not, however, an interpretation that I consider accurate or useful. The whole purpose of the Sabbath day is to focus the individual's mind on what God has done for her, not to set up a series of traps so that she spends the entire day focused on the possibility of doing something wrong. In that light, the use of *eruvin* strikes me as a practical solution to the problem of living among human beings—and yet another example of how a human tool like a property line is all too easily mistaken for a distinction handed down from on high. Moreover, Jews are permitted—indeed, actually required—to violate Shabbat rules in order to preserve human life. A Jew can therefore rush an injured person to the hospital in his car or phone the fire department without worrying that he has broken a divine commandment—indeed, if he *fails* do so, he's broken a commandment.

It's also worth emphasizing that any gentile preparing to criticize Judaism for allowing *eruvin* had better be prepared to consider the mote in his own eye, as more than a few dividing lines seem to have become rather less divisive over the years. There are, for example, plenty of Christian scholars in the world who have justified ignoring the Bible's injunctions against eating shrimp or wearing wool-blend clothing, not to mention its rules requiring tithing and circumcision. Every belief system on Earth alters certain of its standard practices in certain situations. Catholics have a rule about what happens if a supplicant should sneeze while in the midst of receiving the Host, while Baptists receive Communion with a liquid that is not, according to most definitions, wine. (Granted, if left undrunk, it *could* become wine . . . eventually.) Injured or aged Muslims are not required to prostrate themselves for prayer, and even atheists are prone to redrawing the lines at times, most famously when in foxholes.

One of the most fascinating examples of moral delineation, to my eyes, involves the capybara. According to biologists, this South American mammal is a gigantic semiaquatic rodent—in fact, the largest member of that order, reaching a weight of up to 200 pounds. According to the Vatican, however, the capybara is a fish.

Given the animal's appearance—somewhere between a guinea pig, a beaver, and a small hippo—and mammalian features such as lungs, hair, and milk glands, this might appear to be a significant error on the part of Catholic naturalists, but in fact the issue has nothing to do with taxonomy and everything to do with cuisine. The Church's rules about diet are many and varied, but when its influence was first being spread throughout the New World, one caused some concern: the historical injunction against eating meat at certain times, particularly Ash Wednesday, Good Friday, and every Friday between them. According to the U.S. Conference of Catholic Bishops,

> Abstinence laws consider that meat comes only from animals such as chickens, cows, sheep or pigs—all of which live on land. Birds are also considered meat.

By this definition, an observant Catholic, even today, should not only forgo the consumption of beef, pork, and mutton during Lent, but more exotic meats such as venison, rabbit, horse, goat, squirrel, and opossum, not to mention poultry of any sort. Those familiar with the anti-Catholic slur "mackerel-snapper," however, will know that the Church has long permitted the consumption of fish when other flesh is forbidden:

> Fish are a different category of animal. Salt and freshwater species of fish, amphibians, reptiles, (cold-blooded animals) and shellfish are permitted.

For generations, these categories defined the Lenten diet quite clearly for Old World Catholics, but the discovery of the New World also involved the discovery of whole new types of fauna—strange animals like llamas, tapirs, chinchillas, and marmosets. Still, none of these New World mammals are permissible foodstuffs—only the capybara. How did the Church come to give its blessing to the eating of a rodent? Accounts, as the saying goes, vary, but Brian Ellsworth of the New York *Sun* reports that sixteenth-century South American converts had trouble keeping food on the table, let alone deliberately abstaining from some foods during Lent.

According to legend, the clergymen sent a message to Vatican authorities, describing a furry creature that spends much of its time swimming with its webbed feet, implying that it might be a fish—and hinting that permission to eat the animal could save them from possible starvation.

As a result of the Vatican's approval, salted capybara is consumed in great quantities by Venezuelans, especially during Holy Week. This may seem strange, or at least unappetizing, to those of us with smaller rodents in our neighborhoods, but who are we to argue with the interpretations religious authorities deliver to the faithful? If a simple wire can turn an apartment complex into a single dwelling, why shouldn't a papal decree transform a rodent into seafood? The lines drawn by religion between right and wrong, ultimately, are the same as the lines drawn by politics on a map, and often are drawn for the same reasons. Whether you believe that the riverbeds and ridgelines of the world were shaped by divinity or diastrophism, those natural features do not become borders until some human authority chooses to treat them as such. And of course, even if these human authorities change their minds about where the border should go, the river will keep right on flowing regardless.

In fact, some research indicates that the lines between right and wrong are drawn in our brains—specifically, that our most sacred beliefs are considered in particular regions of our brains, but not in others. As Brandon Keim reported in *Wired*, researchers at Emory University asked subjects a variety of questions while mapping their brain activity:

The statements were not necessarily religious, but intended to cover a spectrum of values ranging from frivolous ("You enjoy all colors of M&Ms") to ostensibly inviolate ("You think it is okay to sell a child"). After answering, test participants were asked if they'd sign a document stating the opposite of their belief in exchange for a chance at winning up to $100 in cash. If so, they could keep both the money and the document; only their consciences would know.

When subjects agreed to sell out their earlier beliefs, even with no negative consequences for doing so, their brains showed activity in regions where utility is usually calculated—the cost-benefit zones. Basically, their brains weighed the repercussions of signing such a statement and viewed them as acceptable. But if a subject refused to sign such a statement, the decision was not reached within that same region:

When they refused, activity was concentrated in other parts of their brains: the ventrolateral prefrontal cortex, which is known to be involved in processing and understanding abstract rules, and the right temporo-parietal junction, which has been implicated in moral judgement.

In other words, the part of the brain that considers two possible cuts of meat and says, "The ham's a better value than the beef" is not the same part that looks at them and says, "The ham's not kosher." Once your brain has drawn a moral line, the question of what lies on which side of that line is considered only in the region of the brain where moral lines are drawn. If a principle is held as sacred enough, the rest of the brain literally doesn't consider violating it. "If it's a sacred value to you," Emory's Greg Berns told Keim, "then you can't even conceive of it in a cost-benefit framework."

Obviously, this discovery has some profound implications. If nothing else, it helps explain why disputes between people of different faiths or different political values systems so often seem intractable; what one side views as a completely logical compromise may enter the other side's brains as an action completely outside the realm of utility. And if you were one of those hoping for peace in the Middle East anytime soon, it's the kind of discovery that may drive you to drink. If drinking is acceptable to your right temporoparietal junction, at least.

THAT THERE ARE borderlines for moral judgment within the human brain should not, I suppose, be all that surprising, considering how our lives involve a never-ending series of decisions about which lines to cross and which to leave inviolate. The rules handed down by the various divine powers may involve a bewildering variety of moral lines, some more clear and specific than others, but at least a believer can take comfort in one fact: unlike a true line, these rules are not infinite. It's a practical matter; if they were infinite, no human being could obey them all. Thus, most faiths rely on a short list of fundamental principles or behaviors—the Five Pillars of Islam, the Four Noble Truths of Buddhism, etc.—which is supplemented by additional more specific rules. If you like, these latter rules can be considered as closer views of the border between right and wrong, just as more detailed maps of small sections of a border can reveal more specific curves and whorls than a small-scale map of a large region can easily depict.

As time passes and the world changes, however, questions inevitably arise about the side of the boundary where new situations belong. The human brain hasn't yet had a chance to settle on a location for considering these situations, so it may not even be clear whether this is a decision of utility or morality. Obviously some kind of outside assistance is needed, but the outside assistance may be equally lacking in clarity. The Torah, for example, has no direct teachings about the telephone; if YHWH has passed down no specific ruling on whether the phone may be used on Shabbat, how can an observant Jew determine what to do?

Enter the rabbi. Like most religions, Judaism is administered by human beings who through study, or insight, or divine selection are considered authorities on the teachings of the faith. These individuals consider any novel situation or behavior and examine it in light of the faith's existing principles; eventually, they make a pronouncement concerning this new development and its permissibility. (In the case of the telephone, it's usually forbidden; most Orthodox and many Conservative authorities consider the use of electrical devices a form of the *melakha* that involves igniting or sparking a fire.)

The rabbi, the priest, the imam, the lama, the priestess, the minister, the mother superior, the shaman, the abbot . . . these are, in effect, surveyors of the moral landscape. Acting as intermediate authorities between the divine and the human, they are called upon to pass judgment on exactly where each border lies, and exactly which territory a given human being is occupying.

Nonbelievers might argue that these surveyors presume too much authority, or that they seek to draw lines where none logically exist—trying to create a Four Corners where the myriad folds and wrinkles of the human landscape defy such simplistic linearity. It is certainly likely that even believers will agree that the *other* faiths' surveyors have drawn lines in the wrong places. The overriding truth, however, is that these moral borders are fundamentally the same as those drawn on the map; they are tools. Whether they have their origins in nature or divine commandment, these lines are still tools used by human beings to give order to human behavior, and unless a human being respects them, God only knows where they actually lie.

Time of the Season

> *The water's not cold, baby, dip in your big toe,*
> *Maybe I'll see you in flagrante delicto.*
> —Jonathan Coulton, "First of May"

THERE IS PERHAPS one place where humanity's scrawl across nature is even more obvious than on the map: on the calendar. Like a map, a calendar is at its base a public recognition of certain truths: that the sun comes up like so, and the moon goes through phases like so, and the seasons change like so. Beyond those universal bits of consensus, however, calendars exhibit only the human desire to impose order on a system— and as on the map, the order being imposed depends almost entirely on the preferences of the entity doing the imposing.

The first thing that entity must provide is a decision about which heavenly body will be the basis of the calendar. Some calendars are based on the rotation of the earth; the fundamental unit of such a calendar, then, is the day. Others are based on the moon and its changing face, thus giving primacy to the month. And still others focus on the seasons, which are based on the position of the earth in its orbit around the sun, making the year the fundamental unit. To some degree, that decision may be based on scale—how big a unit do you want to consider in your measurement of time?—but no matter which of these natural cycles you choose, you cannot ignore the existence of the other two. Unfortunately, if you try to take the other two into account, you quickly discover that your calendar won't let you. As Stephen Jay Gould drily observes in *Questioning the Millennium*:

> God—who, on this issue, is either ineffable, mathematically incompetent, or just plain comical—also arranged these primary cycles in such a way that not one of them works as a simple multiple of any other . . .

This sounds complicated, but it's actually fairly straightforward: nature can do whatever it wants, but people need numbers that divide evenly. America's monetary system, for example, depends upon the fact that we can evenly divide one unit (the dollar) into smaller ones. There are exactly 100 cents in a dollar, so if you're at the movies, trying to buy Milk Duds for $4.39, you can quickly determine which bits of your pocketful of change will give you the 39 cents you need. Now imagine trying to make that same quick calculation if a penny was worth 1.2 percent of a dollar, rather than exactly 1 percent, or if there were eleven dimes in a dollar. If you can figure out how to pay 39/100ths of a dollar in time to get to your seat for the opening credits, you're some kind of wizard.[1]

What's the mathematical issue with the calendar? Again, the problem is a lack of divisibility. For example, a year is not 365 days long. It takes approximately 365.25 days for the Earth to complete an orbit around the sun. A solar calendar, like the Julian calendar established by the Romans, is based on the day, but even the Romans weren't disciplined enough to work with a six-hour discrepancy every year. They were, however, disciplined enough to create the leap year, which combines those six-hour discrepancies to make an extra day every fourth

---

1. I mean this literally. The monetary system devised by J. K. Rowling in the Harry Potter books is based on prime numbers—numbers which cannot be evenly divided by any number other than one—making it completely impractical for muggles like you and me. The basic unit of the wizard economy is the Galleon; there are 17 Sickles in a Galleon, and 29 Knuts to a Sickle. In other words, if your lunch tab is 26 Galleons, 11 Sickles, and 19 Knuts, the only way to calculate a fifteen-percent tip before the dinner rush is with a magic wand.

year. Not that the leap year was enough. That 365.25-day figure is only an approximation; the actual length of the year is a little over eleven minutes shorter. Eventually, at a rate of nearly an hour per five years, that kind of error adds up. By the time Gregory XIII took up the papacy in 1572, the calendar was some ten days ahead of the earth's orbit. Astronomical events like equinoxes and solstices were now occurring long after their predicted dates, making the determination of the arrival of Easter even harder than it is today.

Gregory's solution was two-pronged. Some minor adjustments of leap years (namely, dropping them in years divisible by 100, but keeping them in years divisible by 400) would keep the calendar from going any farther astray, but there were still those extra ten days to get rid of. And as Gould describes it,

> Pope Gregory did so—just like that, and by fiat! In 1582, October 5 through 14 simply disappeared and never occurred at all! The date following October 4 became October 15, and the calendar came back into sync.

This elegant, if drastic, solution to the problem was not universally accepted. Though the Catholic world recognized papal authority to eliminate a whole chunk of the year, it would be 170 years before the British came around, and by that time, there was an eleventh day to delete. (This is why British subject George Washington's birth was recorded as the Julian February 11, but was later celebrated by Americans on the Gregorian February 22.) The Eastern Orthodox Church ignored Gregory's excision until 1923, when it adopted a new liturgical calendar based on the Julian calendar, but in the process eliminated thirteen days, thus bringing it in sync with Rome, at least temporarily.

The solar calendar, then, seems to have some issues. Maybe it would be wiser to go with a lunar mode, which both Islam and Judaism follow. Of course, some problems arise fairly quickly, because there are roughly 29.5 days between new moons—a *synodic month*. Twelve of these "months" therefore take a little over 354 days. Thus, if you're trying to observe something on the same lunar calendar date every year, it's going to happen almost two weeks earlier in the solar year each time. The holy month of Ramadan, for example, is observed by Muslims annually, but it moves gradually from season to season; in 2011 it began on August 1, in 2012 in mid-July, in 2013 in early July, and so on. After 32 years, it will once again start on the first of August. Some celebrations, however, are strongly associated with a particular season, rather than a precise date. The observance of Passover, clearly a spring festival, was not one that Jewish authorities would allow to move throughout the year. If necessary, they would insert what was basically a leap month (actually a repetition of the month of Adar) into the calendar in order to keep Pesach in sync with the seasons.

It's this last that I find telling. Regardless of astronomy, these complex epicycles of time develop because of human needs—politics, or religion, or simple convenience. And it's not as though everyone needs exactly the same thing from the calendar, either; this is why even today you can find people—well-meaning, thoughtful, even enthusiastic people—doing their damnedest to make the calendar more sensible.

"Sensible," however, is a purely subjective term, and one that can collide with another subject's definition with a crunch that is almost audible. Consider, for example, the calendar devised by Johns Hopkins University professors Steve Hanke and Richard Henry; Hanke is a professor of economics, Henry of physics and astronomy, and in their mutual desire to find a system where heavenly bodies and human activities can both operate with ease, they have created The Hanke-Henry Permanent Calendar.

Inspired by the business-minded reform efforts of Eastman Kodak founder George Eastman, Hanke and Henry sought to bring more regularity to the calendar, so that dates and days would no longer rotate independently. As described at the libertarian Cato Institute's website, their calendar attempts to be "simple, religiously unobjectionable, business-friendly and identical year-to-year."

This last is a crucial element of the HHPC, ensuring that July 4, for example, will always fall on a Wednesday, while December 25 will always be Sunday. This would make many business calculations simpler, though it would doubtless irritate some NFL players who would prefer not to work on Christmas every year. In order to achieve this regularity, Hanke and Henry give each month 30 days, except for March,

June, September, and December, which have 31. A quick calculation, however, will reveal that this year lasts only 364 days, which threatens to cause the same creep through the seasons that Pope Gregory had to stop. Not to worry, though: the HHPC takes care of this by adding an extra week at the end of the year. In some years. Which years? Perhaps I should let Hanke and Henry explain it themselves:

[E]very five or six years (specifically, in the years 2015, 2020, 2026, 2032, 2037, 2043, 2048, 2054, 2060, 2065, 2071, 2076, 2082, 2088, 2093, 2099, 2105, . . . , which have been chosen mathematically to minimize the new calendar's drift with respect to the seasons), one extra full week (seven days, so that the Sabbath is unaffected) is inserted, at the end of the year.

This leaves me with a few questions. Who chose these years, and by what "mathematical" criteria were they chosen? Why are leap years sometimes five years apart and sometimes six? How can one predict whether there will be a "leap week" in a given year without a copy of the list above? And if you're born during that week, when do you celebrate your birthday? Wouldn't we be creating an entire class of people whose lives play out like *The Pirates of Penzance*?

Hanke and Henry are not trying to do anything drastically different from what other calendar makers are trying to do, but they do demonstrate a fundamental truth: humanity and Mother Nature are working with two different sets of concerns. No matter how carefully considered a calendar may be, or how eminent its designers, there comes a point where we have to acknowledge that she's simply not going to sync her activities up with ours. At that point, a certain resignation may settle upon us, or we may search for a view of time that ignores complex astronomical observations and numerical trivia and gets down to a more basic question: Is it cold out?

I FOUND MYSELF considering this particular question in the spring of 2011, when I spent two months as an intern on *Living Bird* magazine. The magazine is a publication of the Cornell Lab of Ornithology (CLO) in Ithaca, New York, which left me living roughly seven hours north of my home in Virginia, but in a place of no small natural beauty. Ithaca, a classic college town, sits at the upstream end of a deep glacial lake some forty miles long and roughly two miles wide. Over millennia, as highland streams have made their way to the basin of Cayuga Lake, they have cut a variety of channels, some steep enough to create the town's most famous feature: a variety of scenic gorges, several of which drop away in the middle of Cornell's campus. The best known of them is the gorge of Falls Creek, which plunges 150 feet over Ithaca Falls into a natural amphitheater. The Falls have been celebrated in graphic form as the initial "I" in the ubiquitous *Ithaca Is GORGES* T-shirts and bumper stickers sold all over town, not to mention in the numerous parody slogans reading *Ithaca Is GANGSTA*, *Ithaca Is HIGH* (with a prominent marijuana leaf), *Ithaca Is BRAAAINS* (featuring a zombie theme), and (my favorite) *It's Spelled* Gorgeous, *Assholes.*

The most relevant parody slogan, however, reads simply *Ithaca is COLD.* This is something no resident will deny, and indeed, many of them will regale the listener with tales of temperature extremes and unlikely weather developments, including horizontal blizzards and the occasional May snowfall. The National Oceanic and Atmospheric Administration reports that temperatures in January and February average a high of over 32 degrees Fahrenheit—barely—and a low of just over 13, while the record low is 25 below zero. In a typical year, Ithaca will get a whopping 68 inches of snow, starting in November and extending through April, but it will be distributed unevenly. The lakeside community is about 400 feet above sea level, while the hills around the lake valley rise to about 1100 feet, meaning that there is often a significant thermocline between the downtown area (at lake level) and the CLO's headquarters (up on the highlands). It is thus not uncommon to find rain howling down on the lower side of Triphammer Road, while at the uphill end snow is falling—a form of binary precipitation known to the locals as *ithacation.*

When I left for New York in mid-March, my home in Virginia was well past the end of winter, not that we'd had an especially hard one; the average snowfall there is about 18 inches, and I'm not sure we'd made our average. I knew in my head that I was moving into a very different region, but that fact wasn't settled in my gut until I woke up on my first morning in Ithaca and discovered the light dusting of snow

that had fallen during the night. Indeed, snow continued to fall inter-
mittently for my first three weeks at the CLO, culminating in the unexpected "blizzard" of April 5. (That was the term at least two different
Ithacans used to describe it to me, but since the total fall was under
five inches and melted rapidly away, I can't repeat it without the scare
quotes.) Skies remained cloudy for another week, and the temperature
remained below 70 degrees (a number my hometown had topped back
in February) until April 11. At that point the heat became so oppres-
sive to the other interns working with me in the Sapsucker Lounge that
we had to open the windows.

As you can imagine, in a place with a winter of such intensity, the
population is focused with similar intensity on the arrival of spring,
and the human population is hardly the only one so focused. The pond
behind the Lab, almost completely frozen over when I arrived, was by
mid-April home to the activity of muskrats, mink, and turtles, while
the local Canada Geese had been pairing off and building nests for
several weeks.

None of this is especially different from spring in the Southeast,
though we don't have mink and our thirst for good weather isn't so
intense that we break out the shorts and T-shirts at the first sign that
the high might top 45 today. In Virginia, spring is marked by the
blooming of daffodils, the arrival of Common Grackles in great numbers, and the accumulation of yellow pine pollen on every flat surface.
Though we may get a snow flurry in early March, the trees are always
well on their way to full leafing by St. Patrick's Day, and the arrival of
spring migrants is viewed as a pleasant surprise—sure, we knew they
were coming at *some* point, but we hadn't really thought about the
matter much.

In Ithaca, however, they've thought about it. For months. From the
first meaningful snowfall in November through the grim darkness of
December, through the icy grip of January, through all seventy-four
godforsaken days of February . . . oh, yes, they've thought about it.

Spring arrives in Virginia as a welcome change, a shift in ward-
robe and attitude that's anticipated, but never in doubt; it's like waiting thirty minutes after you eat to go swimming. In Ithaca, however,
spring is more like a pardon from the governor: a reprieve from a fate

dreaded at great length. Its arrival is desired desperately, and it's made worse by the underlying fear that *it's not going to come.*

As a result, birders in Ithaca view migration very differently from those in Virginia. For an Ithacan birder, spring is a matter of belief: to get through the winter, you must keep your faith that it will end, that the sun will come back out and the bright birds of summer will return to the shores of Cayuga Lake. As a result, the common birds that spend the winter in Virginia—Hermit Thrushes, Yellow-rumped Warblers, Carolina Wrens—are greeted like liberators when they arrive in the Finger Lakes region, even if there is still ice on the water and snow in the air. On the morning of April 2, the CLO's Robyn Bailey and I spotted a Northern Mockingbird on a wire at our birding group's first stop. Robyn, a native Alabaman who had been in Ithaca for only three months, thought no more of it than I did, as mockers are abundant throughout the year where we come from. When we mentioned it in passing to the others in our group, however, there was actual agonizing that they had missed it.

In truth, I should not have been surprised to find so many Ithacan birders impatiently waiting to see The First ___ of the Year. It should have been obvious from a list compiled and distributed by the Lab's community outreach program, a document titled "Average Spring Arrival Dates" showing 72 migrant species and when to expect them in the area, starting on March 5 (Wood Duck) and ending on April 28 (Wood Thrush). Here, in black and white, was a clear example of the northerner's powerful yearning for the end of winter. In this place, battered by snow and ice in a way no Sun Belt community could appreciate, such a list was almost holy writ.

Nor did it take me long to get caught up in the excitement of the oncoming season. The Sapsucker Lounge, which has a variety of donated optics lying around, fills with CLO researchers, artists, editors, and administrators whenever a new bird arrives on the pond behind the Lab, and since I was already stationed there, I took it upon myself to keep visitors up to date on the latest developments—the Tree Swallows that came in on March 30, the Belted Kingfisher's arrival on April 4, and so on. Mind you, the favor was returned; when a Northern Pintail landed out back, outreach manager Charles Eldermire bounded into the room to announce the fact to the lounge. I immediately dropped what I was doing and followed Charles to the Arthur Allen tower over-looking the pond in order to observe the drake's handsome plumage from up close. *Spring* was coming, dammit.

SCIENTISTS, NOT SURPRISINGLY, are interested in migration, and thousands of pages have been devoted to answering the question of how birds manage to find their way from place to place over distances greater than many humans travel in a lifetime.

Somewhat fewer pages, however, have been devoted to the question of *why* birds migrate. The three leading contenders for answering this question are 1) changes in the availability of food, 2) changes in the vulnerability of birds and nests to predators, and 3) direct effects of the seasonal changes on birds' physiology. In layman's terms, we can call these starvation, predation, and exposure.

In their 2007 examination of bird migration (titled, sensibly, "Why Migrate?") Alice Boyd and Courtney Conway of the University of Arizona considered these issues by examining the New World birds known as the Tyranni. For Americans, the most familiar birds of this very large group are probably the flycatchers, kingbirds, and phoebes, most of which are both insectivorous and migratory, but other Tyranni, including manikins, cotingas, and becards, can be neither, or only one of the above. Boyd and Conway restricted themselves to the 379 species on which significant data was available in journals and field guides, then divided the birds by migration activity, habitat (including elevation), diet (four groups, ranging from primarily insect-eating to primarily fruit-eating), foraging habits (whether alone, with other conspecific birds, or in mixed-species groups), and body mass. The scientists then started crunching the numbers, revealing that bird migration, like so many other natural activities, is a complex, non-linear thing.

The birds most likely to migrate were insectivores—but only the ones living in open country or broken scrubland. Among birds of the forest and the thicket, insectivores were somewhat less likely to migrate than frugivores (those eating fruits, nuts, and seeds), and fewer such cover-loving species did so. Birds that foraged alone were more likely to migrate than those foraging in mixed groups, but both were more likely than those who foraged in pairs with others of their own species. Finally, birds with smaller body masses tended to be less migratory than larger birds.

Clearly, though they are certainly more plentiful in warmer weather, insects are not the sole force driving migration. Some birds are able to alter their diets with the season, switching from insects to a more plentiful food source. Tree Swallows, for example, spend the winter dining on the berries of the wax myrtle, which grows in such places as Florida and the Gulf Coast. As a result, they need not travel as far as other American swallows, many of whom winter in South America. This shorter migration works to the Tree Swallow's advantage on the northward journey as well, since they can return to their breeding grounds earlier in the year than other spring migrants, and find. nesting sites before they must compete with other birds, such as the Purple Martin, which typically arrives in Ithaca several weeks later.[2]

Another migrant, however, may be more dependent on insects than is commonly thought. The Ruby-throated Hummingbird is a familiar sight all across the eastern part of the country, darting through gardens to insert its long thin bill deep into a blossom to enjoy the nectar. It is natural, then, to assume that the ruby-throat's absence during the colder months (it arrives in Ithaca in late April) is due to a lack of blooming plants, but an article by Jack Connor in the autumn 2010 issue of *Living Bird* suggests that flowers are only part of the story. Connor examines a variety of studies ranging from 1946 to 1995, all of which indicate that the popular view of hummers as primarily nectar-eaters is mistaken. The 1995 study by F. G. Stiles is given particular emphasis, as it indicates from research over an 18-year period that over half of the feeding done by hummingbirds is done on arthropods— spiders in particular. Indeed, hummers will sometimes go to a web not just to eat the spider, but also to dine on the prey that the spider has already captured in it. No matter which food the ruby-throat prefers,

---

2. The Purple Martin's own insect diet is somewhat misunderstood. Many people put up martin houses under the impression that the birds will serve as a natural form of mosquito control. According to Steve Kress of the National Audubon Society, however, martins rarely eat insects so small, preferring instead to feed on larger prey, such as dragonflies—which *do* eat mosquitoes.

however, Ithaca has little of it during the winter, which explains why the bird spends its winters in Mexico.

Luckily for the species heading north in the spring, and not coincidentally for the birders that long to see them, the Ithaca area is rife with natural features that appeal to birds. Over a dozen state forests lie within fifteen miles of the downtown area. At the northern end of Cayuga Lake is an expanse of marsh and mudflats, some 7000 acres of which lie within Montezuma National Wildlife Refuge. Finally, there is the not-inconsiderable appeal of the lake itself, the waters of which attract loons, grebes, ducks, geese, swans, cormorants, gulls, eagles, herons, and other birds that specialize in aquatic living. Perhaps because of all these features, as well as its position relative to the ridgelines of the Appalachian Mountains, Ithaca sits along the Atlantic Flyway, one of America's four major channels for migrating birds, so any eastern species heading toward Canada are likely to put in at least a brief appearance en route. Factor in the numerous small ponds and streams feeding into the lake, and it's easy to see why even an amateur like myself can easily spot forty species of water-loving birds over the course of a few weeks in the spring—not to mention another fifty ground birds—without traveling more than a few miles from Cornell.

Mind you, some birders *do* travel more than a few miles, and I spent the spring in motion almost as constant as that of the birds. Some of this I did on my own, making trips to places like Upper Buttermilk Falls and Taughanock State Park in hopes of viewing new species and/or scenery, but the majority of it I did as part of the CLO's Spring Field Ornithology course.

My enrollment was, to say the least, unplanned. When I first contacted editor Tim Gallagher about interning at *Living Bird*, he told me up front that he had no idea what to do with an intern, having never had one before. Since I had never interned before, I didn't have a much better idea than he did, but we agreed that we'd both be willing to improvise. I thus arrived in mid-March and happily took on the job of copy-editing several articles that Tim was planning to run in the next few issues. I enjoyed this part of the gig quite a bit, primarily because proofreading the work of skilled writers like Pete Dunne, Mel White, and Jack Connor is both easier and much more enjoyable than proofreading dozens of eleventh-graders' essays on "Why Jay Gatsby Had It Made." Unfortunately, years spent reading the latter have increased my reading and editing speed quite a bit, which meant that I was soon finishing assignments faster than Tim could set them up for me.

Luckily, a few days after my arrival, Tim had a brainstorm: he'd give me a pair of long-term writing projects to work on whenever there were no pressing editorial or indexing tasks for me. I could do as much research as I wanted, either around the Lab or down in the library, and I could work on the writing whenever I had the time, even after I returned home. To make the jobs easier, there was even a bit of overlap between the assignments: both were focused on anniversaries, both dealt more with observing birds than with birds themselves, and both involved one of the best-known figures at the CLO: Steve Kress.

Dr. Stephen W. Kress is best known as the founder of Project Puffin, the catchier name for what was originally called the National Audubon Society Seabird Restoration Project. My first article would examine the thirtieth anniversary of the project's first great success: the re-establishment of a breeding colony of Atlantic Puffins off the coast of Maine. This would be fairly well-traveled ground, addressing the same subject that had been covered in past articles for *Smithsonian*, *Down East*, and even *Living Bird* itself, and would involve my spending a bit of time in conversation with Kress once he returned to his office at the CLO.

His return would mark the start of my second writing assignment: an article on the thirty-fifth anniversary of Cornell's Spring Field Ornithology class. Offered to the greater Ithaca community through the Lab, the non-credit SFO course lasted eight weeks, combining Wednesday-night lectures by Kress with weekend field trips to a variety of local (and not-so-local) birding hotspots, and culminating in an overnight trip to Cape May, New Jersey, at the height of the spring migration season. To help me write my article on this course, Tim informed me, he was enrolling me in it.

Naturally, I begged him not to throw me into that briar patch.

FILLING OUT the enrollment forms was not a complex or onerous task, particularly since Cornell and *Living Bird* were splitting the cost of my tuition, but one prompt did leave me momentarily flummoxed, and the flummoxer was, as you might expect, a matter of drawing a line. The item in question was this:

Rate your level of birding expertise:

A) Beginner
B) Intermediate
C) Expert

I immediately ticked B, but then I was seized with a moment of doubt. I had, after all, been birding actively for nearly twenty-five years. I'd even written a book about it. Would it be reasonable to consider myself an expert? Or had I really not crossed the line into expertise yet?

This question is one that matters to me. My wife can attest that I Like To Be Right (Quite A Bit, Actually), but when there's no real chance of my knowing the right answer, I feel compelled to admit the fact before I'm caught giving the wrong one. I don't *mind* when people think I know more than I do, but when my ignorance absolutely has to be put on display, I want to be the one who puts it there.

Aside from that basic insecurity, I had another reason for weighing the question of expertise: I was, after all, preparing to take a course at the Cornell Lab of Ornithology.

And the birders at the CLO are *scary.*

This was something I had to face daily. Right outside the door of the lounge was the office of the Lab's Director of Communications, Miyoko Chu, the author of *Songbird Journeys: Four Seasons in the Lives of Migratory Birds.* Next to hers was the office of Tim Gallagher, my immediate supervisor, a lifelong falconer, and one of the rediscoverers of the Ivory-billed Woodpecker. Just down the corridor was Ken Rosenberg, like Tim a former member of the Sapsuckers, the CLO's World Series of Birding team, which won the event in 2001, 2002, 2006, and 2007. And around the corner was current Sapsucker Jessie Barry, whose team set a North American record on April 22, 2011, by logging 264 species in a single day . . . and then broke it in 2013 with *294* species. Plainly put, the joint was crawling with birders who were not just experts, but among the greatest ornithological minds in the world.

I knew this, of course; it was why I'd come to Ithaca in the first place. But it was truly driven home on the third or fourth day of my internship when Kevin McGowan (a Sapsucker for the 2001 and 2002 WSB championships) made his customary early-morning appearance in the lounge to get a quick look at the pond before settling in at his desk and getting to work. On this particular morning, the milky grey March sky was filled with strings of northward-bound waterfowl, mostly Canada Geese, heading toward their namesake in their familiar V formations. Kevin looked out the window and scanned one skein. "Hmm," he said. "Looks like they've got a cackler."

I sat upright immediately. The Cackling Goose is a smaller, shorter-necked version of the Canada, identical to it for all practical purposes unless you've got them side-by-side for comparison, and I had never seen one. As Kevin stepped to the Zeiss scope to confirm his identification, I peered out at the geese in hopes of spotting some telltale sign, but the distance was simply too great. If they hadn't been in a V, I wouldn't have even known for sure that they were geese.

"There we are," said Kevin after a moment. "Cackling Goose."

"Mind if I take a look?" I said casually.

"Sure," said Kevin, stepping back from the scope. I brought my eye to it and discerned the same series of distant silhouettes I'd been looking at. They were larger now, yes, but in the diffuse light of the cloudy sky, they still betrayed no field marks whatsoever. Flapping gamely away at the trailing end of the line, however, was a bird that seemed somewhat smaller than the others. I squinted, unable to see so much as the familiar white chin marking, or the line of division between the goose's black neck and grey-brown body. I couldn't even really say for sure that its neck was shorter than those of the birds in front of it.

I raised my head from the scope, shook Kevin's hand, and thanked him for getting me a life bird at such great distance, but after he went back to his office, I started having second thoughts. Eventually I came to the decision that I couldn't really put it on my life list. I hadn't identified it myself; all I had done was lay eyes on a bird that he had identified, using indicators that only he could see. It wasn't really my bird.

My focus on the moral ramifications of this decision was so tight that it took me several hours to appreciate what I had actually witnessed: Kevin had walked into the room, looked for a brief moment at a moving bird in poor light, and had identified it from probably a mile away. *With his naked eyes.*

So. "Intermediate" it was.

THE FIRST WEEK of the SFO class didn't quite cement my intermediate status in my mind. The opening lecture dealt with issues of no small significance—choosing a field guide, operating binoculars, etc.—but they were issues that I had long considered, and I had a pretty good idea of what to carry with me in the field.

In fact, over the past 25 years I had progressed through field guides in basically the order Steve Kress suggested. For beginners, he recommended the Peterson guide, the same one that had launched me into birding for good back in the mid-1980s. Intermediate-level birders would find the National Geographic guide helpful, particularly because its thumb tabs and range map placement (on the same page as the species description) were handier in the field. And finally there was the Sibley field guide, whose clarity and numerous illustrations of varied plumage made it most useful for experts. I took satisfaction in looking down into the backpack under my chair and seeing both my NatGeo and Sibley guides, thereby assured that when the time finally came, I had the proper tools to make the transition from journeyman birder to master.

The field trip three days later, however, did little to dispel my uncertainty about my expertise. What it did make me sure about was my habitat. I was not in the South anymore.

It was Saturday, March 26, nearly a week after the vernal equinox, and we were freezing. I was the lone male in this particular group, as well as the only person over five-foot-five. As a result, I had a clear view of the top of everyone else's hat, each one of which was pulled down as low as possible to keep out the cold. Dancing from foot to foot to generate warmth, we waited for Meena Haribal, the leader assigned to guide Group Three for the day, to set up her spotting scope on the side of Snyder Road. With the sun barely over the horizon and a brisk northerly wind howling at us over the open expanse of the Ithaca Tompkins Regional Airport, there was no one among the six of us who felt there was anything springlike about today's field ornithology; the temperature here by the airfield was hovering at about twenty degrees, not counting the wind chill. Meena had brought us here to look for what she hoped would be the year's first Eastern Meadowlark, and for the rest of the group, this was viewed as a goal well worth the intense cold. I was clearly out of my comfort zone, in both a personal and geographical sense.

Still, I had to admit this was a great teaching opportunity. With a mix of intermediate birders in her group, Meena could not make assumptions about our varying levels of expertise, and she wanted to be sure we had all internalized the principle that a bird's voice is as important as its appearance. For this purpose, the Eastern Meadowlark's song is close to ideal; it's a distinctively slurry whistle, one which Meena said she remembers by the mnemonic "Spring is here."

And that, of course, was exactly what she was trying to convince us of. And herself. No matter what heavenly body astronomers may consult, no matter what lines human beings may draw on the calendar, birds remind us that time passes at its own pace. We must accept that our wishes for spring warmth, however sincere, have no power.

But somewhere in the tall grass, carried by the frigid wind, there was a whistling, and before long the yellow breast of the meadowlark could be seen at last: as welcome as Noah's rainbow, as uncontrolled as the wild geese, the first sign of winter's end.

PART TWO

Arts and Sciences

Life is short, Art long, opportunity fleeting, experience treacherous, judgment difficult.
—*Hippocrates,* Aphorisms

Just Lines on Paper

Not on the ground—Nearly touching the chicken—A really stupid ques-
tion—Nothing whatsoever about lines or paper—All in the gutter—
What happens in between—This Is So Lame

Give the chalk here—quick, thus the line should go!
—Robert Browning, "Andrea Del Sarto"

WHEN LINES ARE not drawn on the ground, it is somewhat
easier to remember that they were drawn by human beings
for human purposes, but remembering all the different purposes isn't easy in the slightest. The arts, in particular, are rife
with lines of all sorts. Writers (especially poets) sweat over the
task of composing lines of text, while actors must absorb lines
from a script and turn them into speech and action. Composers worry about melodic lines, recording them on staves made
of parallel lines. In the plastic arts, sculptors and painters
must consider the lines that give their work shape, while illus-
trators who use pen or pencil or brush may place lines on a flat
surface with a care that even Euclid might find exaggerated.

One such artist is Ursula Vernon, author and illustrator of
such titles as the children's book *Nurk: The Strange Surpris-*
ing Adventures of a (Somewhat) Brave Shrew, as well as an experienced painter, collagist, and digital manipulator. Vernon
knows a good deal about how lines function in visual art, as
well as the ways in which an image may follow a line its creator never intended. One of her paintings, "The Biting Pear of

Salamanca," a whimsical bit of surrealism featuring a green fruit with a large mouth full of oversized teeth, went viral and turned into an Internet meme; you can now see the pear posted on discussion threads all over the web, typically in situations where the poster is mocking the idiocy of a previous comment, accompanied by "LOL WUT."

Within the confines of an image, though, Vernon's lines go pretty much where she tells them to, and with remarkably little prodding from me, she points out several ways in which they can affect the composition of a drawing.

"One is 'activated' space. For whatever reason, if you have something—and lines are the worst—that is almost but not quite touching something else, the little gap in between is suddenly VERY charged. The viewer's eye is dragged to it. So if you've got a blade of grass that stands out against the background and it's nearly touching the chicken, but not quite, people will find themselves staring at that little space between the blade of grass and the chicken.

"Likewise, if you have a horizon line across the middle of the painting (or the comic panel) and nothing breaks up the line, the viewer's eye doesn't go naturally across it. Might as well be a brick wall. Hacks the piece in half completely. You either have to have something running across that stark line to give the viewer a kind of bridge across it, or make something so shockingly bright on one side that the eye will jump to it.

"And finally, a line running off at the exact corner of the page yanks the viewer's eye right off the page. Feathers, for example. If you've got a wing breaking out of the frame, great, dynamic, wonderful—but if one of the lines happens to run off at the point of the corner, the whole composition gets borked."

Vernon obviously knows lines, but as you might guess from her observation about feathers, she also knows birding. She fills her various websites (including her blog, "Tea with the Squash God," at www. redwombatstudio.com/blog) with running commentary on the birds and other wildlife she encounters in her North Carolina garden, and she is now well beyond the vague embarrassment that afflicts many novice birders. This becomes clear to me when she admits to having experienced that realization, near universal among veterans, that one has been running around the house naked, looking for binoculars in order to identify a bird outside the window. "I did once do it while my boyfriend was on the phone to a priest," she adds, "but since the bird was a Pileated Woodpecker, who could blame her?

Birding informs her art in a variety of ways, including her choice of subject matter. Vernon's preferred bird? Not what you might expect. "I love painting chickens. Chickens are one of my default settings. It would probably be cooler if they were a wild bird, but for sheer variation—and grumpiness—there is nothing quite like a chicken." She has also discovered, however, that even when the subject is a chicken, some viewers insist on drawing a line between different art forms—or in their minds, between Art and Not-Art.

The "Not-Art" in question is the medium of comics, a medium that Vernon has explored in several works, including her Hugo Award-winning webcomic, *Digger* (now available in six collected print volumes as well as a new omnibus edition), and *Dragonbreath*, an ongoing series for children. Her non-comics work is at times informed by her comics (and vice-versa), but she has come across some viewers who resist the whole notion of comics as an art. "In traditional comics, you're kind of lucky—if you want to draw a chicken, you draw a line around the chicken. Realism, not so much. I've actually seen people say that something isn't *real* art because there's a line around it, which is sort of baffling, but there you are."

It is indeed baffling, but perhaps there is an explanation: comics is an art form where the line has long been the most important means of expression. The majority of comics artists employ pencils and pens to create their images, and even those who do not typically use their digital equivalents. It is often considered compliment enough to say of a comics artist, "She's got a good line." The writers and letterers, meanwhile, concern themselves primarily with the lines of text, leaving only the colorists (assuming the publisher can afford color printing) to consider the fields between the lines. No definition of comics has ever been more succinct than R. Crumb's: "It's all just lines on paper, folks."

That statement is largely accurate, but it's equally accurate, and equally reductive, to say, "Painting is just globs on canvas." Oddly, though, no one ever denies that painting is *"real* art." The question of whether comics should be considered *real* art is raised on a regular basis; it has also been answered in the affirmative on many occasions, including by one authority who also felt compelled to preface his answer by pointing out that it is "a *really* stupid question."

This particular authority is writer/artist/blogger Scott McCloud, whose online journal's title, *I Can't Stop Thinking!*, is as pithy a statement about his own work as Crumb's was about the form. McCloud first came to prominence in the 1980s as the creator of the whimsical independent comic *Zot!* and the hilarious super-hero fight-scene parody *DESTROY!!*, but it was not until a decade later that he found his true niche as a theorist. His 1993 book, *Understanding Comics: The Invisible Art*, was part history, part dictionary, part manifesto, and part example; the book uses the comics form, rather than text, on every page but the acknowledgments and the index. A serious and thoughtful work which explored the myriad ways the medium of comics could be used, it also served as a terrific showcase for McCloud's wit, imagination, and artistic skill. It won comics' two highest awards, the Harvey and the Eisner, was named a *New York Times* Notable Book for the year, and was praised by every comics creator from Neil Gaiman to Art Spiegelman to Matt Groening. Almost immediately, *Understanding Comics* became one of the most influential works ever written on the medium of comics, one that framed the discussion of the form for years to come, and McCloud's own cartoon doppelganger became as recognizable to readers as many of the characters he discussed, even to the point of being parodied in online comics like *Penny Arcade* and *PVP*. That awareness in the online comics community stemmed partly from his next book, *Reinventing Comics* (2000), in which he examined the impact of digital technology on the creation and distribution of comics. He then put together a how-to book, *Making Comics* (2006), for those interested in pursuing comics as an art and/or career. He has traveled many miles explaining his ideas to audiences all over the world and all across the web, including a 2005 TED Talk which can be viewed at www.ted.com.[1]

---

1. Some years ago I was lucky enough to get McCloud to come speak at Woodberry Forest School, where he proved a delightful guest and repaid our hospitality by explaining the meaning of the Queen song "'39," which had puzzled me for years. Admittedly, its

Needless to say, consulting McCloud's work to learn about lines in comics is not unlike knocking the plug off a fire hydrant, but he shows where the main stream of his thinking will be blasting right in the first chapter of *Understanding Comics*, in which he sets out to define the word *comics*, eventually arriving at this:

> **comics** (kom´ iks) **n.** plural in form, used with a singular verb. **1.** Juxtaposed pictorial and other images in deliberate sequence, intended to convey information and/or to produce an aesthetic response in the viewer.

As McCloud explicitly points out, this definition says nothing whatsoever about lines or paper: "There is no mention of black lines and flat colored ink. No calls for exaggerated anatomy or for representational art of any kind. No schools of art are banished by our definition, no philosophies, no movements, no ways of seeing are out of bounds!"

But that mention of boundaries suggests that lines *are* on his mind, though not the lines that commonly make up the images; images, after all, can be created with a finger, a spray can, or a camera, not just a pencil or pen. No, the most important lines are instead those that create the "deliberate sequence" necessary in comics. To have a sequence, there must be at least two images, and those images must be separated. And what tool do human beings tend to favor for the job of separating two things on a flat surface?

THE BORDER BETWEEN images on a comics page isn't always a line; sometimes it's simply an indefinite empty space, or an element of the backgrounds depicted in the images, or even a carefully demarcated vacancy. Still, the standard comics sequence, whether in a comic strip or a comic book, is divided into individual images called *panels*, each of which is typically contained inside a set of lines. These lines are frequently arranged in rectangles and drawn with a straight edge, but such traditions have often been violated. *Pogo*'s Walt Kelly added a rustic feeling to his strip's swamp setting by drawing his panel borders

---

thematic link to Einstein's Twin Paradox would have been more apparent if only I'd paid attention to the fact that songwriter/guitarist Brian May got his degree in astrophysics.

freehand, sometimes with deliberate whorls or dents, while comics master Will Eisner might eschew panel borders entirely, or else work them into the architecture of a city scene. But whatever lies between the images, be it a thin black penstroke, a vague white space, or an ornate frame, it acts like a borderline separating those images, and it goes by a name: the *gutter.*

In that place between the images depicted in the panels, Scott McCloud argues, lies the fundamental aspect of comics: "Here in the limbo of the gutter, human imagination takes two separate images and transforms them into a single idea." This process is called *closure,* "mentally completing that which is incomplete based on past evidence." By imagining that something occurs in the gutter, we connect one image to the next, and create meaning: a chronology, a cause and effect, a change in perspective, a complete sequence—in short, closure. As McCloud puts it, "In a very real sense, comics *is* closure!"[2]

McCloud's pronouncement is a bold one, just as Crumb's was, but neither claim should pass unexamined, and Ursula Vernon (who has herself earned an Eisner Award nomination to go along with her Hugo win) is one comics creator who is willing to give both an examination. "Lines on paper is, if nothing else, still one of the fastest and most efficient ways to do it," she notes. She concedes that Crumb might be right about his own comics, but in the end, she considers it too narrow a definition. "A great many comics use color and shading and other things rather more extensively—I have a friend who painted each panel of her comic—and there are even some very good photo comics out there. In the early days, though, it was definitely all linework, although I suspect that was caused as much by the requirements of cheap printing as anything else, and there's a lot of that still grandfathered into the field."

When it comes to closure, however, Vernon is more than willing to view it as a central element in the medium of comics. As she puts it, "I might disagree with R. Crumb, but I wouldn't have the cojones to disagree with Scott McCloud!" There might be comics that get along

---

2. Without that closure, we don't have comics; all we have is a single image. That image can still be a cartoon, and in the hands of a Gary Larson or a Charles Addams, it can be a wonderful form of art in its own right, but it's not really *comics* if there's not a sequence. As McCloud observes, a still photo of Humphrey Bogart is not a film.

without closure to some degree—single panels repeated three or more times, for example, giving the reader no pieces to assemble into a whole—but as a broad definition of comics, it works for her.

It's also a definition that she considers different from the definition of reading. "My kids' books are marketed to kids who find reading intimidating, because all the pictures make it much less scary to pick up, but I still occasionally want to grab somebody by the ear and go, 'It's not quite the same! Comics aren't just easy chapter books, really! They're a whole thing by themselves!'"

Still, if there is in fact a dividing line between comics and chapter books—and I agree with Vernon that there is—it seems appropriate for an art form so rife with lines. It's also rife with paradox. Comics isn't really all just lines on paper, but the medium depends on the reader's ability to achieve closure by crossing panel borders, even though the images separated by those borders may not use lines themselves. Without a dividing line, there's no such thing as closure . . . and without closure, there's no such thing as comics.

NOR IS COMICS the only art form that depends on the act of closure across borderlines. Mosaics, for example, consist entirely of small, distinct pieces, each of which has its own clearly defined border, but the various tiles (or "tesserae," to use the technical term) are arranged by the artist in a configuration that makes up a larger whole. If the viewer is far enough away from the mosaic, he may not be able to distinguish the individual tesserae, or even realize that there *are* individual tesserae. He must be able to perceive the whole, but the closure between separate pieces may be entirely unconscious, as it is when we watch a movie.

Like mosaics and stained-glass art, comics depends upon the existence of borders, but that doesn't mean that the borders between the images are of more concern to a comics artist than the images themselves. "The space between takes care of itself for the most part," says Vernon, though she did play with that space somewhat while working on *Digger.* "I did find it useful to vary the color of the gutters—black for cave scenes, light for aboveground—and played around with more experimental uses in some of the shorter and more experimental bits of the comic, but I suspect that most readers barely notice that, except as an atmospheric thing, and the set-up of the gutters becomes nearly automatic after you've been doing the comic for awhile." Nor is the gutter always used to separate the same kind of territories. "I've used it at least two ways—sometimes to arbitrarily force a sense of the passage of time on what would otherwise be a single image on a page, sometimes to express that this little inset bit here is happening, but in a different place than this big image around it." Sometimes the gutter lies between times, sometimes between spaces, sometimes between ideas.

To a large degree, then, Vernon believes that the medium of comics demands that the reader cross a line separating two distinct territories. "Learning to read comics is a specific skill," she says. "It's an easy jump from reading, you can pick it up in a few seconds, but you do still have to learn how to process pictures and word balloons together and figure out how to interpret what happens in between the various panels." It's this central idea that makes me wonder about my longtime love of the comics medium. If the act of reading comics demands that I use my imagination to connect the distinct images it presents, it must also demand that I acknowledge the distinctions between them. A comics reader who can't tell one panel from another cannot comprehend what he's seeing.

And if that's how I've grown up, habitually thinking about the borders between panels, has the experience left me more acutely aware of the presence of other borders?

It can be argued that a birder who can't distinguish one species from another isn't likely to understand what he's seeing, or that a traveler who can't tell one place from another may not even know she's traveling, but I'm not at all certain that the process of closure is as central to ornithology or geography as it is to comics. One need not cross the borders that lie between places in order to understand those places; indeed, a determined investigator can learn an awful lot about a place he has never been, developing expertise in an area's history, language, culture, and landscape—potentially more expertise than some of the people living there. But still, can an observer *truly* understand a place without firsthand observation? At a gut level, I think crossing that border may be necessary, if only so that the observer can directly compare where he is with where he's been.[3]

In the same vein, is it really true to say that birding *requires* the observer to make a whole out of separate pieces? In the strictest sense, no; one can look at a bird and observe its actions without any need for closure. When it comes to identifying the bird in question, however, I think it's entirely possible to argue that the field mark system devised by Roger Tory Peterson depends on assembling a whole out of well-defined parts. There have been instances where I had to identify a bird using only a handful of individual field marks—a glimpse of color here, an impression of shape there, a recognition of habitat there—so maybe the extra familiarity with closure that I've obtained from years of reading comics has made me a better birder in some ways.

Ursula Vernon, however, does not consider comics and birding especially similar, and that's the way she likes it, even though she insists that most of her birding, like much of her artwork, is done from indoors, looking out the window with her binoculars. "If I am staring through the binoculars, I am definitely not working on the comic. Frequently I am avoiding working on the comic. If it wasn't a change of pace, it wouldn't be so useful for procrastination."

Away from the drawing table or the computer, the distinction between the two activities remains. "Comics, however awesome they are, are basically at your control," Vernon points out. "Birds aren't. You will never get up at five A.M. and drive two hours to draw a comic and have it stubbornly not appear on the table. You can always draw *something*. It may suck, it may be nothing you want to show anyone, it may be a chicken holding a sign that says 'This Is So Lame,' but if you persevere, you'll get a comic.

"Birds, eh. You can hire guides and go in the proper season and spend three days memorizing the call of the Fulvous Whistling-Duck

---

3. This is the line of argument I have been using with my wife, who recently completed her master's degree in Library and Information Science, using a program conducted online by the University of Wisconsin-Milwaukee. Neither she nor I have ever set foot in Wisconsin, but from day one of her enrollment, I have insisted that we must go there, on the basis that it would be wrong to accept a degree from a place where one has never been.

and still come away empty-handed, and your friend will say 'Oh, that? I got that one out behind a gas station on the way back from Disney World.'"

I can't argue with that logic. I also have to consider that it's probably unwise to consider a form of art as a model for a science, or vice-versa. But there's no question that lines are present in most forms of art, even if it's only in the way we divide up the periods and genres that help us find the particular art we're interested in. In comics, however, the line is not only part and parcel of the art (at least in most cases), but is in fact a bedrock requirement of the art. If the artist can't divide the images from one another, the reader's mind cannot create closure between them; in comics, and maybe in other forms of art as well, the artist decides where the endpoints will be and draws them in whatever position and at whatever distance he chooses, but only the observer can draw the line.

Bricks and Mortar

A new kind of pain—I am not the only one thinking about it—"Pixels were the only way I knew the world"—Vultures eating obsolete technology—Between 1 and 0—Spoiled by jagged edges—Compressed and rarefied air—A much more complex set of skills—Exchanging fidelity for convenience—Chaotic interactions

> *The creation of a world view is the work of a generation rather than of an individual, but we each of us, for better or for worse, add our brick to the edifice. —John Dos Passos*

IT IS RARE to invent a new kind of pain. Most forms have existed for centuries, if not longer; Shakespeare knew the paper cut and Charlemagne the saddle sore, and Lucy walked the Olduvai Gorge in full awareness of the stubbed toe. When a person experiences the results of such an injury personally, she can at least take some solace in the knowledge that she is not alone, that billions of others have been there before, that humanity as a whole is in perfect sympathy.

Alas, this was not true of the first person ever to step barefoot on a LEGO® brick.

The distinctive agony of putting the full weight of one's body on the sharp plastic corners and edges of a LEGO is only about half a century old, but what it lacks in history, it makes up in ubiquity. According to LEGO.com, over 30 billion "elements" were manufactured by the company in 2010, each one of which was compatible not only with the previous year's elements, but with the original blocks made by the company in 1958. The company's headquarters is in Denmark, but LEGO toys are sold in over 130 countries, and they are enormously popular throughout Europe and America. With the total number of LEGO elements in existence approaching half a trillion—roughly 70 of them for every human being on earth—and facing neither obsolescence nor biodegradation, it is perhaps easy to understand just how many people have discovered them the hard way: with a bare foot coming down on an unlit floor.

Like most people, I first encountered this pain as a child, hoisting myself by the common petard of the American eight-year-old by treading painfully on one of the scores of LEGO bricks I habitually left lying around in half-constructed forms on the carpeting of our family room. Nor was it a singular occurrence; I played with LEGOs so much that I probably had tiny indentations in the soles of my feet until after I hit puberty. But that was hardly the end. No, long after I had hung up my bricks, I was reintroduced to the harsh consequences of careless floor inspection when my sons began leaving their own LEGO pieces around the house. The only satisfaction I have is the knowledge that when the boys' own children someday begin strewing their toys around the room, Ian and Dixon will come to understand the pain they visited upon their father, and the cycle will begin anew.

Why am I confident that this will take place? Because despite its relatively recent origin, I believe the LEGO system speaks to something primal, even eternal, in human beings. It's a desire to see the world in discrete and manageable units—to draw clear and distinct lines. The genius of LEGO is that its lines exist in three dimensions, but in effect, a LEGO block is still a set of twelve line segments defining a shape: the part of the universe enclosed by those lines is the LEGO, and on the other side, there's everything else. But once we've got the first brick defined, we can combine it with another brick to make something larger. If we're willing to add in some slight variations in shape, we can assemble enough bricks in enough configurations to make a wall, or a house, or a castle, or Wembley Stadium. But when we create that structure, we remain aware at all times that the whole is made up of clear and identifiable parts. And as complex as the interrelationships between those parts may be, when we break the system down to examine its components, each component is simplicity itself.

I am far from the only person to think about this issue, and I know that perfectly well. Nonetheless I was jolted when I came around a corner in Washington, D.C.'s Renwick Gallery in February 2013 and was brought up short by physical evidence that I wasn't the only one thinking about it. That evidence came in the form of a sculpture, one constructed out of small wooden blocks, each colored by hand and then affixed to others to create a larger form. When you stood up close, it was a sprawling assemblage of tiny, brightly colored rectangles—basically three-dimensional pixels—but when you backed away and could focus on the system, rather than the components, the overall shape became clear and obvious: it was a campfire.

The creator of this piece was Shawn Smith of Austin, Texas, an artist whose mind and imagination sprawl over an eclectic variety of places. Though he attended Dallas's Arts Magnet High School, he was planning on a career as a scientist. Smith lays the responsibility for this plan at least partly on a book: "This was just about the time James Gleick's *Chaos* came out. My physics teacher talked about it: aspects of physics, Schrödinger's cat, small bits making up a larger whole . . ." Nor did the visions of quanta and Mandelbrotian images dancing in his head go away after graduation. He was living at home, working full time, and taking classes at Brookhaven College while he took care of his father, who had undergone heart surgery (and soon after would be diagnosed with lung cancer). "I thought I'd work at the superconducting supercollider in Texas. Smashing atoms sounded fascinating—bits of information flying around. That's where I started—but then I had math limitations. The enthusiasm was there, but not the math to speak that language."

As a result, when Smith went off to Washington University in St. Louis for his junior year, it was to study not physics, but printmaking and sculpture. Even with this change, however, his interest was engaged by books, though this time not as inspiration, but as raw materials. "I cut them up with a bandsaw," he says cheerfully. "I did one series called *Deep-fried Southern Authors*—literally deep-fried. I worked at a restaurant with a sympathetic sous chef who would let me fry works in the leftover grease."

A less fattening use of literature, however, was a 2002 project called *Re-Frankenstein*, which drew Smith increasingly into the realm of the digital. "I was interested in how Google Image search works; what rises to the top of the image search? It's usually by popularity. Open-ended nouns like *car* are big and make sense. But if you search using the word *the*, what's the popular image?" With the help of a computer-savvy assistant who created a "webscraper" to find images, Smith used Mary Shelley's novel to search the web word by word for raw material, creating a string of images based on the text. The results? "There was lots of porn," he reports, with the knowing tone of the web-savvy, but he was also being exposed to a new and unfamiliar territory. "With all the natural elements of *Frankenstein*, a lot of images of nature popped up. It dawned on me one day that I knew nothing about the natural world—I'd never seen a real campfire, never spent the night outdoors, and I ended up thinking about humans' relationship with nature." What he did know about nature, he realized, was actually just what appeared on his computer screen: "Pixels were the only way I knew the world—or certain parts of it."

Soon Smith was off to San Francisco to pursue a master's degree in sculpture at the California College of the Arts, and two lines of thinking finally crossed. "In grad school, they tried to break you down and see where you gravitate back to," he recalls. "I was ready to leave and become a parapsychologist." But along came another book—in this case Carl Zimmer's *Parasite Rex*—and suddenly the relationship between the small and the large, the component and the system, began to resonate again. "I started reading about string theory and the way the world was broken up by different lines, into different bits of info." And by the end of his last year of grad school, Smith had found a new form of art: Re-things.

As he describes them on his website, ShawnSmithArt.com, Re-things are "whimsical sculptures that represent pixelated animals and objects of nature"—campfires, say, or vultures, or antelopes. "I find images of my subjects online and then create three-dimensional sculptural representations of these two-dimensional images." By doing so, Smith is investigating the lines between the organic and the inorganic, between digital information and reality, and between the observer and the surrounding world. And in making his investigations, the key tool in his kit is the voxel.

Much of the information we take in today comes to us in pixels—neatly delineated polygons on a two-dimensional screen. So neatly delineated, and so convenient, are these polygons that we may not even recognize them as human creations. But when Smith makes those pixels three-dimensional, they become *voxels*—"volumetric pixels"—and force us to recognize the line between the natural and digital worlds. "I definitely think my work asks people to cross that line," says Smith. In his *Vicious Venue* (2009), the voxels are shaped into scavenging birds and set in a strikingly mundane setting: an office. "You've got vultures eating obsolete technology, a collision of digital and non-digital worlds. It's a weird space with the whole room looking like Sam Spade's office, a 1940s world, and dead technology being food for vultures." The vultures are not particularly naturalistic; their pixelated corners are visible from a good distance away. At the same time, they're unmistakably vultures, painstakingly assembled with the shape and color of each feather rendered in hand-dyed wooden voxels. The audience cannot help but see both sides of the border: digital here, natural there.

That border is defined most clearly when it takes a shape that a voxel cannot: a curve. "I definitely like the curvatures of the animals—that roundness that's difficult to achieve with little volumes," says Smith, who notes that his move to Austin has given him greater access to the curvy denizens of the natural world—especially to one of his favorite subjects for Re-things, birds. "I'm in a hillier part of Austin, and a green belt is literally across the street. Late at night I'll hear owls and go outside to look. Birds are always up to something. When the mating cycles are going on, there's this idea of dancing and showing colors to the female, and her saying *no, yes, okay*. That's actually kind of what got me interested in biology—the colors. And the movie *The Birds* was inspirational; I love the idea of birds as a collective consciousness, saying 'We don't like this, and we're going to fix this.' And the anatomy—their hollow bones and their feet are fascinating. So many types of feet, and so specific to their evolutionary heritage."

Still, he has explored other curves as well, including those of the Stanley Cup—"It didn't quite work"—and another recent subject, one that he lifted from video games. "I made a yellow mop bucket," he reports. "They're so innocuous—if that's the right word—but they're *everywhere*. Ninety percent of first-person shooters have mop buckets in them. It gives a sense of place, so that when you're running through a room from a monster, you get the sensation that this building seems familiar."

I ask Smith point-blank whether he might attempt to work with a higher-resolution image, one where the curves might be smoother and the blockiness of the pixels might not be so obvious. He doesn't dismiss the idea, but really, working with low-res images is the whole point: "I like the abstraction that begins to happen with that." He enjoys turning information into volume, in what he calls "a perverted $e = mc^2$," where m is still mass, but instead of energy, e represents information.

Deciding what will be m and what will be e, however, can be a challenge. "Once I decide on what I'm going to make—and sometimes I'll futz around in Photoshop, change the resolution, et cetera—some information is going to be lost." From that original image, Smith will distill the colors and make his own image: a pencil drawing on graph paper. "Our culture's moving toward digital, but I'm moving the other way," he observes wryly. "I'll make a drawing, maybe two or three that show the front, side, top view. All of them have to match up, like an architectural drawing. With a pencil line, I'm defining what's positive space; I'm making visual choices at that point."

Those positive pixels on the page become voxels in space through a lengthy process that involves cutting plywood or fiberboard into half-inch strips ranging from one-half to two inches in length. Each piece is then hand-colored, with an eye toward creating more depth and vividness. Then comes the gluing. I can't tell from his description how much of this is fun and how much is drudgery, and Smith explains why: "It's a little of both—a place to play, and a place to grit my teeth. Because a lot of these things I don't know—I'm using the Internet as my model." Sometimes it requires math, sometimes just dedication, but it always stems from one basic question that Smith asks about our world: what is its smallest unit?

Like me, he recognizes that he is not the first to ask this question. "You can go back and consider pointillism, cubism, and so on. There are a lot of blogs that consider my work 'cubism come to life.' But it's also minimalist: what's the kernel?"

THE SHAWN SMITH sculpture that first captured my attention is titled *Between 1 and 0*—a provocative name for a work in which simple parts make up a complex system. The genesis of that sculpture, and that title, can be found in a system far more widespread, more complex, and more varied than any taxonomist ever dreamed—and yet the bricks that make it up are even simpler than the voxels of Smith's creations, or the more venerable tesserae that make up the mosaics of Minoan civilization, or even the humble LEGO elements of my childhood.[1]

I speak, obviously, of the Internet, a.k.a. the interwebs, the inner-tubes, the Web, and a host of other catchy names invented by people who've been using it long enough to get bored with the ordinary name. (If you've ever heard a House Sparrow referred to as a "McDonald's Warbler" or a "Black-throated Brown," you'll know that birders fall into the same habit.) Despite the fact that the Internet now reaches into billions of human lives, tying together everything from Bank of America's financial records to field recordings of Tuvan throat-singers to pictures of Lolcats riding invisible vehicles to blog entries about which actress should play Black Canary in a theoretical *Justice League* movie, the entire structure is built out of only two simple elements: ones and zeros.

The reason all those ones and zeroes can successfully reproduce the face of a swimsuit model, or the motion of a skateboarder, or the voice of a humpback whale, is scale. Human beings can see and hear things with only a certain degree of precision, and if we use tools small enough to fall below the threshold of ordinary perception, we detect only the larger system and not the tools working within it. Nor is this exclusively a digital phenomenon. The human eye can be tricked into

---

1. And please, if you're trying to describe Shawn Smith's voxel sculptures to someone, don't just casually say, "Oh, they're like LEGOs." He knows all about LEGOs and approves of them as a toy, but take it from someone who's seen his work up close: even if LEGOs are a useful analogy for trying to explain the concepts underlying a Re-thing, a Re-thing is *not* a toy. Even the most whimsical Re-thing is a serious, meticulously designed, hand-cut, hand-dyed, hand-assembled work of art. You can't make a Shawn Smith sculpture out of LEGOs any more than you can make a Ming vase out of Play-doh.

seeing motion where none exists through the simple method of show-ing it many static images very quickly, as a visit to any movie theater will demonstrate; when twenty-four frames flash by in a second, the audience sees them as a continuous flow. Newspapers have for years used a similar trick to make collections of carefully arranged dots ap-pear to be photographs of people and objects, and the screen of a TV is essentially nothing more than a series of dots lighting up in an in-credibly rapid sequence, creating the illusion of movement. This illu-sion is entirely satisfying to most people in most situations, but there are cases where the jagged edges of the building blocks become notice-able and spoil it.

Consider a Canada Goose swooping down into a pond. The impact of its body on the water creates a disturbance, and the previously smooth surface is reshaped into a series of vertical waves, each moving away from the goose at a certain rate, until they gradually fade back into flatness. If it's a small goose—perhaps the Lesser Canada, or even the diminutive Cackling Goose—and it flies more slowly and lands more softly than a big, fast, heavy bird would, then the waves it pro-duces may differ from the big goose's. The crests may be more distant from one another, the speed of the waves may be less, or perhaps the sheer height of the waves will be smaller. These are phenomena that anyone close to a body of water can observe.

What cannot be seen, however, is that what is happening to the water is also happening to the air. The goose's impact creates waves in the atmosphere, invisible curves that behave much as the ones in the water do. The height of the wave is still referred to as its amplitude, the speed of the wavecrests going past the observer is still called the fre-quency, and the distance between crests is still called the wavelength. The difference is that we can't see what's happening in the air; we can only detect it as sound.

"Sound waves are waves of compressed and rarefied air," explains audio engineer Mike Beard, who studied with, among others, synthe-sizer inventor Robert Moog, and who has spent over thirty years work-ing with every form of sound-related technology from wood blocks to wah-wah pedals. He has installed stereo equipment in private homes and designed public-address systems for churches and concert halls.

At live performances, he has balanced the onstage output of musical performers ranging from solo violinists to punk rock bands, and in the recording studio he has worked to reproduce the sounds of everything from a muted trumpet to a baritone voice to a Dodge van being beaten with a microphone stand. His understanding of sound is thus not just deep, but extraordinarily broad, and when he talks about his profession, or pretty much anything else, his mind ranges far and wide in search of analogies to help the layman comprehend.[2]

"When we talk about wave forms," says Beard, even though I'm not entirely sure we *are* talking about them, "we're talking about how compressed or rarefied the air is—that's how high or how low the amplitude is." Thus the more compressed the air is, the more we notice it, as our ears are particularly sensitive to amplitude—more than to wavelength or frequency. Basically, if the amplitude is higher, we hear the sound as louder. As Beard puts it, amplitude "is really what we hear."

The waves we hear also differ from the waves we see on a pond in another important way: sound waves are much easier to duplicate. This can be done naturally by many bird species, most famously parrots, mynahs, and mockingbirds, and of course by human beings; we do it through a combination of sensory organs (our ears), memory storage, and sound-producing apparatus (our larynx, tongue, lips, teeth, etc.). Basically, we hear something, remember what it sounds like, and use our lungs, throats, and mouths (sometimes supplemented by tools such as musical instruments) to make the same noise. This process is so fundamental to our ideas of communication and culture that we can easily overlook how remarkable it truly is. The fact that I can hear someone singing a tune, recall the combination of pitches and rhythms in it, and then repeat that combination to a third person is nothing short of astonishing. It's also unique to sound; I'm capable of detecting the scent of a rose, and even of remembering it, but I still couldn't use

2. His best analogy ever, in my opinion, came some years ago when I asked him to explain electricity. He paused for only a moment before opining, "Electricity is magic. If you follow the wisdom of the sages and lay out the material components of your spell correctly, the spirits will be pleased and will do your bidding. But if you do not lay them out correctly, the spirits will be displeased and will ignore your plea. And if you lay the components out in a way that actually offends them, the spirits will wreak a terrible vengeance upon you."

any part of my body to duplicate that odor for someone else. In fact, until civilization found ways to create perfumes, there was no way to store a rose's scent in anything but a rose.

Our natural ability for duplicating sounds, however, has been enhanced in a number of ways over the years. One is the method you're using right now: the alphabet. In effect, I'm using these arrangements of letters as a medium for storing the sounds of the words I want to say to you; since you know the sounds these letters represent, you can read them and "hear" what I'm saying. Granted, the fidelity of this medium isn't great; you can't hear the tone or cadence of my voice, and it's likely that some of what I intend to communicate is lost due to my own limitations as a writer.

Luckily, we've come up with other methods of duplicating sounds. The telephone, for example, allows the vibrations created by your voice to be detected by an electrical apparatus, transmitted over a great distance, and recreated almost immediately by a similar apparatus at the other end. From this point, it wasn't a great leap to reach the possibility of replicating sounds en masse—in other words, reproducing them for more than just one listener, as on an intercom. Radio allows sounds to be carried by electromagnetic waves to any receiving apparatus within range, no matter how many listeners may have such a receiver. Sounds can now also be recorded, stored indefinitely, and reproduced multiple times at the listener's convenience. Early attempts to do this with wax cylinders proved less than satisfactory, but once the media of magnetic tape, acetate, and vinyl were invented, people all over the world could listen to sounds that had been produced tens of years and thousands of miles away.

The combination of these last two technologies was responsible for the explosion of a new industry in the twentieth century: the record industry. On the one hand, there was now a network of radio stations looking to fill airtime, and on the other, there now existed inexpensive and portable recordings of music that could be sold in any store and played on any station. It was a marriage made in heaven. The more radio play a record got, the more copies it would sell, and the more popular the music played by a radio station, the more listeners that station could attract.

Popular music as we know it was not merely distributed but actively shaped by this technology; most pop songs are under five minutes in length because that's all the music that can be contained on one side of a seven-inch vinyl single. Similarly, albums have typically come in at about 45 minutes in length because a vinyl LP won't hold much more information than that. Even after the disappearance of the 45-rpm single and the 33-rpm album (not to mention the venerable 78-rpm record), the audience still expects pop music to come in containers of roughly this size.

Despite the widespread popularity of these formats, however, there were definite disadvantages to reproducing sound waves in them. For one, making a good analog recording required the kind of specialized skills that only someone like Mike Beard was likely to have—everything from knowing how each instrument actually produces sound to knowing the physical limitations of magnetic tape to being able to solder together frayed wiring. "It's the difference between developing photos and using PhotoShop," he says. "There's a much more complex set of skills required to work in a darkroom."

And the disadvantages didn't end when the recording process was done. For example, both vinyl and tape are susceptible to heat; a few hours in a hot car can wipe out hours of carefully recorded music, or warp the flat disc of an album into unplayability. Scratches and dirt can interfere with the phonograph needle or the tape heads—the devices that "read" the information on the tape or record—by preventing them from moving smoothly over the surface, leading to hiss, pops, and inaccurate reproduction of the original sounds. And even if great care is taken to keep the system clean, properly cooled, and in good shape, the ugly fact is that every time you play a record, you make it sound a little worse. The grooves on the surface of a record wear down as they move past the needle, gradually becoming so smooth that the music they contain is lost in the sound of vinyl rubbing against a diamond.

With so many problems, it's not surprising that the music industry has largely abandoned the use of metallic particles stuck to pieces of plastic, embracing instead the same approach Shawn Smith sets up on graph paper: one where tiny bits of information are arranged in a much larger system, with each bit serving as either positive or negative space—in other words, digital recording, which uses complex arrangements of ones and zeroes to duplicate the sound waves created by musicians. Mike Beard, for one, sees significant benefits in the change: "In digital audio, I can cut and paste sections. I can fix glitches. I can even re-align drummers to get them to play on the beat." Storing music digitally has "a huge advantage" over using analog means, and interchangeability is markedly better in the digital realm. With analog recordings, "the recording and playback machines must be calibrated identically or you don't hear what was recorded," says Beard. "Taking one tape from studio to studio usually means missing some stuff because one set of tape heads doesn't match another . . . You don't have any of that crap in digital."

The digital reproduction of sound is a huge step forward in technology, avoiding many of the storage and reproduction problems with analog recordings while simultaneously allowing for advances in dozens of other areas. Voice-recognition software allows us to buy tickets from automated phone agents. Family members on separate continents can use Skype to converse with digital interfaces for their voices. Digital recordings of birds, whales, and elephants have spawned dozens of studies about our environment, many of them conducted at Cornell University's BioAcoustics Lab. Computers can even provide prosthetic voices for the mute; clips from his past television shows were spliced together digitally to allow film critic Roger Ebert to speak on camera after his cancerous lower jaw was removed.

Only in a few places does analog audio still dominate, namely microphones and speakers. Digital technology is great at recording and storing sound, but not so good at gathering it or translating it to the human ear. "There's not really a way to digitally sample or digitally reproduce air pressure," Beard notes. He is thus emphatic about the need for speakers that work well, regardless of whether you're listening to an analog or digital recording through them. "They're the interface with your ear, and that's why they're the most important."

Despite these limitations, digital sound reproduction is a huge industry, and it is one that has altered the music business, for good or ill, in a permanent way. This industry's ability to record and play back sound digitally is what allows us to do things like store music on devices smaller than a human hand—music that, recorded on vinyl records, would take up dozens of feet of shelf space. It allows us to transfer music from device to device in moments, and to choose precisely which music we want to hear from a shared central storage unit, rather than keeping copies for ourselves in our homes.

But the one thing digital sound reproduction can't *quite* do? Reproduce sound.

Oh, it can come very close. But the building blocks that make up a digital sound are just that—blocks. They're stacks of ones and zeroes, if you like, and if those ones and zeroes are stacked in a particular way, they can begin to resemble the sound of a flute, or a human voice, or a goose landing on a pond, just as LEGOS can be stacked to resemble a house, or a cathedral, or a life-size Darth Vader. Squint a bit, or stand far enough away, and you might have the temporary impression that there is an actual Sith Lord holding his lightsaber just over there, but if you get close enough, the illusion will vanish and the jagged, artificial edges of the plastic components will become apparent. LEGO blocks, as versatile, as numerous, and as compatible as they are, can never perfectly recreate the shape of a human body; in a nutshell, they can't make curves.

This is exactly the impression created when a set of sharp ears approaches a digitally reproduced sound wave. That reproduced wave may be shaped very much like the one produced by the original instrument (or goose), but if you're sensitive enough, or if you examine it closely enough, you can tell the wave is not a smooth curve. Moreover, what we hear on our iPods and computers is usually incomplete; the most common kinds of sound files are .mp3 and .wma files, which contain only a fraction of the data found on a CD. Most listeners, however, are incapable of detecting the missing information anyway, so its absence has little if any effect on their enjoyment of the music, and the portability and flexibility of the digital format outweigh the loss of data. As Beard puts it, exchanging fidelity for convenience is "a decent trade."

It's not a trade a professional audio engineer would always make, but as technology has improved, a full digital recording now has fewer "corners" than it once did.[3] There are still telling details that distinguish a digital recording, at least for a true audiophile, but they are not necessarily problematic. For Beard, the giveaway is in the background. "If I have a good set of phones, the ambient noise of particles going across the tape head is audible. If I don't hear that, it's digital." That "if" is important, because even the best ears don't always get to listen to music in the best conditions; to enjoy every curvy nuance of a top-quality analog recording, you can't just throw a record on your living room's turntable. "You have to be in a precision listening environment—in lab conditions. And nobody listens to music in lab conditions. If you're at home and your AC or your heat comes on, forget it; those nuances are masked." Basically, as Beard puts it, the difference between the best digital and the best analog recordings can today be masked "with a mouse fart."

IN THE ABSENCE of mouse farts, however, a layman may still be able to detect the difference between analog waves and digital blocks. Audio engineer Ethan Gamache, who has spent most of the last decade recording audiobooks, points out that one thing digital sound doesn't handle well is silence. When a voice stops reading, or when an instrument hits the final note at the conclusion of a movement, there are still a great many vibrations left sounding in the air, often for quite some time. With a digitally reproduced sound, however, those final faint vibrations are more likely to drop below the threshold of reproduction, meaning that to the listener, the noise comes to an end too quickly, rather than continuing to resound. Thus, you might not be able to tell whether a recording is digital while it's playing, but you might well be able to tell once it's over.

Or, if you prefer, listen to the sound of a real piano—a sound that is familiar to millions, but enormously complicated: metal strings of

---

3. This has been achieved, according to Beard, not by taking more samples per second, but by devoting more memory to the amplitude of each sample. Years ago, each of the 44,100 samples recorded in a second was stored with only 16 bits of resolution, which gave each sample a little over 65,000 possible levels of amplitude; today it is more common to find resolution of 24 bits. This gives each sample over 16 *million* possible levels. "There are more corners with 16 bits," says Beard. "Cutting [the sound] finer is better than cutting it more often."

varying lengths and thicknesses, each fastened to a metal frame within a wooden structure, and all being struck by felt hammers attached to wooden rods moved by wooden keys, themselves put into motion by human fingers. There are multiple organic components, the composition of which can vary widely, giving each individual piano a distinctive sound. Moreover, as Beard notes, "They're chaotic in their interactions. When you put the pedal down and play chords, you have other strings vibrating in tandem. Grand pianos are one of the most difficult things to sample."

Now listen to a digital reproduction of a piano. (One early example can be heard during the scene in *Who Framed Roger Rabbit?* in which Daffy Duck and Donald Duck are dueling their way through a duet of Lizst's Hungarian Rhapsody No. 2.) Digital keyboards are typically plastic, with metal components triggering the electrical signal that carries the reproduced sound. There are no wooden levers or rods, no felt or ivory, and only the more expensive keyboards make any attempt to reproduce a piano's variable "attack," which allows a pianist to play a note louder or softer depending on how hard the key is struck.[4] Each key on a digital keyboard, then, is basically an on/off switch— that whole binary thing again—which produces its sound at one volume, and only when the key is pressed down far enough. None of this sounds quite right—or at least, it doesn't sound quite like a piano. The corners are just too noticeable.

Any aficionado will tell you how sound is best reproduced: on vinyl— but it must be vinyl that has been carefully tended and preserved, and played on a system of great sophistication and expense. The best analog recordings, played on the best sound systems, will render the best-reproduced sound, but the process is not an easy one. True sound is wild and difficult to capture, beautiful and extreme.

But digital sound? Digital sound is tame. It is penned up neatly by the lines we have drawn around it, docile and under our control. It

---

4. This feature is in fact the main strength of the piano, as well as the source of its name. Before the piano's invention, the main keyboard instrument was the harpsichord, which plucks each string at exactly the same volume no matter what. By contrast, the pianoforte, to use its full name, allows the player to make a note soft (in Italian: *piano*) or loud (*forte*).

can be stored, carried, and transferred with ease. We have crafted it into discrete units that can be altered, edited, recombined, erased, and reproduced by anyone with a computer—even a child, who can play with its blocks just as easily as he can snap together and break apart a fistful of LEGOs.

To manipulate analog sound requires a degree of control that only a professional can attain. Digital sound, though blocky and imperfect, belongs to the rest of us.

Rock and a Hard Place

"The Sound of Difference"—An illegitimate reason—Scandalized metal fans—The surprising contents of Pandora's box—Dickie defies corporate policy—In search of Beethoven's Third Symphony—High-powered consultants

> *In this country we waste an enormous amount of time and energy disapproving of one another in three categories where only personal taste matters: hair, sports, and music.* —Molly Ivins

IT WAS EARLY in the summer of 1984, I was blasting Prince's "When Doves Cry" to everyone in central North Carolina, and the guy on the phone was pissed.

"Why are you playing this shit?" he barked.

"Because it's *good!*" I replied.

And that, in a nutshell, was the root of the dispute. I was starting my fourth year as a disc jockey at WXYC, the University of North Carolina's student radio station, and both I and my audience were caught up in the tangled web of musical genre. Since its FM debut in 1977, station manager Bill Burton had guided XYC to a status as a model for college radio, giving airtime to artists too abrasive, too avant-garde, or too obscure for commercial stations. We played almost every kind of music imaginable at some point during the week. Triangle Slim's Sunday morning show, *The Orange County Special*, featured traditional music of all sorts—bluegrass, string band, Celtic, and blues, among others—while the four-hour *Jazz on a Sunday Afternoon* opened up the airwaves for fusion, hard bop, big band, and other subcategories. Saturday night was Ken Friedman's legendary *Anarchy in the P.M.*, where punk and garage-band artists took center stage, and Bill's own Thursday-night show was likely to feature a healthy dose of psychedelia and space-rock. The station's playbox was full of new releases of all kinds, but the majority fell somewhere in the burgeoning categories of punk or new wave; long before they broke through on MTV and commercial radio, WXYC was giving regular airplay to groups such as the Clash, the B-52's, U2, the Talking Heads, R.E.M., and the Cure, as well as artists who never quite had that breakthrough: Laurie Anderson, the Dead Kennedys, Robyn Hitchcock, the Roches, Oingo Boingo, and the dB's.

For the most part, however, the station encouraged the DJs to do our own things. We had to play five songs per hour from the playbox of new releases—three from different records in the Heavy Rotation section, one each from Medium and Light—but other than that, we were free to make our own choices about the artists we played. This freedom could have resulted in a display of the worst tendencies of college radio announcers—in other words, hour after hour of demonstrating our hipness by playing nothing but the most obscure material we could find in the station's voluminous library—but the hourly playlist restrained us somewhat by asking for a pair of songs that the station management considered "hits" (which might or might not have made a major impression on the charts at some time) along with four or five reasonably well-known tracks designated "standards."

I began my tenure at WXYC in 1981, when my favorite bands were Yes, the Who, and Steely Dan, but it wasn't long before my tastes exploded in all directions. A typical forty-minute PC set might from the mid-80s might have looked something like this:

(Hit)	Elvis Costello/Accidents Will Happen
(Standard)	Tom Waits/Clap Hands
(Other)	The Bonzo Dog Band/Jollity Farm
(Standard)	Icehouse/Icehouse
(Other)	Bill Nelson/The October Man
(Other)	Suburban Lawns/Flying Saucer Safari
(Standard)	King Crimson/Elephant Talk

(Other)   The Swimming Pool Q's/Big Fat Tractor

(Hit)   Stevie Wonder/Boogie On Reggae Woman

Obviously, there was plenty of room for us to play a wide variety of material, but what we didn't play, for the most part, was the hit music of the day. That caused a certain degree of resentment from listeners, but not always for the same reasons.

Some were like my caller, who objected to hearing a Top-40 Prince single. In his view, the quality of the song itself was not problematic, but its popularity was. If he could hear the song on another radio station, it was by definition unsuitable for WXYC. To him, our "alternative" programming precluded the broadcast of anything with mainstream popularity. My counterargument was that our format did not require us to *avoid* the popular; it simply ignored the issue of popularity altogether. We played songs that had been hits in years past—everything from the Kinks' "Waterloo Sunset" to Brewer & Shipley's "One Toke Over the Line"—whether the performers were still producing new music or not. And since many of the artists we played, including Prince, had been included in our playbox well before they hit the big time, I didn't see much reason to quit playing their music now that the rest of the world had finally caught up with us. Basically, I considered popularity an illegitimate reason to keep a song off the air.

But much of the resentment came from the other direction. Many students felt the student station ought to play what most students liked—what was already on MTV and the local Top 40 stations. When the student newspaper, *The Daily Tar Heel*, printed an editorial criticizing WXYC's musical direction (and thereby Bill's leadership), I took umbrage and fired off a letter. Perhaps ironically, I ended up pointing out what my caller had objected to: that there were already dozens of radio stations where the most popular music of the day could be heard, whereas XYC was probably the only one in the region that could satisfy those who enjoyed Gil Scott-Heron, the Soft Boys, or They Might Be Giants. No benefit would be provided to anyone if we simply duplicated the playlists of the other stations.

In short, my time in the broadcast booth showed me the truth of Molly Ivins's observation, but she and I are hardly the only people to have figured out that the practice of musical categorization can get a whole bunch of burrs under a whole bunch of saddles. One detailed examination of these multifarious burrs is made by sociologist Jennifer C. Lena in her book *Banding Together: How Communities Create Genres in Popular Music*. Her points about genre are many and varied, but one of the most important is her observation that too often we categorize music not for musical reasons, but in order to draw social boundaries. As Lena defines the word, "genres" are "systems of orientations, expectations, and conventions that bind together industry, performers, critics, and fans in making what they identify as a distinctive sort of music." The crucial point here is that the genre definitions are not objective, but rather based on the opinions of the various members of the musical community. In Lena's words, "a genre exists when there is some consensus that a distinctive style of music is being performed."

If a musical genre exists only because people agree that it exists, then there will inevitably be disagreement about what music properly belongs in that genre. That disagreement may prevent inclusion in any genre at all; Lena lists Sigur Ros, Philip Glass, and the Carpenters as musicians who have achieved acclaim and/or popularity while remaining "unclassifiable." More often, however, the battle will be fought over the borderline of a particular genre and which side a particular artist falls on.

Fans of heavy metal music are legendarily concerned with genre boundaries, and lengthy arguments have been made about which artists can lay legitimate claim to metal status. For example, if you type the words "are guns n roses" into a Google search bar (or did so in July 2013, at least), the second auto-fill-in result is "are guns n roses metal." Clearly, the question has occurred to more than a few people. The answer is suggested by the fact that Guns N' Roses won an MTV Video Music Award for Best Heavy Metal Video, plus multiple American Music Awards in the Hard Rock/Heavy Metal category. The very existence of that slash, however, suggests that there might be some overlap between genres, or maybe even that the band is hard rock, not metal at all. There are doubtless plenty of metal fans who would argue that GnR is no more a metal band than Jethro Tull, who in 1989 won the very first Grammy Award for Best Hard Rock/Metal Performance—a victory that so scandalized metal fans (who had largely favored Metallica) that the award category was thereafter split in two. At the same time, there are plenty of metal fans who would love to claim GnR; websites like Metal Insider and Metal Express Radio provide substantial coverage of the band, offering readers interviews with the members and information about shows. But even if we accept GnR as metal, our task is not complete; we now have to consider whether they belong in any of the many, many sub-genres of metal, including speed metal, black metal, death metal, glam metal, alternative metal, thrash metal, and even Christian metal.

Obviously, some listeners may wish their preferred genre was more inclusive, while others may already find it too inclusive for comfort. This issue is typically brought to the fore when an artist tries to alter or violate the boundaries of his/her genre, bringing in outside elements that may or may not please the audience. Run-DMC's adoption of rock guitar (particularly on their 1986 cover of Aerosmith's "Walk This Way") served both to expand the available palette of sound for hip-hop and to bring the genre to the attention of rock listeners, but Bob Dylan's use of electric instruments during his notorious appearance at the 1965 Newport Folk Festival angered some of his fans who favored a traditional acoustic sound. At other times, however, the music itself isn't what's stretching the boundaries uncomfortably, as in one case Lena recounts from a *New York Times* story. The article concerned the online music service Pandora, which uses information about a listener's preferences in order to provide other music he/she is likely to enjoy. Founder Tim Westergren shared with the *Times* the tale of a Sarah MacLachlan fan who wrote a letter of complaint after Pandora offered him a song by Celine Dion:

"I wrote back and said, 'Was the music just wrong?' Because we sometimes have data errors," he recounts. "He said, 'Well, no, it was the right sort of thing—but it was Celine Dion.' I said, 'Well, was it the set, did it not flow in the set?' He said, 'No, it kind of worked—but it's Celine Dion.' We had a couple more back-and-forths, and finally his last e-mail to me was: 'Oh, my God, *I like Celine Dion*.'"

In other words, this listener had drawn a boundary in his own mind between acceptable artists (like MacLachlan) and unacceptable ones (like Dion), but the algorithm used by Pandora did not recognize that boundary. He was thus forced to recognize that the borderline he had drawn not only had no objective existence, but didn't even meet his own subjective requirements. It's a good example of Lena's point that "we have been encouraged to deploy our tastes to categorize music rather than to understand how categories come to define our tastes."

I HAVE LONG SYMPATHIZED with the contrarianism of the legendary writer Roger Zelazny, who once claimed that if he ever came across a working definition of science fiction, he would immediately attempt to violate it. There's definitely something about putting up a fence around a genre that inspires people to try jumping it. Sometimes it's purely for fun, as when Brave Combo turns the Doors' "People Are Strange" into a rollicking polka, but it can stretch our minds in new directions, too, such as in Jonathan Lethem's *Gun, with Occasional Music*, a hard-boiled detective story, but one placed in a science-fiction setting that involves talking kangaroos and portable long-term memory storage units where you can keep the names and faces of people you don't want to remember personally. Indeed, I have found that works of mixed genre are often among my very favorites, whether the mix is planned in advance (as with the western-in-space TV show *Firefly*) or constructed after the fact (as with DJ Earworm's brilliant mash-up "No One Takes Your Freedom," which combines the Beatles' "For No One," the Scissor Sisters' "Take Your Mama Out," George Michael's "Freedom," and Aretha Franklin's "Think" in an inspiring gumbo of song).

But I have to feel that, to some degree, my fondness for crossing genre boundaries stems from my experiences as a clerk at one of Chapel Hill's legendary retail establishments, the Record Bar. From 1987 to 1990, I was in the business of selling compact discs, cassette tapes, and a dwindling number of vinyl albums to the listening public, and that business was not always made easier by the decisions of our head office. Luckily, our store's manager, the estimable Richard K. Layne, known to us as "Dickie," was something of a maverick, and he routinely defied corporate policy in order to make our store one of the most profitable in the chain, despite the fact that our tiny shop on Franklin Street had less square footage than practically any other R-Bar. One of his innovations was to focus heavily on the music played on our local National Public Radio affiliate; since WUNC was primarily a classical station when it wasn't transmitting *All Things Considered*, this plan required Dickie to immerse himself in the study of the classics, which could be a little alarming if you were assigned to a morning shift and arrived to find him blasting Mahler over the stereo system. He also made sure we were well stocked with the artists featured on *A Prairie Home Companion*, *Thistle and Shamrock*, and other NPR shows featuring traditional music, despite the fact that the head office was not, for the most part, terribly interested in catering to fans of folk, jazz, Celtic, or even classical music.

And that, in a nutshell, was where the problem lay. The corporate mission was to sell as much music as possible. To the head office's way of thinking, the proper way to do this was to sell the music that was most popular; to Dickie, the proper way was to sell the most music, period, whether popular or not. The conflict between those two goals was played out primarily in the area of genre.

Every recording we carried had to be displayed somewhere in the store, but the head office sometimes made odd choices about how to do it. The big classical section, at least, was logically arranged, primarily by composer, with a few sections for famous performers like Yo-Yo Ma and Luciano Pavarotti. The soundtrack section, however, was arranged primarily by title; again, this was a sensible arrangement, given that many films, plays, and TV shows use songs by multiple composers and/or performers. And I certainly can't object to the fact that virtually every other section in the store was arranged by artist.

No, the problem wasn't the arrangements within those other sections, or even the nature of all those other sections. The problem was where to draw the lines between the sections. And with many artists, the placement of that line was a vexing question. Should Guns N' Roses be filed under Rock or Metal? (Corporate HQ said Rock.) Should Prince go into Rock or Soul? (HQ said Soul.) And what about all the female singers with acoustic guitars and twangs in their voices? According to HQ, Emmylou Harris belonged in Country, Nanci Griffith in Folk, and Lucinda Williams in Rock. Maybe there were sensible reasons for drawing these distinctions, but they did not always make a lot of sense to either the staff or the customers searching for recordings.

In truth, my daily confrontation with the task of organizing and learning that inventory helped me to recognize a fundamental truth about the lines we draw: in the end, any system of dividing lines has to be one that the user can, well, *use*.

THIS TRUTH BECAME even more sharply obvious when I encountered a group of musical offerings whose organizing system not only failed to be user-friendly but seemed designed to show the user active hostility: the CD collection in the Woodberry Forest School library. Like most of the students (and probably most of the faculty), I spent years unaware that the school's audio-visual collection even had an audio section, choosing instead to focus on the wealth of DVDs and old video cassettes that previous librarians had acquired. As it turned out, there were several hundred CDs on hand, but they were stored in drawers that weren't accessible to users. The only clue to their existence was a three-ring binder containing a printout of the items available—a printout where each disc was listed by title.

And *only* by title.

As Record Bar understood, this is a potentially baffling approach to cataloguing. When the works being catalogued are operas or musical comedies, the titles are often unique, which offers little trouble to the user. Unfortunately, in any other genre, titles are commonly shared. Woodberry patrons in search of Beethoven's Third Symphony could see plainly from the printout that the library did contain a work entitled "Symphony No. 3," but there was no indication whether the piece had been written by Beethoven or Brahms, or for that matter by Arnold, Bernstein, Copland, Dvorak, Enescu, Finney, Gorecki, Haydn, Ives, Kabalevsky, Lloyd, Mahler, Nielsen, Prokofiev, Rachmaninoff, Saint-Saens, Tchaikovsky, Vaughan Williams, Wagenaar, or any of the other seventy-plus composers who wrote a work of that name. The problem was not unique to the world of classical music, either, as the numerous works entitled "Greatest Hits," "Gold," and "Live" clearly indicated. If you were to open up the notebook in hopes of finding the greatest hits of, say, Frank Sinatra, you had no guarantee that the AV clerk wouldn't return with a best-of collection by Dean Martin, or the Temptations, or Bob Dylan.

In addition, since the AV Center had depended heavily on donations rather than purchases, the musical offerings were a bit on the bizarre side. A user would find the classical collection fairly sizable, with multiple complete Wagner operas, but would see no recordings by Elvis Presley, Chuck Berry, or James Brown. He could also check out the second discs (but not the first) of live double albums by both Jimmy Buffett and Peter Frampton, or a near-mint copy of *The Disregard of Timekeeping*, the 1989 debut album from the not-exactly-legendary British hard-rock band Bonham. Each of these CDs was given a unique catalogue number, so that it could sit in the drawer in numerical order for easy location. Unfortunately, the discs were not assigned numbers according to composer, genre, artist, or even title; instead, they were assigned a number according to the order in which they were acquired. The first CD donated to or purchased by the library was listed as CD 0001. The next one became CD 0002, the next CD 0003, and so on.

As a result, when you opened the binder to peruse the AV Center's musical holdings, this is essentially what you saw:

0001	Symphony No. 3
0002	Greatest Hits
0003	Frampton Comes Alive! (Disc 2)
0004	Greatest Hits
0005	Symphony No. 3
0006	Pleasures of the Dance: A Collection of Norwegian Carpenters' Songs
0007	Symphony No. 3
0008	Die Walkurie
0009	Greatest Hits
0010	The Disregard of Timekeeping

As you can imagine, not a lot of CDs were checked out.

Luckily, when Phoebe Warmack became head librarian in 2007, she saw the problems with both this collection and its accessibility; she quickly engaged the services of two high-powered consultants to help realize her dream of a CD collection that would not only contain a broader sample of modern popular music, but would also be arranged in such a way that the students could find what they were looking for. The first consultant, with experience as both a radio announcer and music retailer, provided a list of one hundred discs that could give the typical twenty-first-century student the opportunity to explore the broad strokes of rock, pop, soul, country, and hip-hop from the previous fifty years, from "Jailhouse Rock" to "Mercy Mercy Me" to "Dancing Queen" to "Fight the Power." The second, a professional cataloguer and former copy editor on her way to a master's degree in information science, gave each CD a new catalogue number and created a database where each disc was searchable by number, title, main artist, genre, additional artists (individual band members, if applicable, and guest artists, if any), and track title.

The first expert was yours truly; the second was Kelly Dalton, wife of yours truly. And if you think I was going to contest Kelly's decisions about the placement of Emmylou Harris or Prince, you need to understand that in a successful marriage, there are certain lines you do not cross.

My overall point, however—you thought I'd forgotten about that, didn't you?—is not that it's useless to draw lines between genres. Sometimes those lines provide helpful information, giving the user a way to track down specific information or exclude unhelpful details. Yes, there are always going to be artists who cross those lines, either intentionally or through dumb luck, but so long as there are people who feel strongly that they like epic fantasy and don't like science fiction, those people will find it helpful to have fewer works through which to search for something they like. Granted, they may miss something good that straddles the line (such as Gene Wolfe's brilliant *Book of the New Sun* series), but at least they won't feel adrift in a sea of books with no means of navigation available.

Some lines are confusing, yes. Some are artificial or even capricious barriers. But some are guidelines.

Parts Is Parts

An exercise in double entendre—Bikinis and burkas—A pair of overlapping bell curves—"Sex is biology. Gender is sociology."—I'm thinking of Mrs. Frisby—Elephants do it too—The South's most widespread invasive plant—People who are not typical—Smudging the lines

> *Japonica*
> *Glistens like coral in all the neighboring gardens,*
> *And today we have naming of parts.*
> —Henry Reed, "The Naming of Parts"

THERE ARE THOSE who consider it at least ironic and at worst unworthy that the only Chuck Berry song ever to reach the top of the Billboard charts was a novelty tune titled "My Ding-a-Ling." This exercise in double entendre, recorded in concert, appears on *The London Chuck Berry Sessions*, a 1972 release that was my introduction to Berry's oeuvre. The titular ding-a-ling is described as a toy—"silver bells hanging on a string"—that is played with and carefully looked after by the narrator in a variety of situations, and even at the age of nine I knew enough about Freud to know that sometimes a cigar isn't just a cigar. The first half of the eleven-minute album version consists of Chuck explaining to the audience what they're going to be singing when the band reaches the chorus, and nearly every sentence of his explanation is a sexual suggestion worthy of inclusion in an Aerosmith lyric.

Berry is quite open about this, noting that it's a "sexy" song, but his reasoning is more interesting than the claim itself. He says the song is sexy because "the girls have one part and the boys have the other."

Of course, he's referring innocently to the fact that the girls are assigned the task of singing "my" while the boys follow with a resounding "DING-A-LING!"

Innocently. Riiiiiight.

The doubleness of this double entendre lies in the multiple meanings of the word "part." There is a widespread assumption that there are some parts that belong to males and some to females, and never the twain shall meet. Except, y'know, in a situation that might be described in an Aerosmith song. In general, however, Mother Nature is notorious for smudging borderlines, even in areas where duality would seem to be the norm. And the biological case of sex certainly seems dualistic. For most vertebrate species (and quite a few invertebrates), the existence of two different sexes is a given, a fact acknowledged not just in biology textbooks, but in human languages the world over.

In English, we don't merely have different words for male and female animals (*bull* and *cow*, *buck* and *doe*, *cock* and *hen*) but words drawing a distinction between the human sexes in nearly every walk of life, be it the home (*father* and *mother*), the workplace (*actor* and *actress*), the cloister (*monk* and *nun*), or even the boudoir (*gigolo* and *strumpet*). Romance languages have genders for nouns and adjectives as well. Practically all Indo-European languages recognize sexual differences even at the pronoun level. In other words, you simply cannot speak English or most other Western languages without dividing the world into male and female.

In birds, the differences between the sexes are both more straightforward and more complicated than they are among humans. One complex human issue, however, pops up in only some bird species: that of sexual dimorphism—a visible difference in appearance between the sexes. In the wild, at least, men and women are relatively easy to distinguish, owing to their largely hairless skins and their typically pronounced differences in size, shape, and anatomy. Out of the wild, styles of clothing, differences in behavior, and variations in muscular development can certainly make men and women much harder to tell apart, but in general, making that distinction is something we do easily and immediately, largely because many human societies demand that the line between male and female be made even clearer than nature already makes it. In these cases, socially approved tools may be used to aid the observer; for example, both bikinis and burkas are garments for women only.[1]

With birds, the issue of telling male from female in the wild tends to be a straightforward affair: either you can tell or you can't. It depends on the species.

On my life list, for example, the vast majority of the birds are recorded without any mention of sex because most species are not sexually dimorphic. They may show some variation in size or proportion—female Cooper's Hawks, for example, are nearly a third larger than the males—but from any distance, male and female birds are typically indistinguishable. The exceptions include most species of American ducks, woodpeckers, warblers, and finches, but these make up less than a third of my life list. When the birds in question are gulls, or eagles, or sandpipers, or crows, jays, chickadees, owls, doves, or flycatchers, androgyny is the norm.

Still, to listen to most people talk, you could easily assume that there was a dividing line between male and female as thick and black as the equator on a globe. In fact, however, Mother Nature's crayon has gone over that line repeatedly. Not only are there thousands of people whose self-images are of a different sex than their bodies, but even the most fundamental distinction between male and female can be difficult to draw when we consider that the brains, the bodies, and even the cells themselves sometimes defy duality.

ABIGAIL NORFLEET JAMES has spent her entire life facing that duality. She didn't have much choice. She grew up on the campus of Woodberry Forest, the all-boys boarding school where her parents worked, then went to an all-girls school herself. After she graduated from Duke University, she began a career in education, returning to Woodberry to

---

1. Such garments may of course be worn or eschewed when an individual prefers to appear as a member of the opposite sex, or of neither; an androgynous appearance involves minimizing one's own visible male or female distinctions, while dressing in drag also involves maximizing one's resemblance to the other sex.

teach psychology and basic science (as well as using her theater experience as costume mistress for the school's drama department), but she couldn't ignore the issues that single-sex education brought up for her on a daily basis. Eventually she decided to pursue her Ph.D. in psychology at the University of Virginia, specializing in the study of sex and cognition. Since receiving her doctorate, she has traveled all over the world, speaking to audiences of educators, parents, and students about single-sex and co-ed education, and publishing works such as *Teaching the Male Brain*, which was named ForeWord Magazine's 2007 Book of the Year. Based in central Virginia, James maintains her connection to the classroom by teaching psychology at both Orange County High School and Germanna Community College, and it's clear that the connection remains tight: even when speaking informally about the ways in which males and females are distinguished, she has a legal pad and a pencil ready to help guide the listener to a greater understanding.

The first thing she does after sitting down at our lunch table is pull out her pad and draw a pair of overlapping bell curves for me. "The average woman's height in the U.S. is five foot six. For a man, it's five foot ten." James herself is five-ten, or as she notes, "I'm very tall for a female, but average for a male." This is a pointed illustration of the fact that there will inevitably be specific exceptions to any statement about the general tendencies of men or women. Individuals will fall outside the norm for one sex, but that doesn't mean the statistical norm does not exist. James's own disclaimer is this: "Neurobiology agrees that there are fairly significant differences in male and female brains. They are not dichotomous, they are not universal, but they are statistically significant." (Just like height averages, in other words.)

She has seen scientists worry that teachers will ignore this disclaimer and try to apply their understanding to an individual child, but as she puts it, "That just tells me that they don't know pedagogy. Teach *a* child? That never happens in a classroom." Except in special education or home-schooling situations, teachers work with populations of students—often sizable populations, as I can attest.

She also wants to make sure I understand the terminology. In our culture, the terms "sex" and "gender" are often used interchangeably. In the United States, at least, "gender" is often preferred because "sex" seems awkward, or even dirty. James reports that some single-sex schools have to refer to themselves as "single-gender." If they didn't, computer network filters, which are often set to reject search terms like *sex*, might prevent prospective students from visiting the schools' websites, or even keep current students and alumni from doing research on their own alma maters. In James's line of work, however, there are already enough problems that can appear because of unclear language, so she lays out the difference plainly. "Sex is biology. Gender is sociology," she explains. "Gender is *learned*."

Third, she wants to be clear about what that biology does and does not deal with. "My books are titled *Teaching the Male Brain* and *Teaching the Female Brain*. Not *mind*. The mind is what happens inside the brain. We have no clue what happens inside the mind."

Having assured herself that I know enough to follow along for a while, James turns to the task of filling my head with information on chromosomal anomalies, neuroscience, developmental biology, and education policy. (Final tally: over a lunch lasting roughly 110 minutes, I type up notes comprising just over 2700 words.) She summarizes for me the work of Cambridge professor Simon Baron-Cohen, generally regarded as the one of the world's leading experts on autism. In his book *The Essential Difference*, he puts forth a bold claim on the first page: "The female brain is predominantly hard-wired for empathy. The male brain is predominantly hard-wired for understanding and building systems." Moreover, he sees autism as an extreme version of this systematic male brain, one that has no idea what's going on inside other brains, but tries to systematize and categorize the behavior it observes. There is evidence to support the notion of a correlation between prenatal testosterone levels and autism, and there is certainly a higher incidence of autism in males.

Then it's time for a look at the work of Jay Giedd, a researcher at the National Institute of Mental Health. ("You were thinking of Mrs. Frisby, weren't you?" James asks me, smiling.) But this NIMH work is far from the fanciful tale in Robert C. O'Brien's beloved children's book, though like the titular Rats of NIMH, Giedd ended up learning some things he did not originally set out to learn. His hope was to examine children's brains to detect warning signs of adult illnesses such as schizophrenia. The subjects, mostly the children of his colleagues, were given a functional magnetic resonance image (FMRI) test, meaning that the MRI was set up to show what was firing in the brain not while it was in repose, but while it was working actively. What he discovered, however, was the existence of significant differences in the development of male and female brains.

A single FMRI cannot be used to tell the sex of a brain, but a series of three images—taken over six years of development—almost always shows a distinctive trajectory. "Girls develop the left side of the brain earlier, boys develop the right earlier," says James. "The tricky bit is that the verbal center starts on the left side. Most adult males use only the left side for language and use both sides for spatial skills; adult females use both sides for language, but only the right side for spatial skills."

Why does this happen? That's the big question, and James doesn't have the answer. It may be a matter of education; if we as a society assume that girls *should* learn verbally, we may consciously or unconsciously enrich their opportunities to do so. Alas, we cannot really test this theory in an experiment where we deny girls any external enhancement, forcing them to develop their verbal skills on their own; parents tend to demand that their daughters get every possible form of assistance. Of course, they also push for their sons to get verbal enrichment, and schools are generally responsive. Unfortunately, while they do try very hard to bring boys' verbal skills up to the level of girls', few schools make the same effort to help girls learn spatial skills. "They *can* learn them," James insists, "if you start 'em early enough." Without that extra effort, however, it's possible that girls' brains will remain distinctively developed on the verbal side and underdeveloped in spatial matters.

The distinction between male and female brain development, however, is not the only line of demarcation that Giedd's research uncovered. That line is drawn partially between the sexes, but primarily between adolescence and adulthood. The part of the brain that allows us to control our impulses and apply rational thinking to a situation is the prefrontal lobe; in children and adolescents, that part is not yet fully developed, as any parent will be more than willing to attest. To some degree, then, adulthood can be said to rest in the prefrontal lobe.

"If the prefrontal lobe is the part that allows us to make decisions," says James, "that's the adult part."

But Giedd's research has shown that the prefrontal lobe comes on-line, so to speak, at different times for males and females. "You can see parents deal with this," says James. "Little kids are equally impulsive, but by early adolescence, girls learn to damp it down." In the average girl, the prefrontal lobe reaches full development somewhere between the ages of eighteen and twenty. By that time, most girls have learned not to be so impulsive. The average age for full development in boys, however, is between twenty and twenty-five, and some men may not become fully "adult" until they reach thirty.

With Baron-Cohen and Giedd covered, we turn to one final male/female distinction, one found in a theory advanced in the year 2000 by Shelley Taylor of UCLA. The original research into the fight-or-flight response (done in the early twentieth century at Harvard by Walter Bradford Cannon—and done exclusively on men, according to James) showed that a human brain deals with stress by flooding the body with adrenalin; as a result, the heart beats faster, sugar gets dumped into the system, blood flows to the extremities (including the head), and the breathing rate increases. All of this allows a threatened individual to enter into combat or (more likely, if dealing with a saber-toothed tiger) to run like hell.

But what if this individual is carrying an infant?

Taylor reasoned that if our foremothers had been subject to the fight-or-flight response, we'd never have been born. After all, if you try to fight a predator while holding a baby in one hand, or if your escape is slowed by the burden of a child, you and the kid both are likely to be dead meat. And if neither the mother nor the offspring will survive, natural selection doesn't have much use for fight-or-flight in females.

Instead, Taylor proposed the existence of a "tend-and-befriend" re-sponse, one in which the individual seeks social support to handle the threat—perhaps a wall of spears or a rain of rocks supplied by other members of the mother's tribe. While fight-or-flight is driven by adren-alin, tend-and-befriend is the result of a flood of the hormone oxyto-cin, which produces almost the opposite physiological effects. Blood goes to the center of body, not the extremities, which may cause paleness, or fainting, or nausea; the individual may find it hard to move, or even think.

James has observed tend-and-befriend in animals as well as humans. "Chickens run around like crazy unless they're sitting on eggs; then they won't move—you can go up to them and get the eggs out from under them. I've seen elephants do it too. They put the babies in the middle of a circle, with the female elephants facing outward, and there's no motion of ears or trunks."

Human females are particularly subject to oxytocin floods before puberty and after giving birth, and James notes that test anxiety begins to show up in female students in roughly third to fifth grade. She recalls one of her own students who went pale and wide-eyed during a test; when she asked why the girl had missed a question whose answer she knew perfectly well, the girl looked at her pitifully and said, "I couldn't remember."

"She couldn't remember," says James, "because there was no blood in her brain!"

That many women are subject to tend-and-befriend responses seems reasonable to me, but there is no question that some women are fight-or-flight responders instead. And some men react to stress by seeking social support rather than standing alone or running for the hills. The stress response, like everything else James has said about male and female wiring, applies only to general populations, not to individuals. As we try to understand how boys' brains both differ from and resemble girls' brains, we must be careful not to deny the existence of observable differences, just as we must take care not to draw distinctions where they don't belong. The brain is simply too complex to be accurately depicted with the tools of Euclid. And even if we could accurately number and measure the myriad traits that make up an individual, we would discover that they do not all fall in the middle of the bell curve. But despite the millions of exceptions to every rule, there is often a fair amount of agreement about the differences between men and women. It's just hard sometimes to put that agreement into words.

As James deadpans, "It's a lot like what the Supreme Court says about pornography."

FIGURING OUT WHAT the Supreme Court might say about the differences between men and women is not a purely academic exercise. In fact, a slew of recent developments in courthouses, statehouses, and polling places have demonstrated just how relevant the question is, and how thorny.

In 2008, for example, the California Supreme Court declared that marriage rights could not be restricted to heterosexual couples alone. In response, voters passed Proposition 8, a measure altering the state constitution to read, "Only marriage between a man and a woman is valid or recognized in California." Though judges later ruled Prop 8 invalid, the subject of same-sex marriage became a hot topic, and most of those debating the topic seemed to ignore one of the fundamental issues of the controversy. Rick Moen, however, looked right at it.

In "Kudzu and the California Marriage Amendment," an essay composed in 2008 and updated in 2011, blogger and self-proclaimed "net geek" Moen examined the legal ramifications of Proposition 8. As the title shows, he believed the new law was analogous to the South's most widespread invasive plant, introduced for what some considered a benign purpose, but then rapidly and uncontrollably spreading its influence over the legal landscape just as the kudzu vine has swallowed trees, vehicles, buildings, and entire homesteads. With clarity, specificity, and no small amount of wit, he pointed out that any ban on same-sex marriage would require the state to define the terms *man* and *woman*. That might seem obvious, but Moen went on to note that such definitions will inevitably have "unintended side effects its proponents haven't anticipated and will find horrific—in that *they're going to end up mandating and legally sanctifying exactly the sort of same-sex marriages they're intending to ban.*"

How could a law banning same-sex marriage end up mandating same-sex marriage? To answer this question, we must start small—inside the nucleus of a single cell: a fertilized egg. It is here that the complex and sometimes messy process of sexual development begins, the same process that will eventually lead to later complications such as puberty, dating, uninspired romantic comedies, fumbling explorations of others' underclothes, and in some cases marriage licenses.

Like every cell in the human body that will eventually develop from it, a fertilized egg carries twenty-three pairs of chromosomes in its nucleus. One pair is special—the twenty-third, typically known as the sex chromosomes. In the typical male, that special pair consists of one X-shaped chromosome and one Y-shaped chromosome; the typical female carries two X-shaped chromosomes in that same location. But there are people who are not typical. Because of copying variance during the fertilization process, sometimes only one of the paired chromosomes will be present in an individual's cells, a condition known as monosomy. In roughly one of every 2000 to 5000 births, the monosomy involves the twenty-third pair, leaving a girl with only a single X chromosome. This condition is known as Turner syndrome, the symptoms of which may include small stature, infertility, a webbed neck, and sometimes cognitive and other health problems.

A more common abnormality in chromosomes is trisomy—the presence of an extra third chromosome.[2] The best-known example of trisomy occurs in the twenty-first pair, where the extra chromosome results in Down syndrome, but there are several forms of trisomy in the sex chromosomes, resulting in a variety of conditions. In most cases, these conditions will not be lethal, but they can cause problems with cognition, with reproduction, and with settling into gender roles.

About one in a thousand girls has triple X syndrome, which is in most cases symptom-free, though XXX women tend to be tall. As a result, relatively few women with triple X will even be diagnosed—in fact, the first report was made only in 1959.

Klinefelter syndrome is seen in roughly one out of every 650 males. It stems from the presence of an extra X chromosome, leaving such men XXY at the cellular level and physically tending toward infertility, breast development, and low hormone output from the testicles, which are typically undersized.

XYY syndrome, on the other hand, seems to have few physical effects on males, other than slightly increased height; sexual develop-

---

2. The presence of four chromosomes in a single cell—tetrasomy—has also been recorded by scientists, though it is far rarer than monosomy or trisomy; only a hundred or so cases of XXXX women have been documented since the syndrome's discovery in 1961, and only one in 17,000 births produces a male with XXYY chromosomes.

ment and fertility are normal. Occurring in roughly one in a thousand boys, XYY was at one time thought to be more common in prison populations, suggesting a link between criminality and "supermale" genetics, but this belief arose due to the fact that research into the syndrome was carried out primarily in prison populations. Unfortunately, misinformation about XYY syndrome was passed along into textbooks. In fact the only behavioral impact the syndrome seems to have is a somewhat increased incidence of learning disabilities.

What goes on in a cellular nucleus can have a profound effect on human life, but bodies can demonstrate a continuum between male and female even if their cells sit on one side of the XX/XY line. Our assumption is that all of an individual's cells share the same genes, but there are cases where a single body develops from the fusion of two fertilized eggs, a process known as *chimerism*. In effect, the body is a mixture of cells from a pair of fraternal twins, though the fusion probably occurs when each twin has only a few cells—four to sixteen of them, according to one source. Chimerism has appeared in animals as varied as marmosets, mice, and hummingbirds, but there are also human chimeras.

The most famous of these is Lydia Fairchild, a 26-year-old Washington woman who in 2002 underwent DNA testing in the course of her application for unemployment benefits. The tests produced one expected result, proof that her ex-boyfriend was indeed the father of the children she had borne, and one wholly unexpected result, proof that she was not their mother. The astonished Fairchild was not only denied government aid but suspected of welfare fraud, despite her doctor's vouching for her maternal bona fides.

The power of DNA testing was such that some attorneys refused to represent her in court, but eventually a lawyer came to the rescue— a lawyer for the prosecution who had come across a relevant article in the *New England Journal of Medicine*. The May 2002 article discussed the case of Boston teacher Karen Keegan, whose entire family had undergone DNA testing because she needed a kidney transplant. Like Fairchild, she was told by doctors that her DNA did not match that of two of her children. The hospital's investigation revealed that Keegan was a chimera, carrying cells from two different sources in different parts of her body.

Armed with this new information, Lydia Fairchild and her family underwent further testing, with surprising but effective results. Her children's DNA matched her mother's, demonstrating that they were kin, while Fairchild's own tests produced proof of both her maternity and her chimerism; DNA taken from her skin and hair did not match her children's, but the DNA taken from a cervical smear did match. In effect, she had given birth to her twin's children. Or vice-versa.

Such chimerism is highly unusual, and since it is apparent only at the cellular level, it is unlikely to be detected except in unusual medical circumstances. There is one case, however, in which it can be made much more visible: when the chimeric twins are different sexes.

In 2006, David Bohlen, Assistant Curator of Zoology at the Illinois State Museum, published his account of a case of chimerism that was not merely visible, but startlingly obvious. In this instance, a Northern Cardinal appeared near Rochester, Illinois, demonstrating the species' sexual dimorphism in a single bird. It looked as though two mating birds had been sawed neatly in half and then recombined into one; the plumage on the cardinal's right side was the familiar bright red of the male, while on the left it was the female's sandy brown. This clean, linear, male-on-one-side-female-on-the-other condition—known scientifically as *bilateral gynandromorphism*—made for great photographs, but it was not new to Bohlen. Not only had he seen a similar cardinal in 2002, but in 1986 he had studied the internal organs of a dead Eurasian Tree Sparrow and discovered both a testis on the right and an ovary on the left. The sparrow's intersexuality was unknown to him until that moment, however; unlike that of cardinals, tree sparrow plumage does not differ by sex.

THE TREE SPARROW example is probably the better one when discussing the lines between the human sexes. In cases where traits of both sexes appear in a human being, they rarely do so in the clear and linear fashion seen in Bohlen's cardinal. Some children are born with genitalia described as, in the technical language, "ambiguous." Instead of the clearly external penis-scrotum-testicle configuration or the clearly internal vagina-uterus-ovary set-up, these individuals' genitals have traits from both categories—an enlarged clitoris (which might be considered a "micropenis" by some experts) may or may not have a ureter located at the end, and there may or may not be a vaginal opening. These various individuals are now commonly known by the term *intersex*, rather than the more judgmental Victorian terms "pseudohermaphrodite" (if their bodies had gonadal tissue of one sex and anatomical traits of the opposite sex), or "true hermaphrodite" (if they possessed gonadal tissue of both sorts).

There are even men and women whose genitalia may look perfectly male or female (at least at birth), but who nevertheless smudge the dividing line between the sexes. One example is the group affected by congenital adrenal hyperplasia: genetically, these individuals are perfectly normal females, but in utero, their mothers' adrenal glands produced huge amounts of androgens (testosterone and other male hormones). The girls' ovaries, wombs, and even upper vaginas are usually unaffected, but their external genitalia can be altered by the hormone bath; the clitoris can be enlarged and the labia shaped more like a scrotum (though without testicles), leading to the possibility of a sexual misidentification. Once the proper diagnosis is made, the physical issues can be treated with hormones or even surgery, but psychologists report that these girls, though perfectly fertile, intelligent, and otherwise unaffected, may for the rest of their lives prefer to play with toys and dress in clothes that are typically used by boys.

Another condition that defies male/female duality is androgen insensitivity syndrome (AIS). An individual with this condition has a clitoris, a vagina, breasts, and all the secondary sexual characteristics typically displayed by a woman, but has neither ovaries nor uterus, which may affect the vagina's depth; moreover, this person has the standard male XY pairing and may have a set of underdeveloped and undescended testes. Odds are good that such a person will have been raised as a female and will probably have the self-image of a female, but genetically speaking, this is a male whose cells do not respond to androgens. In fact, despite the genetic masculinity, this immunity to androgens may make the person appear particularly feminine, since most women's bodies produce low levels of male hormones and respond to them by promoting increased muscle mass, body hair, and other male secondary sexual characteristics.

What Rick Moen's essay on the California Marriage Amendment points out, then, is that legally restricting marriage to a man and a woman is not a simple task. For example, he asks us to imagine the case of a woman who has grown up a female and has married a male; in the course of investigating their fertility problems, however, she and her husband discover that she is a genetic male with AIS. As Moen puts it:

> Laws like Proposition 8 might very well cause such a woman's marriage to be retroactively annulled—or prohibited in the first place. Furthermore, if the law decides that this particular citizen is male on account of the Y chromosome, testosterone, and testes, then she *would* be permitted to marry . . . guess who? . . . another woman. So, courtesy of Prop. 8, we are likely to suddenly have *court-mandated same-sex marriages.*

Prop. 8 is now defunct, but Moen's points remain timely, as the majority of states still have laws and/or constitutional amendments forbidding same-sex marriage. With the possibilities of trisomy, chimerism, and various hormonal conditions smudging the line between the sexes, however, it is likely that the only people happy about our nation's hodgepodge of marriage laws will be the lawyers. After all, *somebody* has to tell the people of the United States who to marry.

NEEDLESS TO SAY, trying to impose a simplistic either/or label like "male" or "female" in cases like those described by Moen is likely to end in frustration, but there is immense societal pressure to keep the line between male and female clear, and that pressure has existed for a very long time. Some societies spend a great deal of effort drawing the line between the sexes (and in some cases enforcing the placement of that line), but Abigail James says that in most places such efforts are largely unnecessary. "I travel all over world, and in fact people are really very uniform in what they think of how males/females should look and behave."

But James is careful to make sure I understand that, again, we're talking about the physical differences in general populations and the exceptions demonstrated by individuals. For example, she nods toward me, saying, "You can grow a beard and I can't. Some women can grow one, but not like yours." She asks to look at my hand and comments on my 2D:4D ratio—in other words, the comparative size of my index and ring fingers. A shorter index finger (digit 2) and longer ring finger (digit 4) indicates prenatal exposure to high levels of testosterone, and men as a group tend to have low 2D:4D ratios. Despite my thick and luxuriant facial hair, however, my second and fourth fingers are almost equal in length, with the ring roughly a quarter-inch longer than the index.

I must take pains to emphasize the point that general tendencies do not dictate individual situations. It is purely coincidental that I do this now, just before I mention that the digit ratio has been linked to a variety of physical traits and conditions, including penis size. *Time Magazine* reports that a 2011 Korean study indicates that the lower the ratio, the longer the johnson, while a Dutch study from 2008 indicated a lower digit ratio in women with gender identity disorder (GID). Perhaps the most startling discovery about digit ratio came in a 2001 paper in which Baron-Cohen and three other researchers studied a group of 72 autistic children in the UK, along with their families, and found a correlation between the digit ratio and autism, as well as between the digit ratio and Asperger syndrome (AS):

> We found that the 2D:4D ratios of children with autism, their siblings, fathers and mothers were lower than population normative values. Children with AS, who share the social and communicative symptoms of autism but have normal or even high IQ, had higher 2D:4D ratios than children with autism but lower ratios than population normative values.

James notes that her own digit ratio is typically feminine—a fortunate fact, given the evidence that women with the more masculine ratio may be more susceptible to heart disease than other women—but this is one of the only ways in which she paints herself as typically feminine. Though she is a wife, a mother, and a skilled knitter known to click her needles throughout faculty meetings, she smiles and says simply, "I have the brain of a 14-year-old boy, with better verbal skills."

The study of distinctions between the general population of men and the general population of women, then, is statistically useful for a variety of purposes. For individuals, however, those distinctions can often seem like barriers; a man who stands on the "female" side of the line, either in terms of his physical traits or his behaviors, can easily find himself subject to disapproval, taunting, or even attack. The same is true for a woman who crosses the line into what society has designated "male" territory.

It is thus unsurprising that some medical professionals have attempted to redraw those lines for patients who lie astride them, using hormones and surgery to assign (or reassign) people to one side or the other. Many patients have welcomed such practices, but these are typically in cases where the treatment was voluntary—where the doctor was helping the patient cross the line to his/her preferred side.

Perhaps the most famous attempt to redraw the gender line, however, was made in a case where the treatment was involuntary—and kept secret for over a decade. As recounted in John Colapinto's brilliant book *As Nature Made Him: The Boy Who Was Raised as a Girl*, the parents of an infant boy whose penis had been burned off in a horrifying 1966 accident were persuaded by doctors to raise him as a girl. Despite the removal of his testicles, a regimen of female hormones, and his parents' silence about his infancy, the child then known as Brenda Reimer was never comfortable as a girl, suffering teasing, bullying, and depression for years before his parents finally revealed the truth to him at age fourteen. Adopting the name "David," he chose to live the rest of his life on the male side of the line, even marrying and adopting three children, but that choice did not free him from depression; with his career on the rocks and his marriage dissolving, he committed suicide in 2004.

David Reimer's story is a cautionary tale for anyone who believes that the boundaries drawn by human beings are in any way reflective of some natural order. It is likewise an important lesson for anyone who fails to remember that such lines do not simply lie on a page in a medical text or a law book; they are all too often drawn over real people.

Names Will Never Hurt Me

*The science of names—Interspecies romance—The kind of creature
that would break a taxonomist's spirit—Talking with non-scientists—
The magpie issue—Stupid hybridization*

> *Homo sapiens is the species that invents symbols in which to invest
> passion and authority, then forgets that symbols are inventions.*
> —Joyce Carol Oates

BY NOW WE SHOULD understand the need for caution. It's not
as though we are lacking in examples of the potentially dire
consequences of mistaking a border for a natural phenomenon. Yet on every bird count (for example), in every field
guide, that caution is at best played down, and at worst ignored altogether, all in the name of science—and all too often,
in the science of names.

The modern science of names—*taxonomy*—has its origins
in Carl Linnaeus' 1735 masterpiece *Systema Naturae*, in which
he set down the basic ways in which all organisms were to be
categorized, described, and named. It was an enormous project, and the presence of errors in something so vast should
come as no surprise. Those errors have led to a number of departures from Linnaeus' methods, as well as numerous changes
to the categorizations he originally established; even Linnaeus
himself made some adjustments in later editions, realizing for
example that his initial classification of whales and manatees
as fish was a mistake. Still, he was among other things the first
scientist to recognize that bats are mammals, and the basics of
his system remain in place after nearly three centuries.

Each type of organism in Linnaeus' system is given a particular name—a Latin name, since Latin was the universal language of science in his day. The two-word name (or *binomial*) identifies the organism's genus (always capitalized) and its species (typically in lowercase), as in *Homo sapiens*. These are hardly the only two categories to which an organism belongs, however; biologists now assign each to a particular domain, kingdom, phylum (or division, for plants), class, order, family, genus, *and* species, each respective category becoming more specific. Often, the former category will contain multiple examples of the latter categories. Thus, the phylum Chordata—animals with spinal cords—contains multiple classes: Mammalia, Aves, Reptilia, Amphibia, etc. Within each class there are typically multiple orders, within each order multiple families, and so on, until we get to the most basic unit of taxonomy—the one that has been a source of uproar for centuries, and not merely because Charles Darwin wrote his most famous book about it: *The Origin of Species*.

A species is traditionally defined as a population of organisms that can interbreed and produce fertile offspring, but cannot breed with any other organisms—or at least, that's how the Comte de Buffon defined the word in the eighteenth century. Thus, if two foxes mate and produce little foxes, those foxes can be said to belong to the same species when and if the little foxes grow up to produce little foxes of their own; basically, grandparenthood is what establishes a species. If the original litter is not able to produce its own little foxes, we're dealing with interspecies romance—an occurrence far more common than some staid biologists would like to admit.

How common is it? Common enough that there are numerous words in English that refer to such relations between species—*half-breed*, *crossbreed*, *mongrel*, *mutt*. The technical term, however, is *hybrid*.[1]

Clearly, we would not have such words if organisms practiced any kind of fidelity to their species, nor would we have another very particular English word: *mule*. When a male donkey gets amorous with a female horse, the resultant creature is a mule, but a male and female

---

1. Not all hybrids have parents from different species, but the term is also useful as a description of a creature whose parents lie in different subspecies, or different taxonomic categories of any sort.

mule can engage in all the sex they like without producing another generation of mules. (The offspring of a male horse and a female donkey, known as a *hinny*, is rarer than the mule, but just as infertile.) Though there have been recorded cases where female mules have been impregnated by horses or donkeys, male mules are unable to produce issue, a feature so well known that the word *mule* is applied to the infertile offspring of any two species, animal or plant.

With all this information, one might well suppose that fertility between individuals—*interfertility*—would be a perfectly useful test for speciation. In truth, it's not so great. For one thing, it's slow. Infants take a while to reach puberty, after all, so often we can't check quickly to determine whether an animal is a mule or not. It's also worth noting that, two centuries after Buffon, biologist Ernst Mayr defined *species* a bit differently: "Species are groups of actually or potentially interbreeding populations, which are reproductively isolated from other such groups." The key changes there are the word *potentially* and the phrase *reproductively isolated*. To isolate something, you have to draw some kind of border around it, and what have we been saying about Mother Nature and lines?

Consider, for example, the phenomenon of "ring species." Atop the world, there are many seagulls belonging to the genus *Larus*, and those gulls are spread around the Arctic zone in great numbers and multiple species. In Northern Europe, for example, you will discover two species within the genus: the Lesser Black-backed Gull (*Larus fuscus*), which has a black back and yellow legs, and the Herring Gull (*Larus argentatus*), which has a grey back and pinkish legs. They cannot interbreed. But the Herring Gull can and does interbreed with the American Herring Gull, which itself can breed with the East Siberian Herring Gull. Go west a bit more and you'll find the latter mating with Birula's Gull, which interbreeds at the western edge of its own range with Heuglin's Gull. And Heuglin's Gull is interfertile with the Siberian Lesser Black-backed Gull, the easternmost subspecies of *Larus fuscus*. In other words, gulls interbreed in a continuous line all around the North Pole, suggesting the existence of a single species within the genus *Larus*, but the two gulls at the ends of that line cannot interbreed—which indicates they're not the same species.

This paradox is duplicated around other geographic features such as the Himalayan plateau, and it is but one of the many problems modern science has in defining a species. Consider the issue of geographic isolation. There are two populations of Abert's Squirrels in the Grand Canyon area, one on the north rim of the canyon (known as the Kaibab Squirrel) and one on the south rim. Could they interbreed? Quite possibly. But until one of the groups develops either a) the determination to climb more than a mile down into the canyon, swim the Colorado River, and climb another mile up to the opposite plateau, or b) the ability to fly, they never *will* interbreed. They are geographically isolated, and over time, as each population is influenced by mutation, inbreeding, predation, and other factors affecting its gene pool, they will become less and less likely to remain interfertile, which would eventually make them separate species. But unless we either transplant squirrels across the canyon or breed them in captivity, we will never know when that particular Rubicon has been crossed.

Sometimes, however, animals will not interbreed even given the opportunity. A particularly baroque example of this involves the Italian Sparrow (*Passer italiae*). In 2011, Norwegian scientists published a paper in *Molecular Ecology* showing DNA evidence that *P. italiae* was a cross between the ubiquitous House Sparrow (*P. domesticus*) and the Spanish Sparrow (*P. hispaniolensis*). This in itself had long been understood; my 1999 Princeton Field Guide edition of *Birds of Europe* notes that the parent species hybridize in many places, and it identifies the Italian as a "rather stable hybrid" form, listing it under the Spanish. (Basically, the Italian looks like a Spanish head on a House body, combining the Spanish's brown crown and white cheek with the House's black bib and grey belly.) The 2011 article, however, treats *P. italiae* as a separate species; indeed, Victoria Gill's BBC report, where I first learned of this study, focused primarily on this issue of a "new" sparrow, not on the question of its origins, as seen in the headline and lede:

Italian sparrow joins family as a new species
Scientists in Norway say they have conclusive genetic evidence that sparrows recently evolved a third species.

The most interesting—even bizarre—element of the study, however, is what it says about the turbulent relationship between reproductive isolation and speciation. In effect, the House and Spanish sparrows met in southeastern Italy, and the hybrids that sprang up there have been reproductively isolated from the parent populations long enough to become a separate species. That seems like a clear-cut story of traditional speciation, except for the fact that the populations are not isolated in any physical way. The limited territory of *P. italiae* is largely within the range of both *P. domesticus* and *P. hispaniolensis*. The DNA evidence, however, indicates that the Italian and Spanish sparrows do not interbreed even when they live in the same territory. The exact nature of the reproductive barrier between the birds was not clear, though University of Oslo biologist Glenn-Peter Saetre theorized that either the Italians have evolved some difference in breeding seasons or else they just don't like the Spanish.[2] Whatever the barrier is, however, it does not prevent the Italian Sparrow from interbreeding with the House Sparrow. According to Saetre and his colleagues, "[T]he Italian sparrow hybridizes with the house sparrow in a sparsely populated contact zone in the Alps." In effect, the Italian is a distinct and separate species, except that it interbreeds with its parent species, except that it interbreeds with only *one* parent species.

In her article on the study, Gill understates, "In evolutionary biology, the definition of a distinct species is not entirely clear-cut." I agree, though I personally believe the matter might be more succinctly summed up if science were to rename the Italian Sparrow *Passer oedipus*.

FOR TRUE EXASPERATION in the issue of speciation, however, we need not range into geographical or mythological extremes. We can simply turn to man's best friend. Yes, the domestic dog, dubbed by Linnaeus *Canis canis* and later *Canis familiaris*. It may not look like the kind of creature that would break a taxonomist's spirit, but looks can be deceiving. To begin with, there's the fact that the name *dog* covers

---

2. Increasingly possible following Spain's victory over Italy in the 2012 European Football Cup.

an incredible variety of animals: looming towers of canine grace like Great Danes, wrinkled wads of skin like Shar-Peis, enormous balls of fur and meat like Saint Bernards, slick-coated wisps like Italian Greyhounds, tiny doglets like teacup Chihuahuas, and indescribably odd creatures like English Bulldogs. If the interbreeding test for a species is going to be applied here, comedy is the surest result, even if you ignore the possibility of a whirlwind romance between Lassie and Scooby-Doo. But the ugly fact remains: all these wildly dissimilar breeds are part of the same species. And it's likely not the one you're thinking of. They are all examples of *Canis lupus*—the wolf.

Today, the evidence has persuaded scientists to assign the domestic dog not to the species where Linnaeus first placed it, but to the wolf subspecies *Canis lupus familiaris*. Why did the dog get lumped in with *Canis lupus lupus*, *Canis lupus arctos*, and thirty-odd other lupine subspecies? Because, if a wolf should join a dog in amorous embrace—an embrace that can last for some time, as male canids are equipped with a *baculum*, or penis bone—the resulting offspring will be perfectly fertile. In fact, these so-called wolfdogs are increasingly popular pets, particularly in the U.S., where tens of thousands of the animals are reportedly bred. Both wolves and domestic dogs are, moreover, perfectly capable of hybridizing with other canines, including the Australian dingo (*Canis lupus dingo*), the coyote (*Canis latrans*), and even the jackal (*Canis aureus*). Some experts even claim that the American southeast's native wolf, the subspecies known as the Red Wolf (*Canis lupus rufus*) isn't a true wolf at all, but a wolf/coyote hybrid.

There is some evidence of decreased fertility in the crossbreeds involving coyotes and jackals, but even if we limit ourselves to dogs, wolves, and dingos, we're still talking about a single species that ranges more widely in size, shape, coloration, behavior, and distribution than practically any other vertebrate on earth. Yes, I'll grant you, Queen Elizabeth II may not closely resemble Shaquille O'Neal at first glance, but domestic dogs make them look like twins. Dogs range in weight from under 150 grams to over 150 *kilo*grams—a difference of three orders of magnitude. The heaviest adult human being, Jon Brower Minnoch, weighed in at approximately 635 kilograms (1400 pounds); to match the variability of the species *Canis lupus familiaris*, we'd need to find an adult human being weighing 635 grams—not quite a pound and a half. (The current record holder, a young Nepalese man, is around twenty times that heavy.)

This, then, is the extent of variability within a single species. And frankly, if we cannot use the term *species* to distinguish between Mowgli's brothers and something a socialite carries in her purse, what good does that term do us?

This frustration is not new. Asa Grey wrote about it in a piece for *The Atlantic* in July 1860, in his review of a recent book on natural history by one Charles Darwin:

> It is by no means difficult to believe that varieties are incipient or possible species, when we see what trouble naturalists, especially botanists, have to distinguish between them,—one regarding as a true species what another regards as a variety; when the progress of knowledge increases, rather than diminishes, the number of doubtful instances; and when there is less agreement than ever among naturalists as to what the basis is in Nature upon which our idea of species reposes, or how the word is practically to be defined.

When I open my field guide hoping to identify a bird's species, am I looking for something that doesn't exist? Is there any consensus on what species a bird belongs to? Hell, is there any consensus on what the word *species* means?

Luckily, in searching for the answers to these questions, I was able to find a man who says of his professional role, "I answer questions." Officially, Kevin McGowan is an instructor at the Cornell Lab of Ornithology, but he uses his experience as both professional ornithologist and avid birder to facilitate communication with the curious layman. As he notes, because scientists are trained primarily to talk to each other, the CLO often relies on him to talk with non-scientists like me.

The first thing McGowan wants to make sure I understand is the difference between taxonomy and systematics. These fields are closely interrelated, even interdependent, but they are not identical. Taxonomy is, in his words, "the sorting out of life into parts." In order to make sense of the world, we need to have labels for those parts, and taxonomy supplies those labels; it's not that the parts don't exist without the labels, but rather that we can't really think about them until their labels are affixed. This is a phenomenon I've observed in my students, both indoors and out. Teach them what a symbol is and they start spotting symbolism all over the place; teach them what poison ivy looks like and they'll soon be shocked to discover that even familiar pathways are surrounded by it. Many birders know this from experience as well; once you've seen a bird and learned its name, you suddenly notice it everywhere—and not because it wasn't there before. As McGowan says, "If we don't know the name of it, it's invisible."

Systematics, on the other hand, is the study of how all these parts relate. If there's a question about what to call something, you should ask a taxonomist, but if you need to figure out whether the Black-billed Magpie is more closely related to the other North American magpie (the Yellow-billed) or to the magpies of Eurasia, a systematist should be engaged. Of course, to figure out the relationships, each piece must first be given a name, but sometimes a clearer understanding of the relationships will result in the need to change a name.

In July of 2000 the American Ornithologists' Union decided, as it periodically does, to make a few such changes in the taxonomic conventions for American birds. One was a simple English name change which turned the politically incorrect Oldsquaw into the Long-tailed Duck; others were adjustments in Latin names, such as the one which altered the Black-capped Chickadee's binomial from *Poecile atricapillus* to *Poecile atricapilla*. The change that mattered to me, however, concerned the magpie issue above.

The importance of this change was not immediately apparent to me, nor had it become apparent by March of 2008, when Dad and I spun through the snowy landscape of southern Utah on our way from sunny Zion National Park to our lodgings at Ruby's Inn near Bryce Canyon. Dad was behind the wheel, allowing me to take leisurely looks at the landscape and the birdlife, but while the former was often astonishingly beautiful, the latter was not in the mood for display. I did, however, catch sight of a bird I'd first seen in England a quarter-century before—a Black-billed Magpie, its black-and-white plumage standing out boldly against the muted colors of the winter fields and trees.

Sadly, I felt relatively little excitement about this sighting because I had allowed myself to become caught up in the game of listing: I mean, I had been in Utah for almost *a whole day*, going up and down the Virgin River and all around Zion. But I had not yet spotted a life bird. Hell, I'd gotten two in Nevada just the day before, and one (the Great-tailed Grackle) had been in a Jack-in-the-Box parking lot. Here in Utah, though, I'd spent most of the day in a freakin' national park with no lifers to show for it, and I was a bit surly—for a day. My attitude about the state's birds would be reversed the next afternoon by one of the most spectacular sights I've ever witnessed: my first Prairie Falcon making a full-speed dive—known to falconers as a *stoop*—at a pair of Golden Eagles who were getting too close to its nest. The falcon came so fast, and at such an angle, that Dad and I were able to hear the wind ripping through its plumage. Despite a marked advantage in both size and numbers, the eagles vacated the premises as fast as their massive wings could carry them.

Contrasted against that lifer, my magpie was merely a pleasant sighting—the first in my home country, at least—and I promptly forgot about it for nearly two years. But one February day in 2010, as I was flipping through my *Peterson's Field Guide to Western Birds* in preparation for a trip to west Texas, I happened upon the page containing the black-bill and noted for the first time that its Latin name was given as *Pica hudsonia*. What the hell?

The magpie's gloriously repeated specific name, *Pica pica*, was bestowed upon it in 1758 by none other than Linnaeus, and I was astonished that any modern taxonomist would dare to trample on that beautiful, echoing bit of nomenclature. My dander was fully risen and a nasty letter to the editor of *The Auk* was halfway written in my mind when suddenly something occurred to me: the bird in this book was an American bird. Linnaeus' bird was a European bird.

A bit of quick research revealed that while *Pica pica* was still a going concern, the AOU had split the American magpie from its Eurasian cousin after systematists examining the DNA evidence concluded that the black-bill is more closely related to the Yellow-billed Magpie of California than to the magpies of the Old World. Where once there had been one species, now there were two, and I had seen both. Without having so much as looked out my window, I now had a life list of 350 birds when I'd woken up with only 349.

Or, looked at another way, I now had 350 *names* on my life list. Kevin McGowan is very firm in pointing out that these names are not decided upon, or changed, in any arbitrary fashion: "They don't change names willy-nilly." But he is equally clear in pointing out that the decision to place two organisms in a single species, or to place them in two different species, is made for human reasons. As he puts it, "It depends on the questions you're asking."

Linnaeus was, to some degree, asking the same question Adam asked himself in Genesis: "What should I call *this* one?" And, like Adam, Linnaeus was providing a starting point, not a final determination.

As McGowan notes, the problem of Linnaeus' starting point was that it was just that: a point, a unique location, a single place on a vast globe. "Most places, if you sit down and show them stuff, most people will come up with the same species—the same kind of divisions that others do," he points out. But in science, we no longer look in a single place—the perspective is global. "You look out," he says, indicating the Cayuga Lake Basin outside the Cornell Lab, "and you see robin, cardinal, chickadee . . . They're clearly not the same things. But in Seattle, their Song Sparrow doesn't look the same [as ours], and sounds a little different. The Pribilofs [four small islands off the southwest coast of Alaska] have a big honking subspecies of Song Sparrow, bigger than a Hermit Thrush, but it still sings like a Song Sparrow. Is that the same thing?"

For a guy who answers questions, McGowan is not shy about asking them. He does, however, bluntly address my next question: is interfertility a good test for speciation?

"Not really. The process of creating species is essentially finding reproductive isolation, but finding a lack of it doesn't mean much." He points out that warblers often hybridize not only between species, but between genera, while ducks in zoos are notorious for breeding with all manner of exotic waterfowl, producing hybrids that would never appear in nature, but which do just fine where they are. This is the kind of biological boundary violation, he says, that drove one of his colleagues to simply throw up her hands and express her final view on our entire conception of interbreeding: "Hybridization is just *stupid*."

Basically, in McGowan's words, when it comes to separate species, "There must be a divergence, but that doesn't mean they can't come together again . . . If they don't produce fertile offspring, they can't be the same species, but the reverse is not necessarily true." As convenient as it might be to have Nature draw the line between species for us, she won't. If we really want those lines, we're going to have to draw them for ourselves.

Rite of Passage

A certain degree of frustration—The commercial engine of our culture—Where no heads roll—Not by maturity, but by age—The biggest myth about adolescence—Considerable upset—Thirteenness—Right at the edge of the nest—An entirely different animal

Don't bother me, leave me alone.
Anyway I'm almost grown.
—Chuck Berry

BIRDERS ARE OFTEN seen as somewhat outside the mainstream, but in truth, our views on life can be very close to the middle of the bell curve. Like most people, we generally think puppies are cute, look forward to vacation days, and enjoy sex more than paying taxes. Another thing we often share with most people is a certain degree of frustration with adolescents—just not necessarily those of our own species. Sub-adult human beings are well known for devising clothing, hairstyles, and body modifications specifically to annoy their parents' generation, but sub-adult birds are not so deliberate about their appearance. They simply don't look like their parents.

This in itself wouldn't be a problem if there weren't so many people trying to identify them by sight. Practically all field guides illustrate the plumage of adult birds, but they are far less helpful in showing the feathers found on a freshly-fledged young one. If an unfamiliar juvenile turns up in a nearby tree, you can spend a very long time flipping through pages in search of a picture that doesn't exist in your book.

(I've done it with species ranging from the Blue Grosbeak to the Brown-headed Cowbird to the Red-shouldered Hawk.) Worse, the plumage of a juvenile bird is almost always duller and more cryptic than that of an adult—presumably to help make the youngster less visible to predators—leaving fewer obvious field marks by which a birder can identify it. And if you try to avoid the frustration of plumage by attempting ear birding, good luck; immature birds' voices may not resemble those of their parents at all. The young Northern Mockingbird, for example, makes a piercing squeak so unlike the delicately mimicked calls of the adult that it may as well be wearing a black T-shirt with the logo of a death metal band on it. I once spent a good ten minutes trying to penetrate the branches of an overgrown boxwood in order to see what was making that godawful *SHTREEP!* sound before I realized that the dull grey bird in the shrubbery was probably related to the adult mocker that was flapping around me in an attempt to drive me off.

This type of frustration with human adolescents is most acute among parents, but it is far from unknown in the general population. Our society has a great many beliefs, rituals, and even laws concerning people between childhood and adulthood, and these are often so widely shared that they're fodder for comedy. Movies, books, and comics about the communication gap between adolescents and adults are commonplace, perhaps because adolescents are often the people driving the commercial engine of our culture; a movie that excludes teenagers from its audience is a movie that is giving up a significant amount of cash at the box office, which is one reason why filmmakers often work hard to avoid the R rating.

That R is assigned by the Motion Picture Association of America, a film industry organization known primarily for its rating system for movies. The system is voluntary—no studio or producer is legally required to submit its film to the MPAA. A film without a rating, however, is unlikely to be handled by distributors or shown by theaters for fear of violating the fundamental assumption on which the MPAA is built: that there are certain words, images, and concepts inappropriate for people below a certain age. In other words, it's a system based on lines; until a viewer crosses a certain chronological boundary, the MPAA feels she should not encounter these words/images/concepts in a motion picture. The same sort of timeline is a common feature in many other areas of our culture; minimum ages exist for driving motor vehicles, for voting, for attending school, and for playing Little League Baseball. The movie-rating system, however, is perhaps the most interesting of these linear systems because of the way its lines are placed.

Since 1968, each movie rated by the MPAA has displayed its rating on its promotional materials, as well as on a blue screen after the final credits. The ratings have been tweaked over the years, but they have held steady since 1990. According to www.mpaa.org, the ratings are G (all ages admitted), PG (some material may not be suitable for children), PG-13 (some material may be inappropriate for children under 13), R (under 17 requires accompanying parent or adult guardian), and NC-17 (no one 17 and under admitted). The ratings are applied in order to give parents some idea of what they're letting the kids see, or in the case of films rated R or NC-17, what they *can't* let their kids see. The potentially objectionable contents identified are theme, language, nudity, sex, and violence, and the tool used for determining when these become objectionable is a bright, clear line. It is one of the very few things about movie ratings that qualify as bright or clear.

Vague and timid terms abound. "Adult themes" and various mysterious subcategories of violence ("sci-fi violence," "fantasy violence," "graphic bloody violence") are often cited in MPAA ratings, but the most pervasive euphemism, by far, is the use of the word *language* to refer to profanity. In fact, profanity in general isn't the issue so much as a single profane word: *fuck*. The precise formula by which the MPAA judges films remains a trade secret, but at least one part of that formula is both clear and public. A quick visit to http://www.mpaa.org/ratings/what-each-rating-means will leave the reader in no doubt about how the word *fuck* is to be handled: as though it were dripping with radioactive Ebola-ridden ape feces.

> A motion picture's single use of one of the harsher sexually-derived words, though only as an expletive, initially requires at least a PG-13 rating. More than one such expletive requires an R rating, as must even one of those words used in a sexual context.

In short, the MPAA will allow only one use of the word *fuck* in a film that might be seen by unaccompanied adolescents. Even in an old-fashioned biopic like *The King's Speech*, where no heads roll, no blood flows, and no breasts are bared, the simple depiction of a frustrated Colin Firth working through a lengthy string of curses was enough to require an R rating. Moreover, though a PG-13 film may contain a single use of the word, it cannot be used in its literal sense, as a reference to sexual intercourse. It can be used idiomatically ("What the fuck is that?"), as an interjection ("Oh, fuck! It's a vampire!"), or as a participle ("That fucking vampire is sparkling!"), but that's about it. The audience for a PG-13 film may watch a man threaten a woman with "I'm going to fucking kill you," but under no circumstances can such an audience see a happily married man gaze adoringly at his wife and say, "I love you, darling. Let's fuck."

What the fuck is going on here?

Perhaps to help the viewing public better understand its reasoning, in 1990 the MPAA began offering what it calls "rating descriptors," a few words of explanation for the rating of a particular film, words which often accompany the rating on the cover of the DVD as well. Reading these descriptors is illuminating, and occasionally amusing, for those interested in seeing how our culture and our lives are viewed through the lens of the film industry. For example, the third *Lord of the Rings* movie, *The Return of the King*, was rated PG-13 for "Intense Epic Battle Sequences and Frightening Images," which is certainly true enough, albeit a bit inexact.[1] Still, the terminology here raises concerns. If the MPAA is really interested in keeping young people away from inappropriate films, I think it should probably avoid using the same slang terms that teens use for giving their highest praise:

"Dude! Did you see that snowboard crash on YouTube? It was *epic*!"

"Oh, hell yeah! That was *intense*!"

While I have so far found no descriptions of battle sequences as *hep, cool, hip, with it, groovy, awesome, bitching, phat, dope, fly,* or *sweet*, I have found the MPAA's justifications for its ratings puzzling at times,

---

1. I would certainly consider the fire-breathing balrog in the first film a potentially scary image for a child, but I also have a friend—a responsible, tax-paying adult—who is unwilling to see any movie with a hobbit because he's creeped out by their hairy feet.

even when it isn't appropriating the language of the audience whose money it is ostensibly rejecting. Sometimes the issue is terminology, sometimes it's more of a logic problem. Consider these examples of helpful advice for concerned parents:

Eternal Sunshine of the Spotless Mind (R): "Language, Some Drug and Sexual Content." Well, yes, there is language in the film. I believe the language is English. And "some drug"? Couldn't they have been specific about which one?

Holes (PG): "For Violence, Mild Language and Some Thematic Elements." What is mild language, exactly, and how does it differ from regular-strength language? And doesn't any movie with a theme contain thematic elements?

Shaun of the Dead (R): "Zombie Violence/Gore and Language." This may be another use of *language* to mean *profanity*, but I prefer to imagine that the film features scenes in the zombie language, which has over 200 words for *brains*.

South Park: Bigger, Longer, and Uncut (R): "For Pervasive Vulgar Language and Crude Sexual Humor, and For Some Violent Images." Specificity at last!

But the irony here is that the MPAA saves its precision for a satire of the MPAA's rating system. *South Park: BLU* is, at its core, a movie about using the word *fuck* in a movie. In the opening scenes, a quartet of American fourth-graders sneaks into *Asses of Fire*, the new R-rated movie by their favorite Canadian television stars, Terrance and Philip. Why did this film within the film get an R? Because it is filled to the brim with profanity—no, actually, it's even fuller than that. Terrance and Philip insult each other onscreen in a jaunty ensemble number that somehow contains more profanity than it has room for—a TARDIS of *fuck*. When the schoolkids emerge from the theater cursing like sailors, the town of South Park erupts in indignant outrage, eventually leading to the use of chips in children's brains, war with Canada, and the beginning of Satan's rule on earth—everything the MPAA wants to prevent, really. But the fundamental issue on which the film builds its satire is the belief that lies at the foundation of the MPAA rating system: that the proper audience for a movie is determined not by maturity, but by *age*. Would providing parents with clear information about reasonable and consistent standards help them decide what their kids are mature enough see? Probably. But drawing a line on the calendar is a lot easier.

In early 2012, the MPAA found a way to wrap the logic of this foundational idea into an even greater Mobius strip, this time through the simple application of an R rating to the documentary *Bully*. In the film, children and adolescents discuss the very real dangers they face in school on a daily basis—but they discuss this subject in language that the MPAA considered inappropriate for them. The violence they endured wasn't too much for the young people in the audience, nor were the suicides they'd seen among their peers, but the fact that kids onscreen were using the same language used by kids in every elementary and middle school in the country every day was considered so traumatizing that those under 17 had to be kept from hearing it without parental accompaniment. Linda Holmes of NPR.org responded to the news about the rating thus:

> There's a grotesque irony in declaring that what is portrayed in *Bully* should be softened, or bleeped—should be *hidden*, really, because it's too much for kids to see. Of course it's too much for kids to see. It's also too much for kids to live through, walk through, ride the bus with, and go to school with. *That's why they made the movie.* The entire point of this film is that kids do not live with the protection we often believe they do—many of them live in a terrifying, isolating war zone, and if you hide what it's like, if you *lie* about what they're experiencing, you destroy what is there to be learned.

Bully's distributors, the Weinstein Company, initially announced that they would release the film without an MPAA rating, which would have kept it out of most American theater chains, but by April 2012 they had agreed to remove some of the problematic language. The cuts, according to the *Los Angeles Times*, consisted of dropping out the audio for two "F-words" and "an obscenity that begins with the prefix 'mother.'" A new rating of PG-13 (for "intense thematic material, disturbing content, and some strong language—all involving kids") was given to this version, which is the one later released on DVD and Blu-Ray.

The protection of young people from troublesome ideas and images is not the goal of the MPAA alone. In Great Britain, movie ratings are assigned by the British Board of Film Classification, formerly the British Board of Film Censors, which was formed by the film industry to provide in-house regulation of its content, a tactic useful in situations where outside regulation is feared.[2] Though the BBFC operates with different criteria and different ratings than its American counterpart, it operates under the same fundamental assumption: that a viewer should not encounter certain images, words, or concepts until reaching a certain calendar age.

As we have already observed, to work with this assumption is to court absurdity, and you can see it not merely courted, but wedded, bedded, and pregnant, all within the pages of *Monty Python and the Holy Grail (Book)*, the hilarious historical documentation of the classic Python film's production. Early drafts, thumbnail sketches for animation, photos from the movie, and a facsimile reproduction of the script make up the bulk of the text, but also included are publicity posters, script pages from deleted scenes, and even a copy of the accountants' final cost of production statement.

Obviously a book about this film is likely to be absurd, but few would expect the BBFC to be as adept at creating absurdity as the Pythons themselves. One of the most surreal pages in the book is the copy of a letter from producer Mark Forstater to writer/actor Michael Palin, explaining how the film might be edited in order to receive an "A" rating, which would have allowed those under 14 to see it. As I'm sure the Oxford-educated Palin realized, he was in the presence of greatness. Truly, there have been few English sentences to achieve the glory seen in this one:

> I would like to get back to the Censor and agree to lose the *shits*, take the odd *Jesus Christ* out and lose *Oh fuck off*, but to retain 'fart in your general direction', 'castanets of your testicles' and 'oral sex' and ask him for an 'A' rating on that basis.

2. The American comics industry did much the same thing in the 1950s when it introduced the Comics Code Authority in response to Dr. Frederic Wertham's Congressional testimony of about the dangers of comic books.

DESPITE THE SEEMINGLY endless entertainment offered by censoring organizations, they are for the most part motivated by a common and not illegitimate impulse: to protect the innocent. Unfortunately, such censors often do a sloppy job of defining innocence, and worse, their attempts at protection show an overreliance on a single tool: the line. If you were born on one side of the line dividing Day X from Day Y, you're innocent and must be protected, while if you were born on the other side, you are mature enough to make your own decisions about what content to view.[3]

Why is a line on the calendar not the proper tool for drawing such distinctions? Joan Lipsitz would argue that the problem lies in what that line demarcates—calendar age. And *only* calendar age. "It's possible that the biggest myth about adolescence is chronological age," says Lipsitz, a veteran student of early adolescence whose Ph.D. work at the University of North Carolina at Chapel Hill was published as *Growing Up Forgotten* back in 1977. She went on to form the Center for Early Adolescence at UNC, published *Successful Schools for Young Adolescents*, and founded the National Forum to Accelerate Middle Grades Reform, which later launched the Schools to Watch program to recognize outstanding middle schools. "We base everything on chronological age," Lipsitz continues, "but adolescents are many different ages, not just interpersonally, but intrapersonally." Among the various types of maturity a single adolescent can display are chronological age, social age, emotional age, physical age, and intellectual age, and there is no reason to expect all of them to be equal.

Often, however, no one notices that a young person has aged out of childhood and into adolescence until the most obvious changes appear—and only then do adults decide that he or she has crossed the line into adolescence. "Usually what happens with adolescents is that physical symptoms precede the others—the secondary sex characteristics," Lipsitz explains. "A little hair on the upper lip, a little smell under the arms, and parents say 'Oh my god!' *They* draw the line." A teen-

3. This assumes that the censors believe that anyone at all should be allowed to view the content in question. In some societies, it's more common to avoid establishing a line for age-appropriateness altogether and simply destroy the content and/or punish the creator.

ager's physical age and intellectual age might be similar, but they aren't necessarily so, and they aren't necessarily close to her chronological or emotional age.

A line, however, recognizes only two sides—in this case, *old enough* and *not old enough*. And if the individual in question is old enough chronologically, but not old enough intellectually or emotionally, he can end up, in Lipsitz's words, as "a candidate for considerable upset."

"Usually nature works it out so that you can't perceive things that you can't emotionally understand. If that gets out of whack, you get trouble." Lipsitz pauses in her deliberate, carefully enunciated explanation. She has thought about these issues for decades, but it's clear that she's still thinking about them even as we speak. Even for an expert, it's not easy to tell when adolescence begins or ends. "The only universal thing about adolescence is puberty—the rest is a completely social construction. But if you think that everything except physical changes is culturally determined, then it's kind of like umpiring; what's the strike zone and who's creating it?"

Of course, another problem that Lipsitz identifies is that American culture doesn't really have a strike zone, let alone an umpire, for adolescents; our culture simply lacks a singular rite of passage to signify the change from child to adult. Some American subgroups have retained such rites from their ethnic or religious traditions—the Bar Mitzvah among Jews, the Confirmation among Catholics and Anglicans, and so on—but for the most part, individual Americans draw their own lines on the calendar to mark when a boy becomes a man or a girl a woman. Sometimes it's the day the car keys are handed over, or the Thanksgiving when Dad asks Junior to carve the turkey, or the moment a girl makes the entrance to her Sweet Sixteen party, but these marks are largely drawn by family members for family members. For the most part, America has no clear distinction by which strangers can tell that the adolescent in question is now an adult.[4]

4. Another point Lipsitz makes about rites of passage is that they're not just for the adolescents. They're also important for a society's adults, and particularly for parents—and not always in a positive way. She tells of one such case: "My mother's best friend, Selma, came from an extremely Orthodox family. The line for them was the Bar Mitzvah. After that, the son was taken away from the mother, and he no longer spent time in the kitchen with his mother. He had to—got to—join the society of men." The forced

Unfortunately, it's those strangers who really matter in defining adulthood. "So much of adolescence is derived from the culture," says Lipsitz. "How the culture reacts to adolescents determines in many ways how adolescents behave. There's a strong feedback effect." Or, considered another way, when we tell a thirteen-year-old "Act your age," we're not talking about a particular thirteen-year-old's behavior; we're talking about our own expectations—"a preconception about thirteenness," as Lipsitz puts it. Teenagers who have been through a rite of passage may not stop acting like children, but they are at least aware that their culture will no longer treat them like children. In our culture, however, every time teens make behavioral choices, they have to figure out where the invisible borderline between childhood and adulthood is, and the only way to be sure of its location is to cross it and suffer the consequences.

"As parents and educators, we have to set the line knowing the kids are going to step over it," says Lipsitz. "We set it a bit more conservatively than we want it. We don't want the kid stepping into danger, so we set it at a pre-danger point. But it's our job to set it, and it's his job to step over it."

But what happens if society does not establish that border? If adults fail to do so, the task falls to the only other candidates: adolescents themselves. "The lack of a rite of passage seems to lead to a lot of aberrant behavior," says Lipsitz, "as if kids will establish rites of passage if adults don't take that responsibility in a societal way. Kids do it in packs, in groups, with gangs and gang-like behavior, or sometimes with early sex. I don't think we really know anymore what sex means to kids." She sighs, thinking of her two children, born in the 1960s, and her four grandchildren, one of whom has recently had his own Bar Mitzvah. "Sex used to be 'Oh my God, my daughter will get pregnant.' Now sex is literally, potentially, a killer."

One adolescent experience, however, may well qualify as a rite of passage for at least part of the population: menarche. "It is possible

---

social separation was too painful for Selma to bear, and she withdrew into her room after the ceremony. In her case, the rite of passage celebrated by so many Jewish families was actually "a terrible event."

that menstruation is a rite of passage for girls," Lipsitz muses. "I think, just from watching grandchildren and friends, that this is a bonding moment with mother and daughter." She's also willing to consider the fitting of a girl's first bra as a rite of passage, but she and I agree that there's no male equivalent for either of these. A boy's first wet dream isn't really comparable, being a great deal more private and far easier to keep secret. It's also unlikely that a father will use the occasion to bond with his son or offer helpful advice about nocturnal emission, while a mother and daughter have good, practical reasons to discuss the onset of menstruation.

Another reason to consider a girl's first menstrual period as a rite of passage is the effect the event can have on her mother. Lipsitz still recalls her daughter's first period vividly because it came not at home, but at summer camp. "I felt bereft," she says, and it's possible that her emotional reaction muddled her thinking somewhat. After receiving the news from camp, she put down the phone, turned to her son, and told him, "Don't you *ever* do that to me."

THE ONSET OF menstruation may mark the moment when a girl becomes a woman, but it is important to remember that any mark of this kind must be put there—by the girl, by her parents, or by her culture. In truth, the process of her transformation into an adult has been a long and steady one, and that type of transformation is not unique to human beings. As writer and biologist Bernd Heinrich notes in *Life Everlasting*, "The transitions in our own development from pre-pubescence to adulthood are based on processes roughly similar to those that cause a tadpole to metamorphose into a frog." Granted, the metamorphosis in human beings is comparatively minor, at least in terms of overall form; girls and women have the same kind and number of limbs, breathe in the same way, and consume the same kinds of foodstuffs. There are differences in shape, some rather pronounced, and certain organs start growing and working in ways they did not before, but for the most part, a woman is simply a larger version of the girl she was. The differences between them are for the most part differences in capability.

In this, human beings are somewhat like birds, or at least like a great many species of them. Some species, typically birds that nest on the ground, are *precocial*—almost entirely ready to get along in the world as soon as they come out of the egg. Chickens, quails, plovers, ducks, and geese are among the birds able to walk (or swim) and feed themselves within a day or two of hatching. The young ones can't do everything an adult can do—their flight feathers, for example, don't develop until later—but they can survive with only a minimal amount of parental protection from predators and the elements.

Most birds, however, require a great deal of care after they hatch. Parents must bring them food, keep them warm, and fight off or draw predators away from the nest, in which the young remain for a period of days or even weeks. These young birds have only one job: to grow. To help this happen, the parents must bring in an enormous amount of protein—generally fish or flesh or fowl for the bigger birds, invertebrates for the smaller ones.[5] These species with highly dependent young are called *altricial*, and they include raptors, woodpeckers, flycatchers, and practically all songbirds—birds which, for the most part, do not nest at ground level. It's therefore not hard to see where the dividing line between childhood and adolescence lies for a songbird: right at the edge of the nest. A bird that can fly out of it is almost grown up. A bird that can't remains a child.

Human beings, like dogs, cats, rats, and opossums, are altricial, and their parents must devote long years to taking care of them before they are ready to face the world alone. We may use the term "kick them out of the nest" to describe the process of turning children loose, but we have no line as clear and definitive as that nest's edge for determining when the kicking is done.

---

5. Steve Kress notes two exceptions to this rule: the American Goldfinch and the Cedar Waxwing, both of which feed their young almost exclusively on vegetable matter. The reason is unknown, but one beneficial effect is that these songbirds are relatively immune to nest predation by Brown-headed Cowbirds. The cowbird chicks, which typically mature faster than their nestmates, monopolize food resources and sometimes even push their step-siblings out of the nest entirely. With goldfinches and waxwings, however, the cowbirds never get the chance to wreck their adoptive families; they simply don't get enough protein to survive.

There are, however, creatures for whom the dividing line between sub-adult and adult is as dark and clear as an interstate highway. As Heinrich puts it, in some insects "the metamorphosis truly looks like transformation of one animal into an entirely different one."

Startlingly, this is not just a simile. It is a controversial idea first proposed by British marine biologist Donald I. Williamson: that a larva and an adult insect may actually be two different organisms. To some degree, the idea stems from the theory of endosymbiosis, which suggests that some of the subunits contained in living cells—the mitochondria in animal cells, for example, or the chloroplasts in the cells of green plants—were originally free-living bacterial or algal cells. (This theory would explain, for example, why mitochondria have their own DNA, distinct from that contained in the cell nucleus.) Williamson's own theory is that long ago, when the ancestors of metamorphosing insects were aquatic and fertilization was something that happened in the water around them, they absorbed genetic information from another species. This information, however, can't be activated except in the right conditions, and those conditions don't exist while the original animal is alive. But after the original animal is dead, the new species' genes finally have their opportunity for growth.

It's a wild, even counterintuitive idea, but Heinrich finds it appealing. He tells the story of how this rebirth would work through the example of one of his favorite insects, the hummingbird sphinx moth, imagining how the process took place after the caterpillar had burrowed into the ground before metamorphosis:

> [L]ying there motionless in the dark, it eventually shrank, shed its dead skin, and turned into a mummylike shape with a hard covering. As its organs dissolved, its insides turned to mush, and most of its cells died. However, some groups of cells, named "imaginal disks" (from "imago"), remained. These, like the buds on a plant that can grow into a twig and the twig into an entirely new plant, are like seeds or eggs generating new organs. During this apparent "resting" or pupal stage, the disks secreted enzymes that destroyed the larval cells and incorporated the proteins and other nutrients into themselves. Eventually all of the larval cells

were replaced, and the new cells assembled in an orderly way to produce the moth.

As strange and beautiful as this transformation seems in Heinrich's telling, I have to feel as though growing up is hard enough without the added burden of switching species. Perhaps it's good, then, that human beings remain human beings even after they cross the line into adulthood. Wherever that line may be.

The Undiscovered Country

> *"Cheer up, sad world," he said, and winked.*
> *"It's kind of fun to be extinct."*
> *—Ogden Nash*

As MANY TIMES as I've enjoyed stepping over a line, there is
one border I'm not eager to cross. I'm not alone in this, as
reams of paper and uncountable bits of memory have been
devoted to the proper delineation of this border, the means
for staying on the near side of it, and speculation as to what
might lie on the far side. It's the subject of the most famous
speech in English literature, one in which Hamlet goes on
at some length about it, but it's also addressed in a variety
of pithier statements, the pithiest of which is probably Franz
Kafka's: "The meaning of life is that it ends." The subject is of
course death, a topic so universal that we go well out of our
way to avoid mentioning it.

I realize that the previous statement seems absurd on its
face. The word *death* is not considered obscene or profane,
and it makes its way into many an English idiom: *scared to
death, a matter of life and death, sudden-death overtime,
death of a thousand cuts, death rattle, death spiral, death wish,*
and of course *death by chocolate.* You can *die hard, die off, die*

by the sword, or *die trying.* You can be *dead certain, dead in the water, dead on your feet,* or *wanted dead or alive.* You can observe *a dead cat bounce, a dead giveaway, a dead heat, a dead man's hand,* or *a dead ringer.* You can even listen to the Grateful Dead, the Dead Kennedys, Dead Can Dance, the Dead Milkmen, or And You Will Know Us by the Trail of Dead. Clearly, if I try to claim that we don't mention death, I'm dead wrong.

But my point is that while the *word* "death" and its related terms may be in common parlance, the actual *subject* of death is one that the modern American studiously avoids. We'll talk metaphorically about death when the subject is sports, or bureaucracy, or romance, but when a person actually dies, we have any number of euphemisms handy. During her days on the obituary column of the *Fayetteville Observer,* my wife had to follow a strict formula which required the use of the word "died," explicitly ordered because so many people tried to avoid it. This desire for avoidance was seen clearly in the paper's paid death notices, in which the bereaved employed a variety of terms to suggest death without actually mentioning it: *went to his eternal rest, departed this life, left us,* and numerous variations on *passed,* including *passed on* and *passed away,* were common. People may fall into the passive voice and describe someone who *is lost to us,* or may keep the verb active and say something like *after we lost him.* These examples are of course euphemisms intended to show respect or deference, but if the dead person means little or nothing to the speaker, watch out. There is an entire catalogue of terms available, ranging from down-home favorites like *bought the farm, taking a dirt nap,* and *kicked the bucket* to the Pythonic litany *pushing up the daisies, rung down the curtain,* and *joined the choir invisible.*

Exactly why the subject of death should be handled in such a circumspect manner is a matter of debate. It might be the natural desire to avoid bringing up something that has bad associations for many people; most adults and a fair number of children have suffered the death of a loved one, and speakers may feel that an indirect reference will cause less discomfort than a direct one. Unfortunately, this entirely reasonable desire can lead to unintended consequences. In my teen years I worked at a day camp where one of the other counselors accidentally drowned, but his body was not found until after the campers were gone from the scene. When we gathered with the kids for the opening meeting the next morning, the camp director spoke at length about "losing" Rich and how sad it was and how all the members of the community should be allowed to express their emotions about it, but the campers seemed oddly unaffected by his comments. Finally one brave boy raised his hand and asked, "What happened to Rich?" It was only then that the director realized what we counselors had known for over five minutes: he had never actually mentioned the fact of Rich's death.

Another explanation for such avoidance is the belief that, even if we personally have no bad associations, nobody really wants to think directly about death. It's an uncomfortable fact: each of us will end. Practically every other human experience, even a common one like school, sex, or reproduction, falls short of being universal, but no one avoids the experience of dying. At some point, whether it takes decades or only moments, all of us will lose everything we know, in this life, at least.

That blunt and inevitable truth might explain our avoidance, but it also suggests that the line between life and death is the only truly important line. It's certainly one of the very few in the human experience that can be crossed only once.

It's not a line crossed by every living thing, however. Though all organisms are subject to death by trauma, illness, or predation, there do appear to be some forms of life that are not forced across the finish line by the sheer passage of time. In other words, they do not suffer senescence—the process of aging. If these creatures can avoid being damaged by the world around them, they can live indefinitely.

LIKE SO MANY WORDS in this book, *immortality* is tricky to define. Some biologists believe that bacteria are functionally immortal, since they reproduce by fission. A single bacterial cell—we'll call him "Bob"—splits into two identical cells, each of which splits into two identical cells, and so on ad infinitum; this means that Bob will remain present in the colony indefinitely. In fact, you can argue that Bob *is* the colony. There is another argument, however, that Bob himself is not really immortal; the original Bob cell does eventually die and the remaining Bobs are merely copies. And as anyone who has looked at a ninth- or tenth-generation Xerox can attest, copies aren't always that much like the original, and copies of copies are still more unlike it. If Bob 1.0 is long dead and Bob 675,441.0 is markedly different from his distant ancestor, can Bob really be described as immortal?

Other organisms, however, may be a bit closer to the standard definition of immortality. The common freshwater hydra, a tiny, primitive animal found in streams, ponds, lakes, and practically every high-school biology classroom, has attracted attention from scientists for generations. It was originally described by Antonie van Leeuwenhoek, the world's first microbiologist, in the early eighteenth century, and its reproduction and regeneration were studied at length by Swiss naturalist Abraham Trembley before 1750. At one time it was believed that the animal, like its mythological namesake, could essentially regrow itself indefinitely. Charles Darwin claimed, in *The Origin of Species*, that if a hydra were turned inside out, the interior surface (now outside) would begin respiration, while the exterior (now inside) would begin digesting the animal's food. In *Loss and Restoration of Regenerative Capacity in Tissues and Organs of Animals*, published in the U.S. in 1972, Russian biologist Lev Vladimirovich Polezhaev wrote, "Hydra regenerate even after they are ground through a sieve, while a mouse is not capable of this feat." This sieve experiment has been successfully performed with sponges—one hopes no scientists have felt a need to try it on mice—but despite Polezhaev's claim, it does not seem to work with the hydra. Still, the animal's regenerative powers are remarkable enough that some biologists, including Daniel Martinez of Pomona College and Michael Rose of the University of California–Irvine, believe that the hydra may be immune to the effects of aging.

Like bacteria, a hydra reproduces asexually, by budding a new hydra out of its own body, but unlike a bacterium, a hydra is a true animal—a multicellular organism. If such a creature could extend its life indefinitely, there might be hope that human beings will someday be able to avoid crossing the border of death as well. Unfortunately, there seems to be some controversy about the hydra's theoretical immortality; at least according to one 2010 paper in *Experimental Gerontology*, the older a hydra gets, the less often it buds, which suggests that senescence does have an effect on it after all.

A far weirder form of immortality may be observed in the creature known as *Turritopsis nutricula*, a relative of both the hydra and the Portuguese man o' war. Rather than continuing its earthly existence indefinitely, *Turritopsis* seems to pull off a trick known to no human being save Benjamin Button: it grows younger. In effect, it reverses its metamorphosis into adulthood; as Nina Bai wrote for *Discover* Magazine's blog:

> Once it reaches sexual maturity, *Turritopsis* looks like a tiny, transparent, many-tentacled parachute (only about 5mm in diameter) that floats freely in warm ocean waters. But when times get tough, *Turritopsis* can turn into a blob, anchor itself to a surface, and undergo a sort of reverse metamorphosis back to its youthful form as a stalk-like polyp. That's like a butterfly turning back into a caterpillar.

Lest you think this is a case of a lay writer injecting hyperbole into the staid proceedings of science, take a look at the abstract of the original article, "Reversing the Life Cycle: Medusae Transforming into Polyps and Cell Transdifferentiation in *Turritopsis nutricula* (Cnidaria, Hydrozoa)" in *The Biological Bulletin* back in June of 1996:

> All stages of the medusa *Turritopsis nutricula*, from newly liberated to fully mature individuals, can transform back into colonial hydroids, either directly or through a resting period, thus escaping death and achieving potential immortality.

It is unusual for a peer-reviewed journal to feature a sentence claiming "potential immortality." Then again, there is now and never has been anything that can make humanity set aside objectivity, contentment, and even common sense as quickly as the promise of avoiding or reversing death. Such was the promise that led Gilgamesh to seek immortality in the root of a plant at the bottom of the sea, and drove Orpheus on his ill-fated journey to the underworld. We will travel any distance and cross any border in hopes of finding a way to stave off the grim reaper, as Ponce de Leon did when he crossed the Atlantic in search of a fountain and found himself instead within the borders of Florida. And he was far from the last to do so; the Sunshine State, with a population whose median age of 40 is roughly three years over the national average, is increasingly now a haven for those closest to the end of life.

As Floridians know, sharing the knowledge of mortality with others is an old tradition, founded in the belief that misery loves company. John Donne mused on the universal tolling of the funeral bell, and Tom Lehrer offered Cold War audiences the cheerful nuclear-holocaust-based song, "We Will All Go Together When We Go." Perhaps then, it is comforting to think that the final border, the one that each individual eventually crosses, is crossed by every other member of a species as well. Stephen Jay Gould, like paleontologists in general, considered extinction "the normal fate of a species," but like death, it's a fate most of us are uncomfortable contemplating.

Once you do contemplate it, though, you quickly realize that extinction is much tougher to confirm than death. In the vast majority of cases, settling the question of whether an individual has died is a straightforward matter, evidenced by the presence of a) the individual, or b) a corpse. Even if there is no corpse, there is typically some record of the individual's presence at a particular place or time, one that can help determine where the individual might be—at the bottom of the sea following a shipwreck, say—so that the individual's death can become a matter of official record. Indeed, if we're willing to wait longer than the maximum lifetime, the question becomes academic; at our current distance from 1587, we can safely assume that Virginia Dare is dead even if we don't ever learn how she and her colony were lost.

When we deal with populations, however, nothing so neat and clean is possible. Unlike an individual, a species can survive indefinitely, and even when the last remnant of that species dies, it can be difficult both to prove that it truly was the last and to ascertain that it is dead. Most of the time, the last member of a species dies with no human being around to record the event; often, it has lived that way all along. In other cases, where the human being is the one causing the death, he or she may not even know that the creature being killed is the last of its kind. The quagga, a striped equine animal closely related to the zebra, was once native to South Africa, but was wiped out for food, hides, and grazing space by the late nineteenth century. Because its extinction came before scientists had determined its taxonomic status, however, we don't know if the last quagga was the last of its species or the last of a subspecies of zebra.

We do have the example of Martha, the last recorded Passenger Pigeon, who died in front of witnesses in the Cincinnati Zoo in 1914, but even then, we have to qualify that "last" with the word "recorded." It's not impossible that on the date of her death there was, somewhere in a remote corner of North America, a tiny population of *un*recorded Passenger Pigeons, pigeons unknown to science. It's not even impossible that such a tiny population could survive and reproduce in some inaccessible place, defying the odds and surviving for years. It's not even *completely* impossible that such a population could be lucky enough to avoid detection, predation, and destructive inbreeding—at least for a while. So is it impossible that Passenger Pigeons are still alive today, in some unknown location, a century after they became "extinct"?

Let me be clear: It would require an astronomically long set of odds, odds so long that no sane person would ever take the bet. The Passenger Pigeon fed, roosted, and bred in gigantic flocks, making it hard to imagine how any surviving birds could adapt their lifestyle to a tiny group; conversely, if the flock was large enough to support the birds' lifestyle (as well as the species' long-term genetic stability), it would almost certainly be detected. There's also the issue of where this flock would live, given the inescapable fact that the former woodland habitat of the pigeon barely exists today. Not only have the vast forests of the eastern U.S. been slashed apart for agriculture, housing, roads, and businesses, but the very tree species that used to constitute them have all but vanished. The American chestnut, whose nuts fed millions of pigeons and other wildlife for millennia, is gravely close to extinction itself, thanks to the introduction of the Asian fungus known as the chestnut blight, and the American elm has proved likewise vulnerable to Dutch elm disease. Given the particulars of this case, the chances of the Passenger Pigeon's survival aren't one in a thousand, one in a million, or even one in a billion. They're far smaller than that.

But those odds cannot be—not quite—zero. Proving a negative is famously impossible; even with a great alibi, you can't logically prove you did *not* commit the crime with the candlestick in the conservatory. That's why our legal system doesn't require you to prove you're not guilty; it requires the prosecution to prove (beyond reasonable doubt) that you are. Similarly, the fact that we don't have evidence of a species' presence is not in itself proof that it is not present. As Cornell astronomer Carl Sagan once elegantly put it, "Absence of evidence is not evidence of absence." In terms of logic, we must concede that the extinction of a species can never quite be an absolute.

THIS RESISTANCE to the idea of extinction is not restricted to logicians, however. Indeed, when the concept of extinction first entered the public arena in the mid-1700s, most of the resistance came from scientists and theologians. A few earlier scientists had been prepared to consider the idea of extinction, such as Robert Hooke, the seventeenth-century English polymath who coined the term "cells" to describe the honeycomb-like structures he saw in cork, but the majority dismissed extinction, thanks in large part to the most influential thinker of the day.

This thinker had an understanding of the natural world that was often, to put it courteously, incomplete; he believed, among other things, that women had fewer teeth than men, a belief that could have been tested with a polite request to his wife to say "Aah." But despite his lack of experimental curiosity, not to mention the inconvenience of having been dead for 2000 years, the Greek philosopher Aristotle had enormous influence on eighteenth-century science, and the only kind of extinction in which he believed was the kind where a flame was put out. He also defied standard Christian theology (not a surprise, as he died over 300 years before Christ's birth) by believing in an eternal and continuous universe, rather than one that had a definable beginning or end. His overall conception of nature's stability, however, dovetailed beautifully with Christianity's doctrine that each creature had been created by God in the form and habitat it currently had.

As a result of this seeming agreement between the most credible authorities of the day, many scientists adopted a belief in a natural world that was both perfect and unchanging, a belief called "Special

Creation." The best-known consequence of this belief was opposition to the idea of evolution, a consequence that we still deal with in school board meetings all across America, but another consequence was opposition to the idea of extinction. The thought that one of His creations could be wiped off the face of the earth went directly against the idea of a loving Deity. Further, it suggested that Creation was not perfect—that God had created species too weak to survive, or had arranged the balance of nature with too much weight on one side. Personal death could be blamed on individual human beings—Adam and Eve, in particular—but only God could be held responsible for the extinction of an entire species.

Starting in the 1770s, however, these ideas were challenged as science was forced to consider something new: skeletal evidence of animals never seen by contemporary eyes. Georges-Louis Leclerc, Comte de Buffon, arguably the greatest naturalist of the eighteenth century, tried to find a middle ground. According to Gary Rosenberg, in *The Revolution in Geology from the Renaissance to the Enlightenment*, Buffon was persuaded that the elephantine "Ohio animal" (whose fossils had actually been discovered in the improbably named Big Bone Lick, Kentucky) might indeed be extinct.

The clincher seemed to be the discovery of the creature's distinctive teeth in the Old World as well as the New; Buffon might not know much about the American wilderness, but he felt fairly certain that Europe was no longer populated by such enormous beasts, which we now call mastodons. In 1778, he laid out his theory that the animal was adapted to a warm subtropical climate, and when the earth cooled, it had been unable to survive. Obviously such a climate-driven extinction could be laid nowhere but at the feet of the Creator, but Buffon did hedge his theological bets by claiming the mastodon's extinction as singular—as an aberration from the great plan of Creation, not a fundamental part of the natural world. When he died ten years later, that assertion could still satisfy the scientific community, but the satisfaction would be short-lived. The revolution brewing in biology would be as significant in its way as the one brewing amongst Louis XVI's subjects.

ROSENBERG SUGGESTS THAT the French Revolution's upheaval actually made it easier for the people of Europe to accept the idea that the natural order could be violently upset and reconfigured. It was certainly true that the first eminent scientist to make an in-depth case for extinction was a gifted young French naturalist who had lived through the Revolution and was now ready to bring a revolution to the study of life: Georges Cuvier, who made his case by using the same examples Buffon had considered—the biggest examples possible.

Fossils of huge elephant-like beasts had been turned up in such places as Italy, but they were commonly assumed to be the remnants of the force brought from Carthage by Hannibal to assault Rome. In 1796, however, still three years shy of his thirtieth birthday, Cuvier published a paper detailing the anatomical differences between the Indian and African elephant. He proved conclusively that they were two different species, and further that the mammoths whose bones had been uncovered near Paris were members of a third. And none were the same as those mammoths whose bones turned up in Siberia. He even went so far as to state that a fifth species, the one found in Ohio, was more distinct from extant elephants than the mammoth was, and it was he who would later give it the name *mastodon*. Cuvier made the case that these last three creatures were extinct based on a simple and practical argument: they were too big to miss. If there were still European, Siberian, or American elephants wandering around, someone would have noticed.

More important, if multiple species had gone extinct in multiple places all over the world, Buffon's claim that the mastodon's disappearance was a unique aberration simply didn't hold water. Extinction was not a singular flaw in the natural order—it was an inherent part of that order. It might be theologically comforting to imagine a world where every creature would be specially protected by a loving Creator, but Cuvier felt it was important to face the facts: the elephant in the room, so to speak, was the fact that there was no elephant in the room:

What has become of these two enormous animals of which one no longer finds any [living] traces, and so many others of which the remains are found everywhere on earth and of which perhaps none still exist? The fossil rhinoceros of Siberia are very different from all known rhinoceros. It is the same with the alleged fossil bears of Ansbach; the fossil crocodile of Maastricht; the species of deer from the same locality; the twelve-foot-long animal, with no incisor teeth and with clawed digits, of which the skeleton has just been found in Paraguay: none has any living analogue.

Needless to say, not everyone agreed. Buffon had died in 1788 and wasn't around to raise an objection, but others were more than willing to deny the possibility that the Creator had let parts of His creation vanish. For a modern reader who has long known the truth of extinction, their denial seems almost desperate, particularly given the fact that creatures had been going extinct even during their lifetimes. The historical record accounts for several creatures dying out in the century before Cuvier's birth; the most famous extinct bird of all, the Dodo, vanished in the late 1600s, while the gargantuan Steller's Sea Cow, discovered by science in 1741, had been hunted to extinction within thirty years. The era's conventional wisdom was so powerful, however, that extinction seemed impossible even to a man with full knowledge of the existence of fossils—and Thomas Jefferson was such a man.

He was hardly the most orthodox of Christians, but Jefferson espoused the traditional doctrine about extinction, even though he knew more about vertebrate paleontology than any American president before or since. In fact, he had been introduced to Buffon in 1785 and spent no small amount of effort attempting to disabuse the Count of his belief that New World animals were "degenerate"—smaller and weaker than their Old World counterparts. He is said to have ordered soldiers to kill a bull moose to demonstrate to Buffon what one of America's supposedly small, weak deer looked like, and Rosenberg specifically mentions that he presented Buffon with the skin of a cougar.

Still, Jefferson was in basic agreement with the Count about the subject of extinction. As he wrote in his *Notes on the State of Virginia*, which he composed partly in response to the writings of Buffon, "Such is the economy of nature that no instance can be produced, of her having permitted any one race of her animals to become extinct; of her having formed any link in her great work so weak as to be broken."

This belief had an impact on his famous presentation to a 1797 meeting of the American Philosophical Society in Philadelphia. A group of fossilized bones, including several massive claws, had been discovered by miners in western Virginia and presented to Jefferson. He believed the claws belonged to a species of giant cat, one that might be three times larger than a lion, and proposed the name *Megalonyx*, or "great claw," for the genus. (In 1822, the animal was officially dubbed *Megalonyx jeffersonii* in his honor.) He also put forth the idea that the great cat, along with the as-yet-unnamed mastodon, still roamed the vast unexplored territory of the American West:

> In the present interior of our continent there is surely space and range enough for elephants and lions, if in that climate they could subsist; and for the mammoth and megalonyxes who may subsist there. Our entire ignorance of the immense country to the West and North-West, and of its contents, does not authorise us to say what it does not contain.

Jefferson's errors in this matter were, alas, numerous. Obviously he was wrong about extinction in general, but he was also wrong about *Megalonyx* in particular. Before his APS lecture, he had come across Cuvier's description of a twenty-foot fossilized Paraguayan animal, dubbed *Megatherium*, but while Jefferson admitted its claws were very similar to *Megalonyx*'s, he was reluctant to give up the appealing idea of a gigantic American lion roaming the wilderness. Two years later, however, his find was correctly described by Pennsylvania anatomist and APS member Caspar Wistar as the claws of a ten-foot relative of *Megatherium*: a gigantic ground sloth. (That Wistar went on to succeed Jefferson as APS president is probably just a coincidence.) Still, we must give Jefferson credit for putting his money where his mouth was; when he ascended to the American presidency and organized the Lewis and Clark expedition to explore the newly acquired territory of Louisiana—well after Cuvier's paper on extinct elephants—he specifically ordered Lewis to keep an eye out for *Megalonyx*.

Like Jefferson, many of us resist the idea of a species' extinction because there is, even today, a lot of unexplored territory out there. Until we can penetrate the depths of the ocean, the most isolated mountain valleys, and the farthest reaches of the rain forest with ease, we can be sure that new species yet remain to be discovered. Moreover, we can also hold out the hope that a species currently considered extinct could be rediscovered there.

We know this could happen because it *has* happened. The most famous example of the phenomenon occurred in 1938, when a South African fisherman brought a bizarre and unfamiliar fish aboard his boat. Museum curator Marjorie Courtenay Latimer observed the four-foot lobe-finned fish and suspected (correctly, as it turned out) that it was a coelacanth—a species previously known only from fossils.

A similarly "extinct" creature rose from its grave in the mid-Atlantic. In 1906, Louis Mowbray, the director of the Bermuda Aquarium, discovered an unfamiliar pigeon-sized seabird in the rocks on an island in Castle Harbor. Ten years later another naturalist described to him some fossilized bones that belonged to the Cahow, officially known as the Bermuda Petrel, which had not been observed since 1620. Mowbray now realized that reports of the bird's extinction had been greatly exaggerated, but hard evidence took a while to appear.

In 1935, a visiting American biologist, William Beebe, heard the distinctive "ka-*how*" cry of the petrel near Castle Harbor, but didn't see it. Eventually he was given the corpse of a bird that had struck a lighthouse window and sent it to the Museum of Natural History in New York, where it was identified as a Cahow by Robert Cushman Murphy. Another dead Cahow washed ashore in 1945, but the live birds still eluded scientists. Finally, in 1951, the trio of Murphy, Louis S. Mowbray (son of the aquarium director), and young naturalist David Wingate ventured out to the rocky islets surrounding the main island to hunt for nesting petrels. After investigating the depths of a hole between some stones, they were able to spot a small bird atop a nest, a bird which they were able to snare, examine, photograph, and return to its burrow. It was a Cahow, one of just over a dozen that they found nesting on two islets.

The Cahow, which lays only one egg per year, was down to just 18 breeding pairs when it was rediscovered, and even with careful stewardship, there is no guarantee of its continued survival. The global population today is still under 300 birds, and the petrel will remain on the "critically endangered" list until it reaches at least 1000 breeding pairs. As of March 2012, the number of breeding pairs was barely over one hundred. Still, that's over a hundred pairs more than were believed to exist a century ago.

In fact, it is common enough for a population to be rediscovered after it has been declared extinct that such a population has a name: it's called a *Lazarus species*. Like their namesake, however, these creatures do not negate the reality of extinction for others merely because they have, for the moment, cheated death. Even if we can't prove it, some things have to be extinct.

Why?

Consider the sauropods, a group of dinosaurs including familiar creatures such as *Diplodocus, Brachiosaurus,* and *Apatosaurus.* There are over a dozen known sauropod genera and dozens of sauropod species, each of which is known for its massive size. The smallest sauropods were over twenty feet long, and the bigger ones outmassed an African elephant by a factor of three. If these gigantic creatures had never died out, they'd be hard to miss. And even if the sauropods themselves escaped detection, what of their environment? We're talking hundreds of ten-ton vegetarians wandering through forest, field, and fen, leaving swaths of chomped vegetation large enough to be seen by satellite, not to mention trails of turds beyond human imagination. When even the Amazon rain forest cannot hide the effects of clear-cutting, what landscape could sustain such a digestive force invisibly?

Even if we ignore the most gigantic of history's creatures, at least some of the billions of prehistoric animals would inhabit temperate zones, occupy accessible terrain, and be large enough for human beings to notice. There are people hiking, kayaking, and flying all over the world, and it seems as though most of them are taking cellphone videos. Eventually, some individual would stumble across an Irish elk or a giant ground sloth. They can't *all* be hiding.

Thus, while extinction is not absolute as a logical matter, it is an undeniable fact as a practical matter. As much as we might wish otherwise, it is not realistic to suppose that there is a minute population of Passenger Pigeons gamely hanging on in some undisclosed location. It is even less reasonable to believe that *Tyrannosaurus rex* still survives in some out-of-the-way spot some 65 million years after the Cretaceous period was brought to a close by the impact of a meteorite near Chicxulub, in what is now Mexico's Yucatan Peninsula. Like it or not, extinction is real, and some species—millions of them—have experienced it firsthand.

But that doesn't mean it's real for *all* of them. Not yet, anyway.

We're Not Lost

Hovering right at the brink—Deep in the swamp forest—"I've never felt any doubt"—Bucking consensus—The Romeo error—"It would be insane"—The next mass extinction—The place where we live

Everything changes, nothing perishes. —Ovid

TIM GALLAGHER, a veteran birder, falconer, and writer, works at the Cornell Lab of Ornithology, where he serves as editor in chief of *Living Bird* Magazine. Tall, trim, and genial, with penetrating blue eyes and an easy smile, he has written extensively about ornithological subjects ranging from falconry to seabird nesting habits. He is also one of only a handful of individuals to see a bird that was extinct.

Some may argue that the previous sentence is self-contradictory and therefore nonsensical, but I prefer to think of it as paradoxical, somewhat like a Zen koan: in the oxymoronic nature of the statement, a thoughtful observer can perceive a truth. And the truth is that the line between existence and extinction is not as clear as you might think.

"The borderline we're talking about here is, of course, completely a human construct," says Gallagher. "I think we like to be able to state with rigid certainty that a species is either extinct or it still exists. Realistically, that's nearly impossible to do with a bird that dwells in dark, shadowy places where most people fear to tread—especially a bird that's hovering right at the brink of extinction and may cross over at any time."

The bird in question is the Ivory-billed Woodpecker (*Campephilus principalis*), a spectacular creature of the lowland forests of the American Southeast. Larger than a crow and sporting bold black-and-white plumage (with a red crest on the male), the ivory-bill was a startling sight, earning it the nickname "Lord God Bird," after the oath typically sworn by first-time observers. Unfortunately, these observers form an increasingly rare population; the bird itself began a long decline in the nineteenth century, as the American interior was carved into farmland and living space, and as a result fewer and fewer living witnesses to it were left. In fact, when Gallagher began his search in 2004, he wasn't really looking for the ivory-bill. "It was almost more of an oral history project. I was trying to record the recollections of people who had known this bird in decades past. If the bird was extinct, these people—many of whom were in their eighties and nineties and approaching death—might be our last living connection with the species." And that connection was growing increasingly attenuated. Since 1940, only a handful of sightings had been reported, and many of those were unconfirmed, which led to a dispute over the ivory-bill's continued existence. The reasons for the dispute are many, but they effectively come down to three: rarity, accessibility, and consensus.

Rarity is tied up in any discussion about the edge of existence because, as David Quammen puts it in *The Song of the Dodo*, rarity is "the precondition to extinction." In general terms, a species does not go from abundance to absence overnight. Even when there is a deliberate extirpation going on, as in the case of the smallpox virus, the population will dwindle over time, leaving a remnant. But for that remnant, the odds of surviving, let alone increasing, are far worse than the odds of vanishing altogether. How small can a population get and still survive? That's hard to say. As paleontologist Dave Raup points out in "Death of Species" (collected in editor M.H. Nitecki's *Extinctions*), "[T]here have been very few serious attempts to place actual numbers on the threshold population sizes below which extinction is either assured or highly probable."

One attempt to quantify the matter, however, was made by writer and scientist Jared Diamond, who in a paper titled "'Normal' Extinctions of Isolated Species" (also collected in Nitecki's *Extinctions*) puts forth the seemingly simple equation $e = p^N$, where e is the probability of extinction over a given time, p is the probability that a given individual will die over an equal unit of time, and N is the number of individuals (or breeding pairs) in the population. If the population goes up, e gets very small, but when N reaches 1, the death of the individual will spell the death of a species.

That doesn't give us a hard number, but it does anchor another of Diamond's findings about bird extinctions on islands. He discovered that extinction was more likely among birds whose populations fluctuated widely, sometimes due to harsh winters; a small stable population was in less danger than a large one with a boom/bust fluctuation, where the bust part of the cycle might be disastrous.

Quammen agrees that fluctuation can be a problem, since for any species, population size fluctuates. As he puts it, "[S]mall populations, unlike big ones, stand a good chance of fluctuating to zero, since zero is not far away."

A species close to extinction is therefore very likely to be rare, and it is generally much harder to find something when it is rare. Proving that an animal exists is simple if you can produce a specimen, or at least physical, photographic, or audio evidence, but the sheer proximity of the edge of extinction means such proof will likely be in short supply.

Moreover, obtaining that proof is not just a matter of running down to the local library or booting up Wikipedia; you've got to go where the animal is. As Gallagher notes, "In the case of the Ivory-billed Woodpecker, it's so difficult to explore thoroughly all the places across the South where these birds could potentially still exist. Very few birders ever spend time deep in the swamp forest. At best, most will just walk a few hundred feet out on a boardwalk to find the species that interest them. And it's also difficult for those who do venture deeper into the vast morass of a swamp. You often have to spend as much time looking out for poisonous snakes and other dangers as you do birds."

Still, the ivory-bill's rarity and inaccessibility were not the only reasons why settling the issue of its existence was so difficult. Tim Gallagher discovered a third issue at work: consensus.

At around 1:15 P.M. on February 27, 2004, he was canoeing through the flooded forest of the Bayou de View near Clarendon, Arkansas, along with his friend Bobby Harrison, a teacher of art history and photography at Oakwood College. They were there to investigate a report posted on a canoe club listserve by Gene Sparling, a kayaker who had seen an unusual large woodpecker on a cypress tree out in the bayou. The description of the bird's plumage, ranging from the large white patches on its lower back to the pointed crest atop its head, had impressed both men as similar enough to that of an ivory-bill to warrant investigation, and they'd headed to Arkansas within the week. By midday on the 27th, they'd been following Sparling's kayak around the bayou for a day and a half, and he was now well in front of them, invisible among the distant trunks.

At that moment, as reported in Gallagher's book *The Grail Bird*, a large black-and-white woodpecker flew out of the trees and across the open water in front of the canoe, showing the distinctive white patches on its wings and back as it went. It had vanished before either of them could train a camera on it, but both of them had made the identification; it was an ivory-bill.

By the time I interviewed Tim Gallagher about the sighting, I had known him for several years, read his work extensively, and had the chance to observe his birding prowess in the field. Thus, when I asked bluntly if there was any doubt in his mind about the species he saw in Bayou de View, there was no doubt in mine what his answer would be. His response: "We were absolutely stunned when we saw that bird, because the field marks were so vivid, and it was so unlike anything else either of us had seen in our birding careers. I've never felt any doubt in my sighting."

That certainty, however, wasn't enough. Even with three witnesses, two of them expert birders—and one of those a member of the Sapsuckers, the Cornell Lab's world-class competitive birding team—testimony alone was not enough to change the consensus that the ivory-bill was extinct. Some kind of hard, objective evidence would be required, not just the subjective reporting of Sparling, Harrison, and Gallagher.

The irony here is that the evidence for the bird's extinction was itself purely subjective: no one had reported seeing it. Or rather, no credible scientist had published such a claim. And because no credible scientist had done so, publishing such a claim could damage one's own credibility. "I've had a couple of scientists say to me that they received seemingly credible reports of ivory-bills and didn't follow up on them for fear of being labeled a crackpot," says Gallagher. "One person I know of actually had an unmistakable sighting in the 1950s and didn't report it."

In other words, the existence of consensus was itself a significant obstacle to proving the existence of the ivory-bill; accounts that might have cast doubt on its extinction weren't shared because they violated the standard view. As Gallagher puts it, "If the scientific consensus is that a species is extinct, it's very difficult to buck that idea. Careers have been ruined." One was that of naturalist and author John Dennis, who in 1966 reported hearing and seeing ivory-bills in an area of east Texas known as the Big Thicket. Subsequent searches of the area, however, produced no further sightings and no other evidence of the birds, and Dennis's reports were dismissed by the mass of ornithologists, including Jim Tanner, widely regarded as America's greatest authority on the bird. A different kind of claim was made in the summer of 1971 at the annual meeting of the American Ornithologists' Union, when former AOU president George Lowery produced a pair of snapshots. Taken that May in the Atchafalaya Basin of western Louisiana, each picture showed a different tree, but both showed a male ivory-bill perched high on the trunk. Despite the date stamp on the photos and the unequivocal field marks of the bird in them, they were regarded by the majority of Lowery's colleagues as fakes—pictures of a stuffed bird that had been mounted on a pair of tree trunks. Lowery insisted that the pictures were real, and that the anonymous photographer was trustworthy, but he later expressed regret that he had ever publicized the sighting.[1]

In the wake of such incidents, the fear of challenging consensus was very clear in Gallagher's mind when he broke the news of his sighting to his own colleagues in Ithaca. "Reporting the sighting to Lab director

---

1. It was not until after Gallagher began his search for the ivory-bill that he was able to determine the identity of the photographer, a man named Fielding Lewis, who had gone on to become Louisiana's Boxing Commissioner. One question has never been satisfactorily answered: since Lewis insisted on anonymity for over thirty years, what would have been his motive for faking the photos he gave to Lowery?

John Fitzpatrick was one of the hardest things I've ever done. But what Fitz did, putting his own reputation and the reputation of the Cornell Lab on the line when he launched the Arkansas search in 2004, was an incomparable act of courage for a serious scientist like him."

The search Fitzpatrick launched put the considerable resources of the CLO squarely against the idea that the ivory-bill was extinct. Without publicity, teams of researchers were sent into the Cache River area around Bayou de View in hopes of turning up conclusive evidence: a video, a still photo, a recording, a feather, a nest site, *something*. If only they could capture the bird somehow—on camera, on tape, in a net— then there would be no doubt in anyone's mind of what Gallagher and Harrison had seen.

Perhaps Fitzpatrick should have remembered how much good George Lowery's photographic evidence had done him.

FOR BETTER THAN a year, the CLO's efforts to confirm Gallagher's report were kept under wraps, but at the end of April 2005, the story became public in a big way. The official peer-reviewed ornithological statement appeared in an article published in the journal *Science*, but the lay version appeared everywhere: in the New York *Times*, in the Washington *Post*, on NPR, and of course in *The Grail Bird*, Gallagher's own account of the rediscovery, published in May. Even non-birders were marveling at the word that the ivory-bill was back from the far side of the edge of extinction.

Nor was Gallagher exaggerating the degree of support given him by Fitzpatrick. On the day after the *Science* paper broke the CLO's official silence, Fitzpatrick appeared at a news conference in Washington, D.C., flanked by the Secretary of the Interior, and said of the rediscovery, "This is confirmed. This is dead solid confirmed."

The confirmation which Fitzpatrick announced had come in the form of several additional sightings in the spring of 2004 and one in February 2005, totaling seven (along with the Sparling and Gallagher/ Harrison sightings), as well as several reports of the woodpecker's distinctive "double-knock" display drumming. Personal accounts alone, however, were not what the CLO's efforts were intended to generate . . . and as it turned out, they were not the only things it had generated.

On April 25, 2004, two members of the search team, University of Arkansas–Little Rock researcher David Luneau and his brother-in-law, Robert Henderson, were canoeing through the Bayou de View when both caught a brief look of a large black-and-white bird flying away from their boat. Neither had a particularly good look at it, but when Luneau checked the tape in the camcorder he'd had running, the bird could be seen flapping straight away from the canoe. Though the camera had automatically focused on Robert, rather than on the trees behind him, even the brief, blurry glimpse revealed that the bird had been clinging to the trunk of a tupelo tree, as a woodpecker would. Moreover, this woodpecker's sudden launch into flight revealed not only a rapid nine-per-second wingbeat, but a significant amount of white plumage in its wings—both features that point toward an ivory-bill, rather than toward its nearest living relative, the smaller Pileated Woodpecker. Further analysis of the Luneau videotape would reveal other points of distinction between the bird on the tupelo and the pileated, the only extant bird that could possibly be mistaken for an ivory-bill.

In short, Fitzpatrick's claim of confirmation was hard to dispute. Qualified and experienced observers representing multiple institutions of learning had spent over a year reporting sightings of the Ivory-billed Woodpecker. Bobby Harrison had gotten another look in June, and in April, a sighting was reported by Fitzpatrick's own brother Jim, a bird-bander with more than thirty years' experience. With the addition of the Luneau videotape and its subsequent analysis, the case for the ivory-bill's survival must have seemed ironclad.

Consensus, however, was not so easy to alter. Yale ornithologist Richard Prum was among the first to voice skepticism about the bird in the videotape, though he was later persuaded by the CLO's audiotapes that the ivory-bill still existed. In January of 2006 Prum was one of several scientists to challenge the identity of Luneau's bird in *The Auk*, the official journal of the AOU. That shot across the bow was followed by a paper in the March 3 issue of *Science* in which a team led by renowned ornithologist and field guide creator David Sibley dismissed Luneau's bird as a Pileated Woodpecker, concluding, "Verifiable evidence for the ivory-billed woodpecker's persistence, however, is lacking."

The Cornell Lab's response to Sibley et al. appeared in the same issue, offering additional analysis of the videotape, as well as a detailed discussion of the results produced by building several life-sized models of the two woodpeckers and attempting to duplicate the original tape. It was not enough to settle the issue for good, however, as British journal *BMC Biology* published another critique of the Luneau tape, this time by the University of Aberdeen's J. Martin Collinson, in which the bird was once again identified as a pileated.

Undaunted, the CLO maintained its efforts to obtain more evidence of the ivory-bill in Arkansas, and occasional sightings and reports of double-knocks were reported during the searchers' 2007–08 season (during which they were joined by one of my former students, ecologist Leighton Reid). But nothing more concrete appeared. People were seeing and hearing the bird, but no indisputable evidence of its presence was obtained. Finally, in 2009, the Lab suspended its search. If there was additional proof of the ivory-bill's continued existence, it would have to come from somewhere else.

AND WHERE DOES this leave Tim Gallagher now? In most respects, he's exactly where he was. "The one thing I'm certain of," he says unequivocally, "is that I saw an Ivory-billed Woodpecker on February 27, 2004." What has changed, however, are his feelings about the bird's chances for long-term survival. "I was a lot more optimistic in 2005," he admits, though he ultimately dismisses the nagging idea that he and Bobby Harrison spotted the last ivory-bill on earth. "I mean, what are the odds we would stumble upon something like that? I had hoped that bird was part of a locally nesting pair, but I think it's probably more likely to have been a young bird dispersing up Bayou de View from who knows where." In that regard, he agrees with John Fitzpatrick, who said about his ivory-bill, "This bird had parents."

He's also acutely aware that *extinct* isn't just a word; it's a statement that alters the way human beings think and act, and one that has profound consequences, both for humanity and for the creature so labeled. CLO researcher Mindy LaBranche spotted a bird in April of 2004 and told Gallagher she was "99 percent sure" it was an ivory-bill. The reason for her one percent of doubt? "Because the bird is freaking extinct! For years I've been convinced of that." When consensus says *extinct*, even the evidence of one's own eyes is called into doubt.

Consensus also influences social behavior. Ron Rohrbaugh, a CLO scientist who spotted an ivory-bill in Arkansas on April 5, 2004, said in 2010 that the lack of more recent corroborating evidence for his and others' sightings shouldn't be used to make hasty judgments about the ivory-bill's existence:

> Declaring that a species is extinct before all of the data are in, a phenomenon known as the Romeo error, has profound negative consequences. When a species is moved from the "critically endangered" list to the "presumed extinct" list, it loses protection from direct harm, and more importantly, habitat loss. It is important that we not give up on species based on an incomplete understanding. Decisions about extinction should be guided by science, not perception.

Like me, Tim Gallagher has an English degree, and he too sees the literary as well as the scientific validity of Rohrbaugh's statement: "Yes, if only Romeo had waited for Juliet to awaken, they both would have lived!"

Does he feel frustrated that there isn't a huge pile of corroborating evidence for the Cache River sightings? I couldn't blame him if he did, and I've heard him muttering about David Sibley's skepticism on at least one occasion, but it's important to remember that the Luneau videotape isn't what his certainty is based on; it's the memory of what he saw with his own eyes in the Bayou de View.

Well, that and another thing. After *The Grail Bird* was published, Tim's interest began drifting south, where it eventually settled on another bird. Like the ivory-bill, this one was a woodpecker, the largest that has ever lived: the Imperial Woodpecker (*Campephilus imperialis*). And like the ivory-bill, its close cousin, the imperial was now sitting squarely on the edge of extinction. A native of the high forests of western Mexico's Sierra Madre Occidental, this Mallard-sized bird was hit particularly hard by the logging of its home territory, not to mention a bounty put out by a number of timber companies who feared it might damage their raw materials. And as a result, Tim Gallagher once again found himself traveling south to talk with people who still remembered seeing a now-legendary bird.

This time his companion was Dutch ornithologist Martjan Lammertink, a woodpecker expert who in the 1990s had tracked down a treasure: the only known photographic evidence of a living Imperial Woodpecker, a 16-millimeter film shot by a visiting American dentist named William L. Rhein. After the film was donated to the CLO by Rhein's nephew, Lammertink decided to accompany Tim on a 2010 trip to the site where Rhein had filmed the bird.

Both of them knew going in that the odds were against their seeing the imperial. According to Tim, Lammertink was "very pessimistic," but "open to the possibility" that it still existed. Tim himself framed the question this way: "You have to be optimistic to even go searching for an imperial, because it's so dangerous. It would be insane to venture into those remote parts of the Sierra Madre Occidental these days if you thought the bird you were chasing was extinct."

The dangers in question are considerably nastier than the healthy population of snakes found in the Cache River area; indeed, a few hostile water moccasins might have been almost welcome. Instead, the two woodpecker-hunters were faced with the machine-gun-toting drug growers who have taken over the Sierra Madre Occidental. After a number of narrow escapes, the two returned to the U.S. without evidence of the imperial's continued existence, but with a wealth of harrowing tales and a pessimistic view of the bird's chances for survival. Says Gallagher, "I did not believe it was extinct when I started and I still feel that way, but I'm not optimistic about being able to save it, because the situation in Mexico is so bad—with drug growers massively destroying forest habitat and the government helpless to do anything about it."

The tales of their adventures are detailed in Tim's book *Imperial Dreams: Tracking the Imperial Woodpecker Through the Wild Sierra Madre*, but in some ways the most important part of the search for the imperial was what it revealed about the Ivory-billed Woodpecker. The Rhein film, showing several foraging imperials flying about the upland forest, offers a clear look at the behavior and flight patterns of a large member of the genus *Campephilus*—exactly what you'd need for comparison with the bird in the Luneau videotape. And based on the wing-flap rate and body posture, says Tim, "I think the Rhein Imperial

Woodpecker film clearly supports our hypothesis that the bird in David's video is an ivory-bill."

What do I think? Let's just say that I've seen and read *Romeo and Juliet*. Many times. And I paid attention.

A SURE WAY to make yourself sleepless is to read up on the prognosis for earthly lifeforms in the coming centuries. I myself am lately aroused from my rest by David Quammen's "Planet of Weeds," a 1998 article for *Harper's* in which he predicts a decline in biodiversity not seen since the end of the Cretaceous Period. In a sweeping survey of everything from island biogeography to the prospects for a global human class war, Quammen turns his eloquence toward the conclusion that our best-case scenario, in a world subject to rapid deforestation, unrelenting population pressures, and a wholesale opening of territory to invasive organisms, is a loss of 35 percent of current species. Then again, perhaps we're headed toward a scenario more like the extinction event that followed the impact of the Chicxulub asteroid, which took out 75 percent of existing plant and animal species and is most famous for writing *finis* to the dinosaurs. And that's not the worst-case scenario; if we're really unfortunate, we might be pushing toward an echo of the Permian extinction, some 250 million years ago, which wiped out 95 percent of known animal species.

I have long been of the opinion that Quammen's somber and beautiful account of the death of the last dodo, in his masterful *The Song of the Dodo*, is perhaps the finest bit of American science writing ever, but his description of what lies beyond the borders of the next mass extinction has a similar, and equally chilling, power:

> Wildlife will consist of the pigeons and the coyotes and the whitetails, the black rats (*Rattus rattus*) and the brown rats (*Rattus norvegicus*) and a few other species of worldly rodent, the crab-eating macaques and the cockroaches . . . the mongooses, the house sparrows and the house geckos and the houseflies and the barn cats and the skinny brown feral dogs and a short list of other species that play by our rules . . . Having recently passed the great age of biogeography, we will have entered the age *after* biogeography, in that virtually everything will live virtually

everywhere, though the list of species that constitute "everything" will be small.

I have neither the scientific chops to challenge Quammen's conclusions nor the literary chops to improve on his depiction of them, but I do take some comfort in understanding that they show a short-term viewpoint. Okay, yes, granted, he's talking about a vision of a future than neither he nor I will ever see, the year 2150 or so, but it's important to remember that the future is a much vaster thing than that. Even if we lose 95 percent of our biodiversity in the next two centuries and are left with only rats, House Sparrows, and crabgrass, the extinction of one species, or a dozen, or thousands, is not a line drawn across the entire future of life on Earth. The planet has millions of years ahead of it, regardless of which organisms are around to witness them. Species may vanish, but ecological niches will not, and natural selection is nothing if not dogged in its attempts to generate new forms of life to fill them.

This is not much comfort to those who worry about the fate of the California Condor or the flowering dogwood, and it's hard to dispute Gould's point that mass extinctions "are decidedly unpleasant for species caught in the throes of their power." If some ancient saurian scientist were somehow present on the day the Chicxulub meteorite plowed into the Yucatan Peninsula, watching from a safe distance, I could hardly blame him for lamenting the destruction of the world he knew. A planet without the improbable profile of the triceratops, the graceful ram's-horn spiral of the ammonite, the gargantuan wingspan of the pteranodon . . . this would be an undeniably impoverished place.

But it's the place where we live.

None of us have seen the lost Cretaceous world, one we know only through the careful examination of the rocks on which our own biome rests. And I suspect that we today would not trade the wonders of this remarkable world, the flying frogs and bristlecone pines, bowerbirds and giant sequoias, mountain gorillas and humpback whales, to get back those of the Cretaceous.

So yes, I do believe that we may well end up mourning the loss of these and many other species, just as some other species, perhaps our distant descendants, will ultimately end up mourning our own. But I also believe that Charles Darwin was right. Though the next mass extinction may leave only creatures we might consider weeds, those weeds will flourish on the Earth's tangled bank, finding new ways to exploit the possibilities of the air, the water, and the sunlight, giving birth to offspring with genes and forms not quite like their own. And one day, millions of years from now, standing or soaring or slithering over the resting place of the last lion or the final rhino, there will be a fantastic creature whose form we cannot even guess at, born from the surviving remnants of our own age.

But don't take my word for it. You can see the process in action yourself if you'll just spend a winter's day in the Yucatan, standing on the cenotaph of the dinosaurs. Listen for a faint humming sound. Then look up and see their tiny great-great-grandchild hovering just beyond your fingertips, its ruby throat gleaming in the sun, a drop of nectar still clinging to its long, long bill.

Epilogue

I Don't Know Where I'm Going, but I'm on My Way

Close to the end—Failure to quote Dorothy—Repeatedly denied—There's Kirwin

WE WERE CLOSE to the end—of the day, of the state, of our patience. We had maybe two hours of the first left, about twenty-five miles of the second, and an uncertain but not enormous amount of the third.

It was the first of July, 2011, and I have to say I was frustrated. The frustration might have been partly due to the summer temperature. At Tallgrass Prairie National Preserve, it had been over 85 degrees before 9:00 A.M., which made for an uncomfortable environment even in the shade. I was also irked by the high wind, a southerly blast coming over the Flint Hills at somewhere between 15 and 20 mph, which tended to keep a lot of birds down in cover and drown out the calls of others. But my frustration was mainly due to seeing nothing but the birds we'd seen before: a bunch of Dickcissels, Eastern Meadowlarks, and swallows. It had been a very hot morning of looking unsuccessfully for a life bird in Kansas. Even the astonishing beauty of the preserve (and of the countryside in general) couldn't ease that frustration.

With the heat rising, Dad and I had decided to go to the coolest place we knew—the car—and head for one last target in Kansas: Kirwin National Wildlife Refuge, about four hours away, high in the northern part of the state, only two dozen miles short of the Nebraska line.

Kirwin has a small lake in the middle, and that lake, when we finally drove in sight of it, was crawling with waders: Great Blue Herons, Great Egrets, Snowy Egrets, and at least forty Cattle Egrets were lurking in the shallows near the visitor's center (which had closed roughly four minutes before our arrival). Pelicans, cormorants, and a few unidentifiable ducks patrolled the waters, while a couple of overheated Great-tailed Grackles lurked nearby as well. After a long day of almost nothing but roadside birding, it was simultaneously relaxing and exciting to get to a place where we could not only see but identify the birds. And when I saw a hawk flying overhead, just beyond a row of roadside cottonwoods, I thought it might be my Kansas lifer. I got Dad to stop the car and jumped out for a better look, but even as I was disembarking, I caught in the branches a glimpse of something pale yellow with a dark tail.

I'm happy to say I made the ID immediately: "Kingbird!" And yes, it turned out to be exactly that: my first Western Kingbird. Three or four were flitting back and forth out of the trees, with a number of Eastern Kingbirds making for helpful comparison. I had been worried that I'd get skunked in Kansas after missing Kentucky on our way out west, but now, with the Sunflower State checked off and the promise of new birds in Nebraska, we jetted toward our hotel in North Platte. My only regret is that I missed my first-ever chance to legitimately quote Dorothy until well after we crossed the Kansas/Nebraska border.

But I think about that stop at Kirwin often, and really, it's because of the lines. For one thing, it's a refuge, carefully bounded off from the rest of the state by the federal government, but I think it's important to me because of the lines I brought there myself. I'm still a long way from my goal, with life birds now recorded in 35 states; Georgia and Mississippi have repeatedly denied me, and I've still never even visited Alaska, Minnesota, Oklahoma, Oregon, Washington, Wisconsin, or the Dakotas. Even if I get lucky and see a new bird everywhere I go, there's a lot of traveling left to do.

Nor are state lines the only ones I think about. I'm fifty years old as of this writing, and my father is seventy-six. Time's winged chariot is audible now, the wind tearing through its feathers like those of the Prairie Falcon Dad and I saw stooping in southern Utah. Every time I slide into the passenger seat and see him out of the corner of my eye, I can't help wondering how many more miles we have.

But as I said, there's Kirwin: close to the edge—almost close enough that you can see it—but still full of things that are beautiful, unfamiliar, and unexpected. And there's a bit of daylight yet. The line is near us, yes, but what matters is what still lies on this side of it. We may as well keep looking around.

Bibliography

Maps and Legends

De Blij, H. J. *Human Geography: Culture, Society, and Space*. New York: John Wiley, 1977.

De Chant, Tim. "Redrawing the United States of America"—http://persquaremile.com/2011/11/17/redrawing-the-united-states-of-america/

Weisstein, Eric W. "Line." From *MathWorld*—A Wolfram Web Resource—http://mathworld.wolfram.com/Line.html

Driver's Education

Camp, Greg, interviewed July 8, 2013.

Edwards, Haley Sweetland. "It's Complicated: 5 Puzzling International Borders"—https://www.mentalfloss.com/blogs/archives/104762.

"Nearly 80% Of Passenger Cars Are Sold With Manual Transmission in Europe"—http://prlog.org/10000955

History's Greatest Monster

Rabkin, April. "Gerrymandering: Why Your Vote Doesn't Count"—http://motherjones.com/politics/2006/09/gerrymandering-why-your-vote-doesnt-count

Tabak, Jessica. "Acts of Omission: Fiona Brideoake examines 19th-century censored Shakespeare"—http://www.american.edu/cas/success/literature-brideoake-091102.cfm

The Four Corners Offense

Munroe, Randall. "Weekend"—http://xkcd.com/1073/

What God Has Put Asunder

Boese, Alex. "The Blue Laws of Connecticut"—http://www.museumofhoaxes. com/bluelaws.html

Cowell, Tom. "PA's Disgraceful Liquor Laws"—http://www.philadelphiaweekly. com/news-and-opinion/PA-disgraceful-liquor-loaws.html

Ellsworth, Brian. "In Days Before Easter, Venezuelans Tuck Into Rodent-Related Delicacy"—http://www.nysun.com/foreign/in-days-before-easter-venezuelans-tuck-into/11063/

Keim, Brandon. "Profit vs. Principle: The Neurobiology of Integrity."—http:// www.wired.com/wiredscience/2012/01/neurobiology-of-sacred/

Occhiogrosso, Peter. *The Joy of Sects.* New York: Image Books, 1996.

"Questions and Answers about Lent and Lenten Practices"—http://www. usccb.org/prayer-and-worship/liturgical-resources/lent/questions-and-answers-about-lent.cfm

"The 39 Melachot"—http://www.torahtots.com/torah/39melachot.htm

Time of the Season

Boyd, W. Alice and Courtney J. Conway. "Why Migrate? A Test of the Evolutionary Precursor Theory." *The American Naturalist.* Vol. 169, Issue 3, March 2007.

Connor, Jack. "Not All Sweetness and Light." *Living Bird.* Autumn 2010, 34–35. http://www.allaboutbirds.org/page.aspx?pid=2031

Hanke, Steve H. and Richard Conn Henry. "Changing Times"—http://www. cato.org/pub_display.php?pub_id=13940%3Cbr%20/%3E

Rock and a Hard Place

Walker, Rob. "The Song Decoders"—http://www.nytimes.com/2009/10/18/ magazine/18Pandora-t.html

Parts Is Parts

Bohlen, H. David. "Illinois Sightings of Bilateral Gynandromorphism in Birds"—http://www.idaillinois.org/cdm/compoundobject/collection/ism/ id/5411

Manning, JT et al. "The 2nd to 4th digit ratio and autism"—http://www.ncbi. nlm.nih.gov/pubmed/11263685

Moen, Rick. "Kudzu and the California Marriage Amendment"—http:// linuxmafia.com/faq/Essays/marriage.html

"She's Her Own Twin"—http://abcnews.go.com/Primetime/story?id=2315693

Szalavitz, Maia. "Penis Size: It May Be Written in the Length of His Fingers"— http://healthland.time.com/2011/07/06/penis-size-it-may-be-written-in-the-length-of-his-fingers/

Wallien, MS et al. "2D:4D finger-length ratios in children and adults with gender identity disorder"—http://www.ncbi.nlm.nih.gov/pubmed/ 18585715

Yu, Neng et al. "Disputed Maternity Leading to Identification of Tetragameteic Chimerism"—http://www.nejm.org/doi/full/10.1056/NEJMoa013452

Names Will Never Hurt Me

Gill, Victoria. "Italian sparrow joins family as new species"—http://www.bbc. co.uk/nature/14947902

Gray, Asa. "Darwin on the Origin of Species"—http://www.theatlantic.com/ magazine/archive/1860/07/darwin-on-the-origin-of-species/4152/

Hermansen, Jo S. et al. "Hybrid speciation in sparrows I: phenotypic intermediacy, genetic admixture and barriers to gene flow"—http://onlinelibrary. wiley.com/doi/10.1111/j.1365-294X.2011.05183.x/abstract

Rite of Passage

Heinrich, Bernd. *Life Everlasting: The Animal Way of Death*. Boston: Houghton Mifflin Harcourt, 2012.

Holmes, Linda. "'Bully' Problems: The MPAA Gives a Scarlet 'R' to a Thoughtful Documentary"—http://www.npr.org/blogs/monkeysee/ 2012/02/24/147347673/bully-problems-the-mpaa-gives-a-scarlet-r-to-a-thoughtful-documentary

Motion Picture Association of America. "What Each Rating Means"—http:// www.mpaa.org/ratings/what-each-rating-means

Zeitchik, Steven. "'Bully' rating: Some, but not all, profanity cut to get PG-13"—http://latimesblogs.latimes.com/movies/2012/04/some-f-words-but-not-all-cut-from-bully-to-get-pg-13-rating.html

The Undiscovered Country

Bai, Nina. "The Curious Case of the Immortal Jellyfish"—http://blogs. discovermagazine.com/discoblog/2009/01/29/the-curious-case-of-the-immortal-jellyfish/

Diamond, J. M. "'Normal' extinction of isolated populations." In *Extinctions*, edited by M. H. Nitecki. Chicago: Univ. of Chicago Press, 1984.

Glausiusz, Josie. "Michael Rose Beating Death"—http://discovermagazine. com/2001/may/breakdialogue

Jacobs, Francine. *Bermuda Petrel: The Bird That Would Not Die*. New York: William Morrow & Company, 1981.

Jones, Simon. "Cahow population reaches 'critical milestone' with 100 nesting pairs"—http://bermudasun.bm/main.asp?FromHome=1&TypeID= 1&ArticleID=57556&SectionID=24&SubSectionID=898

Piraino, Stefano et al. "Reversing the Life Cycle: Medusae Transforming into Polyps and Cell Transdifferentiation in *Turritopsis nutricula* (Cnidaria, Hydrozoa)"—http://www.biolbull.org/content/190/3/302.full.pdf+html

Quammen, David. *The Song of the Dodo*. New York: Touchstone Books, 1996.

Raup, D. M. "Death of species." In *Extinctions*, edited by M. H. Nitecki. Chicago: Univ. of Chicago Press, 1984.

Rowland, Stephen M. "Thomas Jefferson, extinction, and the evolving view of Earth history in the late eighteenth and early nineteenth centuries." In *The Revolution in Geology from the Renaissance to the Enlightenment*, edited by Gary D. Rosenberg. Boulder, Colorado: Geological Society of America, 2010.

We're Not Lost

Brown, David and Eric Pianin. "Extinct? After 60 Years, Woodpecker Begs to Differ"—http://www.washingtonpost.com/wp-dyn/content/article/2005/04/28/AR2005042802121.html

Fitzpatrick, John W. et al. "Ivory-billed Woodpecker (Campephilus principalis) Persists in Continental North America"—http://www.sciencemag.org/content/308/5727/1460.full

Leonard, Pat. "2007-08 Ivory=-billed Woodpecker Search Season Summary"—http://www.birds.cornell.edu/ivory/pastsearches/07_08season/07_08updatesstories/0708summary

Quammen, David. *Natural Acts: A Sidelong View of Science and Nature*. Rev. ed. New York: W. W. Norton & Company, 2007.

Sibley, David A. et al. "Comment on 'Ivory-billed Woodpecker (Campephilus principalis) Persists in Continental North America'"—http://www.sciencemag.org/content/311/5767/1555.1.full?sid=bcb9c6fb-1164-415f-b061-73caf7536f7f

Acknowledgments

I OWE AN ENORMOUS debt of gratitude to those kind souls who let me pick their brains for insights I could never have made into subjects I could never have understood. In a very real sense, they made this book; I just stirred the ingredients around and plated them. Mike Beard, Matt Boesen, Greg Camp, Tim Gallagher, Ethan Gamache, Greg Jacobs, Abigail James, Matthew Keating, Joan Lipsitz, Kevin McGowan, Shawn Smith, and Ursula Vernon, I owe you one. Several, really.

Much of this book was written during a sabbatical from my job at Woodberry Forest School, and I am very appreciative of the time and the financial support I received from WFS, along with the Joyce Foundation. In particular, I'm grateful for the effort Ted Blain, Brent Cirves, and Dennis Campbell devoted to helping me get away for a while.

That sabbatical was spent in Ithaca, New York, where I served as an intern on *Living Bird*, the Cornell Lab of Ornithology's quarterly publication. My understanding of birds, birding, and publication was expanded enormously during those spring months, and this would be a poorer book by far if not for the help of Miyoko Chu, Rachel Dickinson, Charles Eldermire, Tim Gallagher (again), Sean Gannon, Kevin McGowan (again), Hugh Morris, Jennifer Smith, and a dozen others I'm sure I'm forgetting.

In particular, I must recognize the students, group leaders, and faculty of the 2011 Spring Field Ornithology course, including Robyn

Bailey, David Bonter, Meena Haribol, Elisabeth and Will Harrod, Wes Hochachka, Bob McGuire, Dave Nutter, Dave Nicosia, Erica Van Etten Marx, and of course professor Steve Kress.

If not for Scott Weidensaul's *Seasonal Guide to the Natural Year*, I would never have known Golden Eagles could be seen in Maryland. If not for Michael Chabon's *The Yiddish Policeman's Union*, I would never have known about *eruvim*. If not for Stephen Jay Gould's *Dinosaur in a Haystack*, I would never have known about the calendar work of Dionysius Exiguus. And if not for Jennifer Lena's *Banding Together*, I would never have learned how Pandora forced Celine Dion upon an unwilling listener.

Support and assistance on this decade-long project have come from many sources, some of them online, some of them in meatspace. My English 500 students offered suggestions for improving one chapter opening, which seemed only fair. Russell Galen provided enormously helpful feedback on an early draft and sent me in a direction I wouldn't otherwise have gone. Ta-Nehisi Coates and his Golden Horde have offered hours upon hours of social and intellectual support. Katharine Weber, Lauren Baratz-Logsted, and the folks at BookBalloon.com (especially proprietor Gary Glass) have been especially helpful, and if not for fellow Balloonist Elizabeth McCullough, this book wouldn't have its subtitle. And if not for Jimmy Wales, Larry Sanger, and the Wikimedia Foundation, I would have paradoxically gotten a whole lot less and a whole lot more work done.

I have had many birding partners whose sharp eyes and ears have taught me a lot and whose company has made the time spent far more enjoyable: Alan Barry, Karen Bond, Michael Cope, Cynthia Fox, Kurt Hiester, Wallace Hornady, Shari Jacobs, Nick Morgan, Tom and Hillary Parker, Leighton Reid, Chris Sprouse, Mary Stevens, and Ginger Walker, among others. And I must thank Douglas Wayne Gray and Dave Magpiong for alerting me to birding info in general and crane sightings in Tennessee in particular.

My parents' generosity with their time, their money, and their spare bedroom has been of inestimable value to me. This book would not exist without them. Of course, neither would its author.

My sons, Ian and Dixon, have put up with a lot from me: long hours of neglect while I slaved away over my computer, extended absences from our home every spring since 2003, and an unreasonable insistence that they not only graduate high school, but continue their educations. I am very proud of them.

And as always, my deepest thanks and love go to Kelly Dalton, muse, polestar, and partner.